Annie Besant
(1847-1933)

Struggles and Quest

Published by Theosophical Publishing House, London.
The Theosophical Publishing House Limited, London is the publishing company of the Theosophical Society in England.

Theosophical Society in England
50 Gloucester Place
London
United Kingdom
W1U 8EA

www.theosophicalsociety.org.uk

Originally published in French under the title *Annie Besant (1847-1933) : La lutte et la quête* by Editions Adyar Paris

ISBN 978-1-9998157-0-7

Cover photograph: Copyright © Archives and Special Collections, Dickinson College, Carlisle, PA, USA.
Cover design and text layout by Aldred Design – www.aldred-design.co.uk
Typeset in Minion Pro.
Printed and bound by Biddles.

Annie Besant
(1847-1933)

Struggles and Quest

Muriel Pécastaing-Boissière

Theosophical Publishing House
London

Contents

Foreword

It is impossible to study late-nineteenth- and early-twentieth-century Britain without coming across Annie Besant's name. I first encountered it while researching my doctorate dissertation on the social status of Victorian actresses[1] — because of Besant's connection both with Fabian playwright George Bernard Shaw and with the suffragettes. Later on, as a senior lecturer in Victorian studies at the Sorbonne, I had my students work on Besant's socialist fight alongside the matchgirls on strike in the East End of London at the end of the 1880s. Focussing on the condition of Victorian women in my seminars, I often dwelt on Besant's pioneering struggle in the 1870s for the right to information on birth control. Meanwhile, when preparing classes on the British Empire, I realized that Besant's election as president of the Indian National Congress in 1917 had been almost completely forgotten in the West.

My interest in Annie Besant intensified when I decided to refocus my academic research on the underestimated links between the late-Victorian socialist movement, the contemporaneous fight for women's rights and the spiritual and occult revival. I then began to work on understanding the full extent of Besant's personal evolution. I discovered that in the main two biographies of Besant — the first by Arthur Nethercot in 1960-1963[2], the second by Anne Taylor in 1992[3] — her conversion to Theosophy is described as yet another fracture in a life these two authors thought to be fragmented to the point of incoherence. Neither managed to establish a link between

[1] Published as *Les Actrices victoriennes: entre marginalité et conformisme*. Paris: l'Harmattan, 2004.

[2] NETHERCOT, Arthur Hobart. *The First Five Lives of Annie Besant*. University of Chicago Press, 1960; and *The Last Four Lives of Annie Besant*. University of Chicago Press, 1963.

[3] TAYLOR, Anne. *Annie Besant: a Biography*. Oxford University Press, 1992.

Besant's freethinking, socialism, feminism, criticism of the Empire, and conversion to Theosophy. To make matters worse, both works suffer from gender-biased interpretations and prejudices regarding Theosophy that are so strong as to impair their reflective abilities.

I therefore decided to try and remedy the situation, and to write a new biography of Annie Besant. My purpose was not to uncover still potentially unexplored archives, but rather to make Besant both better known and better understood by the general public. The logic behind Besant's evolution, leading from an early religious crisis to secularism, feminism, socialism, Theosophy, and Indian nationalism, had barely been addressed, so I hoped to demonstrate the underlying continuities in her long life of struggles. To do so, I chose to recall and to explain Besant's choices and actions in their moral, social, and spiritual contexts, while relying primarily on her own writings.

This book is the result of that decision, which, during five years of research and reflection I never came to regret — so much have Besant's struggles and quest continued to fascinate me.

1

Annie Besant's Childhood, Education and Marriage: From Conformism to Spiritual and Moral Crisis (1847–1874)[1]

'I was born "within earshot of Bow Bells"', Annie Besant pointed out in the first paragraph of the autobiography she wrote in the middle of her long life. With this Cockney phrase, referring to the bells of St Mary-le-Bow, on Cheapside, in the City of London, Besant defined herself as a true Londoner. Her Irish roots, to which she proudly referred a couple of lines later — 'full three quarters of my blood are Irish', she asserted —, only added to this self-definition. In 1847, when Victoria had been reigning for ten years over an Empire 'on which the Sun never set', its capital was a gigantic cosmopolitan crucible, where all social classes, peoples, ideologies, and spiritualities converged — though not necessarily met — and where an uncommon freedom of expression existed, enjoyed by many political exiles.

Annie Wood was born there on 1 October 1847. She was the true daughter of this city of all possible, of this first global metropolis, that provided her with so many crucial encounters, intellectual opportunities, and choices of which a Victorian woman, subjected to middle-class conformity and moral restrictions, could still little dream. It was in London that she sought refuge when she fled her husband, Rev. Frank Besant. It was in London that she met Charles Bradlaugh and Madame Blavatsky, doubtlessly the two most

[1] This chapter is based primarily on the two versions of Annie Besant's autobiography: *Autobiographical Sketches*. London: Freethought Publishing Co., 1885 (republished and annotated by MACKAY, Carol Hanbery, ed., Peterborough, Ont.: Broadview Press Ltd, 2009), and *Annie Besant: An Autobiography*. London: T. Fisher Unwin, 1893.

influential figures in her life. It was in London that, before 1893, she fought her greatest battles, for freethought, women's rights, and the working classes.

Her Father

Like the vast majority of Londoners, then as now, Annie Besant's parents were not born there, but her father, William Wood, had prestigious family ties in London. Besant's great-uncle, Matthew Wood, had been Lord Mayor of the City of London in 1815 and 1816, and had sat in the House of Commons from 1817 until his death in 1843. His support of Queen Caroline during her divorce from King George IV in 1820, and his management of the Duke of Kent's debts, Queen Victoria's father, earned him the title of Baronet. Matthew's second son, Sir William Wood, Annie's cousin, was Lord Chancellor in William Gladstone's Liberal Government between 1868 and 1872.

Besant's grandfather, Robert Wood, however, came from the less successful branch of the family. Married to Emily Truman, an Irish Catholic, he had settled in Galway, where Besant's father was born. William Wood studied medicine at Trinity College, Dublin. One of his rich relatives then offered him a position in the City of London, just when it was becoming the financial centre of the world. The young father barely hesitated and became a businessman, joining the two and a half million inhabitants of the most populous city in the world, as well as one of the largest, spreading over fifteen miles from east to west already. Three hundred thousand newcomers settled in London in the 1840s alone, including William Wood and his family.

With Ireland in a horrendous economic situation, Besant presented her family's move to London as a reasonable career choice on her father's part. Ireland had been experiencing its apocalyptic Great Famine since 1845, as its archaic agrarian system was unable to cope with the potato blight that struck the staple food of its poor rural population. The Great Famine caused the deaths of a million Irish between 1845 and 1852, and the emigration of at least as many. They fled to the United States, Canada or Australia, but also to Britain's industrial ports and cities, and to London, where over 45,000 ended up, most often in much more precarious conditions than William Wood's.

In her autobiography, Besant described her father as keen on mathematics and passionate about classical literature and philosophy. She wrote that he spoke fluent French, German, Italian, Spanish, and Portuguese, as well as rudimentary Hebrew and Gaelic. Despite – or perhaps because of – his Irish mother's strict Catholic principles, William Wood was overtly sceptical of Christianity, and did not hesitate to mock religion. It is obvious that Besant drew on her description of her father, whom she could actually barely remember, when searching in her autobiography for the origins of her intellectual curiosity, love of studies, and rejection of established religions. She nevertheless explained that her father accepted his wife's point of view that 'women ought to be religious.'

This last remark, far from a criticism of her father, was on the contrary Besant's homage to the tolerance and love that existed between her parents. This was doubtless mythologized by William Wood's early death and the memories of his sincerely loving widow. They nevertheless constituted the model of an ideal relationship, against which Besant would later measure not only her own marriage but the institution itself, when she wrote about its meaning and possible reform. Friendship, tolerance, dialogue, and equal rights; such were the values that Besant believed to be indispensable for a successful union she defined as form of companionship.

Her Mother

Annie Besant's mother, born Emily Roche Morris, came from a large Irish Protestant family, penniless despite unfounded aristocratic claims. Although a republican, Besant enjoyed narrating in her autobiography the family saga that she received from the unmarried great-aunt who had raised her mother. The 'Maurices', whose name supposedly dated back to

Charlemagne, considered themselves to be related to the 'Seven Kings of France', whom Besant compared in jest to the Milesian kings of the Celtic legends that she so loved. Emily Morris found in such tales a source of respectability that offset the precarious financial and social situation in which she had grown up. Besant's maternal grandparents 'had merrily run through' what was left of the Morris fortune, she explained indulgently, while having 'a family that grew more numerous as pounds grew fewer.' Though Besant spoke humorously of them in her autobiography, her neo-Malthusianism was partly based on her lucid assessment of such improvidence[2]. She nevertheless described her maternal grandfather with affection, despite his fits of rage that she attributed to his Irish blood. He lived in Clapham, a suburb south of London. The family's relative poverty may explain why none of her three maternal aunts married. Annie Wood was close to the youngest, Marion 'Minnie' Morris.

Emily Morris had developed a rigid system of moral requirements that she would later impose on her daughter, largely through her own example. She was a figure of rectitude, honesty and purity, a model to which Besant adhered, in spite of life choices that would soon radically differ from her mother's. Besant explained in her autobiography that: 'To her [mother] the lightest breath of dishonour was to be avoided at any cost of pain, and she wrought into me, her only daughter, that same proud and passionate horror at any taint of shame or merited disgrace.' This was certainly the reason why Emily Wood never lost confidence in her daughter, not even after the scandal and ostracism that inevitably followed any marital separation in Victorian society, albeit justified and legal.

Emily Wood, admittedly, had tolerated her husband's religious scepticism. Whether due to her own temperament or to his influence, she distrusted Evangelical puritanism, preferring High Church Anglicanism[3], whose art, architecture, and holy music she enjoyed. Emily Wood had also freed herself from some of the most puritanical dogmas, such as eternal punishment, vicarious atonement, and even literal interpretations

---

[2] See Chapter 3.

[3] See Chapter 2.

of the Bible. Besant had also rejected those dogmas when she wrote her autobiography, but only after going through a mystical phase during her adolescence. This concerned her mother, who came to fear that Annie would convert to Catholicism.

Yet Besant's mother, like the rest of her Irish family, firmly believed in the supernatural, especially in ghosts. Emily Wood told little Annie that she had once heard the macabre shriek of a banshee, a female spirit from Celtic mythology, at the exact moment of death of one of their relatives in Ireland. Besant spoke about these family beliefs without any irony in the first version of her autobiography, published in 1885. This is surprising, for at the time she described herself as an atheist, placing her faith in reason and science. So these few lines show that her departure from spirituality was never absolute. As we shall see in the following chapter, Besant actually was agnostic, and did not share in some of the entrenched certitudes of some of her materialist friends.

Besant spoke much more about her mother than her father in the first chapter of her autobiography. She adored her mother — blindly, surely — despite her social and moral conformism, against which she would eventually rebel, but without ever blaming her. In 1891, her friend, the famous journalist W. T. Stead, wrote a 'character sketch' of Besant for his *Review of Reviews*[4], in which he appeared very critical of Emily Wood and her prudishness, typical of the moral constraints of the Victorian middle class, the consequences of which proved disastrous for her daughter.

Did Besant's mother's modesty explain what is missing from Besant's autobiography? We do not know how her parents met and got married, and none of her biographers, including the very exhaustive Nethercot, provided any further information on this subject. Besant explained, in a somewhat distanced but touching manner: 'I have heard that the love between my father and mother was a very beautiful thing.' The couple's respectability and affluence, living in the middle-class residential neighbourhood of St. John's Wood during Besant's childhood, seemed to preclude any

4 STEAD, W. T. 'Character Sketch: Mrs Annie Besant'. *Review of Reviews*, October 1891, pp. 349–67.

embarrassing family secret, in a Victorian Britain that was socially and morally unforgiving on this subject. Besant's parents were married before 1845, the year her eldest brother Henry (nicknamed Harry) was born. A third child, Alfred (Alfie), was born in 1849.

Her Father's Death

Annie Besant's childhood was soon marred by tragedy, to the point that she could only recall glimpses of her happy memories of St. John's Wood in her autobiography. She remembered being disappointed at not being allowed to visit the Great Exhibition of 1851 — the first universal exhibition, dedicated to the glory of the British Empire and the Industrial Revolution — that took place in Hyde Park, in the gigantic Crystal Palace. Besant wrote that she had to content herself with souvenir postcards of this triumphant symbol of Victorianism, but also, unwillingly, of its prejudices and errors, against which she would later fight so ardently.

What would have been Besant's destiny if her father had not died prematurely? It is pointless to imagine, but the financial and psychological difficulties she faced from childhood, as well as the painful choices she had to make, certainly made her a young woman of rare moral strength.

Any premature death seems absurd, and Besant's father's in 1852 was particularly so. William Wood had remained nostalgic about the medical studies he had pursued in Dublin, and he occasionally accompanied his doctor friends on their visits to patients in hospitals, or assisted them in autopsies. During one of these, he nicked his finger on the rib cage of someone who had died of acute tuberculosis. Today, it is difficult to imagine the potential consequences of this type of incident, what with our efficient disinfectants and antibiotics. The wound never healed, and William Wood made the tragic mistake of not taking the advice of those who suggested that he amputate his infected finger. Shortly thereafter, while travelling in an uncovered horse-drawn carriage in the rain, a simple cold developed into pneumonia, a symptom of the same acute tuberculosis for which medicine then had no cure.

Each era has its taboos. While sexuality was an extremely robust one in Victorian society, death was neither denied nor hidden: people died most commonly at home, surrounded by loved ones. After several awful weeks of agony, William Wood died, three days after Besant's fifth birthday. While his children were sent to their grandparents to protect them from contagion, his wife kept vigil by his side day and night. All the same, as well as her terrible childhood sorrow, Besant recalled being brought to him to say her goodbyes. She also wrote, with some pride, that her father refused to see the Catholic priest summoned to his bedside by his mother and sister, and was supported by his wife Emily in his decision.

Besant again obliquely described her parents' deep love: exhausted by her long vigil and devastated by sorrow, her mother locked herself away in her bedroom and emerged the next morning with completely white hair. This extremely rare syndrome, which also affected Queen Marie-Antoinette before her execution, is supported by science. Even more troubling is the following memory, as told by Besant. Emily Wood did not attend her husband's funeral. In her commentary on Annie Besant's autobiography, Carol Hanbery MacKay explains that at the time, women and girls, thought to be too emotional, were generally not present at funeral services. It was only a few weeks later that Emily Wood found the courage to visit her husband's grave. Even though she did not know where it was located in the immense Kensal Green Cemetery in London, she found it without a moment of hesitation, even before the caretaker, though the tombstone had not yet been inscribed. Besant related this strange fact without irony or scepticism in the 1885 version of her autobiography. Nor did she doubt the explanation given by her mother, who said that she had followed the funeral procession in her mind on the burial day. In 1885, by then a self-defined atheist and materialist, Besant confessed: 'this curious psychological problem [...] has often puzzled me.' The absence of definite scientific answer regarding such occurrences, which Besant tried to investigate herself, like many Victorians, constituted one of the reasons for her conversion to Theosophy.

The Wood family soon experienced another tragedy: little Alfie most probably fell victim to the same tuberculosis that had killed his father. He grew weaker during the winter that followed, and died in Emily Wood's arms in March 1853. Even though the Victorian child mortality rate was ten times higher than that of today's developed societies, even among the upper classes, it is a mistake to think that the Victorians were indifferent to the death of a child. On the contrary, at the time children began to hold an increasingly central position in the family and an unprecedented symbolic value of purity and innocence. Victorian novels demonstrate as much, be it Oliver Twist or David Copperfield in the eponymous Charles Dickens novels, or the quality of Victorian children's literature, as famously exemplified by *Alice's Adventures in Wonderland* by Lewis Carroll. At the same time, motherhood began to be idealized, which partly explains why Besant was so insistent about maternal love in her autobiography. All the more so that she herself almost lost her daughter to conditions similar to Alfie's. She therefore described her mother's indescribable pain even more forcefully, recalling that, in his coffin, her little brother still bore the mark of Emily Wood's last kiss on his forehead, bestowed at the moment of his death.

Harrow

In addition to Emily Wood's mourning, now a widow with two young children — Harry, seven, and Annie, five — the family soon encountered serious financial difficulties. Despite earning a comfortable income, William Wood, whether due to imprudence or poor investments (Besant never knew), had left his family almost destitute.

Emily Wood therefore found herself in the situation dreaded by all middle-class women, on whom the demands of the Victorian ideal of womanhood weighed the most. The Victorian era saw a stricter definition of women's role emerge, linked to the strong puritan and conservative reaction to the Regency's aristocratic moral freedom, and to the new values expressed during the French and American revolutions. As a result, a more traditionalist vision of women developed, submissive to men and confined to the family, seen as the cornerstone of an endangered social edifice. A shift nevertheless took place from family and religious matters intended to restrain a feminine nature, thought to be corrupted and corrupting, to their becoming the framework of a specific feminine mission. The representation of women went from that of Eve to Mary, or 'The Angel in the House'[5]. It expressed an ideal of femininity founded on a rigid ethic code with strict rules of modesty, chastity, and submission to the husband, their family, and society at large. This ideal perfectly fitted the puritan revival that developed within the middle classes involved in trade and industry, who then accessed economic and eventually political power, and consequently imposed their values on the whole of Victorian society. It confined women within a domestic existence, as the separation between public and private spheres consolidated. Home became an essentially feminine space, a temple of purity, a haven of peace theoretically protected from contact with the outside world. It was men who were supposed to be active and risk venturing outside of this sanctuary, before returning to their wives' quiet moral inspiration. The woman's task was therefore to take care of their children and create a peaceful and morally pure atmosphere at home, where men could recover from the worries and struggles of the outside world. Victorian society offered young upper and middle-class girls almost no other path. Those who did not marry, or whose husband died, like Emily Wood, found themselves at a tragic social and moral impasse if they did not have sufficient incomes.

Emily Wood relocated to a smaller house in Clapham, close to Besant's grandparents, and the London branch of the Wood family offered her assistance. Sir William Wood, the future Lord Chancellor, offered to pay for Harry's education at one of the City's most respectable schools, before helping him to get started in trade. This was nothing unreasonable, but it did not account for Emily Wood's love for her deceased husband, nor for her pride.

---

[5] 'The Angel in the House' (1854) is a poem by Coventry Patmore, dedicated to his first wife, Emily, that was very popular with Victorians.

On his deathbed, William Wood had made her promise to give 'the best possible education' to Harry. At the time, 'the best possible education' meant a public school, then Oxford or Cambridge. Public schools were — and very often still are — prestigious and elitist private schools for boys, that asked for very high tuition and boarding fees. Lord Clarendon, who inspected the nine most important of them at the beginning of the 1860s, reported that, in all, they only taught around 2700 students aged nine to nineteen[6]. These schools were defined as 'public' because they aimed to form perfect 'Christian gentlemen', supposedly capable of taking part in public affairs at the highest levels. Emily Wood would therefore not be satisfied with a City school for Harry.

Noticeably, Emily Wood hardly concerned herself with her daughter's education, something that was unfortunately usual in the 1850s. Nevertheless, her courage and inventiveness in achieving her goals, with little male support, certainly set an example for her daughter. Harrow, the prestigious public school, accepted deserving students from the small town where it was located with reduced tuition fees, so Emily decided to move there. In 1855, she managed to rent an old vicarage, large enough to turn it into a boarding house for several young boys, who also prepared there with tutors to start at Harrow, a tutoring from which Harry thus benefited for free. Emily Wood gained the trust of Harrow's headmaster, who allowed her to board several day students also, and promised her to accept Harry into the school. She therefore managed to combine one of the rare respectable sources of income available to a young middle-class widow with a means of providing her son with a gentleman's education. Harry made the best of it, and ten years later went on to Clare's College, Cambridge on scholarship.

Little Annie Wood grew up in a very masculine environment, between her mother's boarders and their tutors, in which studying was highly valued. She described the former vicarage and its vast garden as a lost paradise of

[6] See *Report Of Her Majesty's Commissioners Appointed to Inquire into the Revenues and Management of Certain Colleges and Schools, and the Studies Pursued and Instruction Given Therein: With an Appendix and Evidence.* London: G. E. Eyre and W. Spottiswoode, for H. M. Stationery Office, 1864.

freedom and innocence, where she remembered reading *Paradise Lost*[7]. Besant enjoyed provoking the Victorian readers of her autobiography by admitting that, as a child, she performed Satan's speeches aloud. However, it was surely a lost paradise, for this boys' boarding house was soon judged inadequate for a young girl's education. Annie's mother put off the inevitable separation for as long as possible, as she had developed a close bond with her. Thanks to her hesitation, Besant met one of the first essential figures in her extraordinary destiny: Ellen Marryat.

Her Education: Ellen Marryat

Ellen Marryat, whom Annie Besant met at Harrow, at some neighbours' home, was a rich unmarried woman in her forties. She was the youngest sister of the famous naval officer and novelist Frederick Marryat, who had left her a good portion of his fortune after his death in 1848. Ellen Marryat had taken her niece Amy under her wing and decided to offer her a study companion in the person of Annie Wood, who had charmed her during her Harrow visit.

Marryat committed herself to offering Annie a young lady's education, but it was to be on her Fern Hill estate near Charmouth in Dorset. Emily Wood understood that it was in Annie's best interest, and allowed her to leave with Marryat, whom the little girl soon called 'Auntie'. Except for summer vacations, Annie spent five years in Dorset with Marryat and several of her other protégés.

In her autobiography, Besant dwells on her tutor's educational principles, to whom she felt indebted to the highest degree. Thanks to Marryat, Annie Wood escaped those girls' boarding schools that were so severely criticized in 1868 by the Schools Inquiry Commission chaired by Henry Labouchere (Lord Taunton). Those schools were described by the members of the commission (incidentally, all men) as in '[w]ant of thoroughness and foundation; want of system'. They denounced their

[7] By Puritan poet John Milton (1608–1674), written in 1667.

'slovenliness and showy superficiality; inattention to rudiments; undue time given to accomplishments, and those not taught intelligently or in any scientific manner; want of organisation'. Besant also escaped the teachings of a home governess. At the time, governesses were most frequently respectable unmarried women and widows from the middle classes, whose financial difficulties had forced them to seek an occupation. Most of them had no particular training and were generally only able to pass on the superficial education that they themselves had received in preparation for marriage. Not perceiving the irony in perpetuating a system that had kept them in a social impasse — so masterfully described by Charlotte Brontë in Jane Eyre — these governesses taught music, watercolours, embroidery, some French and Italian, and, of course, morality and religion to the girls in their charge. Significantly, governesses educated little boys until the age of seven or so only, who, like Emily Wood's boarders, were then entrusted to male tutors before going off to school, while their sisters remained at home with their governess, in a very sheltered atmosphere.

Contrary to governesses, and even to the majority of Victorian teachers, Marryat, an intelligent and cultivated woman, encouraged creativity in her students. She made them write letters, compositions and book reports in order to perfect their English and introduce them to rhetoric. As a talented essayist, Besant owed a great deal to her. Marryat did not believe in memorizing things by rote either — apart from Bible verses, at which Besant, gifted with a prodigious memory, confessed to excelling. Besant thus developed an intimate knowledge of the King James Bible: she was influenced by its rhetoric, structure and cadences, which often inspired, perhaps unconsciously, the style of her lectures and articles[8]. Besant also used the King James Bible as a source of aphorisms and proverbs, even during her atheist period, when she developed a highly critical exegesis of it.

Marryat educated boys and girls exactly the same: they all learned Latin, French, German, history, and geography, and they all did some

---

[8] See LARSEN, Timothy, 'The Bible and Belief in Victorian Britain', in COSTE, Bénédicte, ed. *Believing in Victorian Times, Cahiers victoriens et édouardiens* 76. Montpellier: Presses Universitaires de la Méditerrannée, October 2012.

needlework as Marryat read aloud to them. Although this egalitarianism did not extend past childhood, as only the young boys continued on to school, it still influenced Besant, who had previously grown up alongside her mother's boarders. Later on, she hardly seemed to be impressed by male authority, and clearly did not believe in men's intellectual superiority. Instead, she developed sincere and deep friendships with those men whom she considered comrades in arms and equals.

In 1861, Marryat, who had travelled a great deal, decided to finish Annie's education along with another young girl's, Emma Mann, with a Grand Tour[9]. This would have been traditional if this Grand Tour had not involved two young girls and their chaperon, at a time when only wealthy young men thus set off to the Continent. Marryat brought Annie and Emma to Bonn, then to Paris. Besant thus discovered the joy of travelling, hardly foreseeing that her life would take her through Great Britain and Europe, then America, India and the British Empire. These first trips abroad allowed Besant, an excellent linguist, to speak German and French nearly fluently, to the point of giving lectures in these languages later on in life, including at the Sorbonne, and of doing translations.

Besant spent seven months in Paris, at the height of the Second Empire. Prudish Marryat did not allow her to go to the theatre, so she made up for it by going to the Louvre museum and to Parisian Catholic churches. She grew fascinated by their decorative richness and their rituals, her favourite being Saint-Germain-l'Auxerrois. She decided to get confirmed on Easter Sunday in 1862, at the Anglican church of Saint George in Paris, and she lived it as a mystical experience.

In fact, while Marryat gave Besant a taste for studying, for personal expression and intellectual horizons beyond the areas traditionally allowed to young Victorian girls, she nevertheless remained an Evangelical Protestant, with demanding and austere values, which marked Besant for the rest of her life. She wrote in her 1885 autobiography:

---

[9] An expression dating to the middle of the eighteenth century, indicating a — supposedly — cultural and educational trip for young aristocrats and upper-middle-class men, most frequently in Italy, France, Germany, and Greece.

> [Miss Marryat] started a Sunday-school, and a Bible-class [...]. She visited the poor, taking help wherever she went, and sending food from her own table to the sick. [...]. Money she rarely, if ever, gave, but she would find a day's work, or busy herself to seek permanent employment for anyone asking aid. Stern in rectitude herself, and iron to the fawning or the dishonest, her influence, whether she was feared or loved, was always for good. Of the strictest sect of the Evangelicals, she was an Evangelical. On the Sunday no books were allowed save the Bible [...].
>
> The strong and intense Evangelicalism of Miss Marryat colored [*sic*] the whole of my early religious thought. I was naturally enthusiastic and fanciful, and was apt to throw myself strongly into the current of the emotional life around me, and hence I easily reflected the stern and narrow creed which ruled over my daily life.

This part of the education that Marryat offered Besant was typical of the values of the mid-nineteenth century Victorian middle classes. In *The Victorian Frame of Mind*[10], Walter E. Houghton explained:

> [...] in all religious quarters, children were brought up to hear such constant emphasis on duty and self-sacrifice, on benevolence and sympathy, and such constant disapproval of any criticism whatever of those they should love and respect [...] Duty [...] was set dangerously high.

Houghton showed the strong connection between this sense of duty and the Gospel of Work:

> In the middle class, where the puritan tradition was strong, the religious theory of work was a commonplace [...]. The arraignment of idleness, the value of work in the development of the individual, and the sense of a mission both to serve society in one's particular calling and to further the larger destinies of the human race.

---

[10] HOUGHTON, Walter E. *The Victorian Frame of Mind, 1830–1870.* Yale University Press, 1957, p. 410.

This work ethic extended even to agnostics, according to Houghton: 'In short, whether to avoid the pain of doubt or to end it, the formula is the same: stop thinking and do some simple duty or useful work.'

In this regard, Besant was no exception, especially after having lost her faith and beginning to fight for freethought. This sense of duty instilled first by Emily Wood and then by Ellen Marryat became for her a powerful humanist requirement, which today we might call a secular spirituality, the limits of which Besant would also come to acknowledge.

In 1863, Besant turned sixteen. At the time, women were not allowed to attend British universities. Queen's College and Bedford College, both in London, were the only further education institutions opened to women, but they were still quite small and could not award degrees. So Besant had basically no other option than to teach herself. Aware of this, Marryat taught her how to work alone, in a structured and organized manner. Besant was infinitely grateful to her for this and paid homage to her in her autobiography: 'No words of mine can tell how much I owe her, not only of knowledge, but of that love of knowledge which has remained with me ever since as a constant spur to study.'

Return to Harrow

Annie Besant spent the winter of 1862–1863 in London with Ellen Marryat, then, lacking an alternative, she returned to Harrow to live with her mother. Like any young girl whose only destiny seemed to entail marriage, she took music classes. A talented pianist, she could play all of Beethoven's sonatas and Bach's fugues, and confessed to loving Mendelssohn. Contrary to what one might imagine, young Victorian ladies did not neglect physical exercise. Besant certainly no longer played cricket with her mother's boarders, but she practiced croquet and archery, as well as horse riding — she would ride until old age.

In her autobiography, Besant detailed an impressive list of books that she read during her teenage years at Harrow, including Homer, Plato, and Dante. However, her knowledge of British literature was limited to poets, such as the romantic Robert Southey or *The Faerie Queene* by the Elizabethan Edmund Spenser, and of course her dear Milton. Following the advice of a mother who was extremely anxious about preserving her daughter's sexual innocence, Besant barely read any novels, and actually devoted most of her reading to theology.

She thus studied the Fathers of the Church, including Origen, St. John Chrysostom, and St. Augustine, as well as the history of the Holy Martyrs. She recalled: 'I read tales of the early Christian martyrs, and passionately regretted I was born so late when no suffering for religion was practicable.' Sunday communion became a near-ecstatic moment and she began to practice fasting. Besant intensely aspired to sacrifice herself for a just cause. Even though this mystical phase led to a disastrous marriage, Besant would retain a fascination for sacrifice, even martyrdom, for the rest of her life — including when she considered herself an atheist — that went further than a mere sense of duty.

First Religious Doubts

The years 1866 and 1867 constituted a prophetic turning point in Annie Besant's life. She glimpsed the vast concerns that would later occupy her existence. In the spring of 1866, she experienced her first religious doubts. Ironically, she had then just met the man who would become her husband, a young Anglican clergyman named Frank Besant. During Holy Week, she decided to meditate on the Gospels. She ardently desired to follow the stations of the Passion of Christ, for whom she expressed an intense mystical adoration. In her autobiography, Besant appeared to have no illusion as to the true reasons for this adolescent passion, which she explained in pre-Freudian terms: 'I was a child awaking into womanhood, with emotions and passions dawning and not understood, emotions and passions which craved satisfaction, and found it in this "Ideal Man".'

She took it upon herself to establish a chronology of Holy Week, based on the Synoptic Gospels. In her autobiography, some twenty years later, she wrote of her naivety: 'With the fearlessness which springs from ignorance I sat down to my task.' The sentence is identical in both versions of her autobiography, for neither the 1885 agnostic, nor the 1893 Theosophist Besant believed in literal interpretations of the Bible, for very different, but not necessarily opposed reasons[11]. The factual contradictions between the Gospels appeared to her clearly. Besant was horrified, for she thought that doubt was a sin — aggravated, in her case, by its developing on the day before Easter. She tried to quash it by convincing herself that contradictions had been put in the Bible in order to test Christians' faith. She repeated Tertullian's sentence: '*credo quia impossible*', 'I believe, because it is impossible'[12]. She also turned to the writings of the then influential Anglo-Catholic theologian Edward Pusey.

Besant's religious fundamentalism during her mystical phase was, in 1866, no longer typical of Victorian Protestantism[13]. Her own mother had stopped believing in literal interpretations of the Bible. The contradictions between the Gospels had been brought to light from the 1770s, in particular by the new Biblical exegesis of German Johann Griesbach. A historical approach to the New Testament had developed, and in 1846 George Eliot had translated *Das Leben Jesu* by David Strauss, a historical biography of Jesus originally published in 1835, around thirty years before that of Ernest Renan. In such an intellectual context, Besant was effectively naïve, if not blinding herself — to the point of refusing to read Arthur P. Stanley, the

[11] See BESANT, Annie. *Esoteric Christianity; or, The Lesser Mysteries*. London & Benares: Theosophical Publishing Society, 1901; or Christian Theosophist KINGSFORD, Anna (with MAITLAND, Edward). *The Perfect Way; or, The Finding of Christ*. London: Field & Tuer, 1882.

[12] It is an apocryphal quote, the real sentence being: '*Et mortuus est Dei Filius: credibile est quia ineptum est; et sepultus resurrexit; certum est quia impossibile est*', in TERTULLIAN. *De Carne Christi* (ca. 203–206), Chapter 5.

[13] This development is based primarily on TURNER, Frank M. 'The crisis of faith and the faith that was lost' and 'The secularization of the social vision of British natural theology', in *Contesting Cultural Authority. Essays in Victorian Intellectual Life*. Cambridge University Press, 1993. See Chapter 2.

Dean of Westminster and one of the great liberal Victorian theologians, who was her mother's favourite. She suppressed her doubts, which consequently resurfaced all the more strongly and painfully during her marital crisis several years later.

Manchester: Discovery of Radicalism and Irish Nationalism

The second event that foretold Annie Besant's later struggles occurred during the autumn of 1867. Emily Wood had just closed her Harrow boarding house, and left the old vicarage where her daughter had so many happy memories. She was looking for a house to rent in the small seaside resort of St Leonards, near Hastings. The Robertses, from Manchester, were friends of hers, and Annie spent the end of the summer of 1867 with them in Switzerland. William Prowting Roberts[14] was nicknamed 'the Poor Man's Lawyer' because he was the legal advisor for the Miners' Association of Great Britain. He was also close to Feargus O'Connor, without doubt the most radical of the Chartist leaders, who fought in vain during the 1830s and 1840s for universal male suffrage and constitutional reform.

It was in a newly tense social and political context that Annie and her mother accepted the Robertses' invitation to come to Manchester in the autumn of 1867. Thanks to popular support, the Second Reform Act had just granted voting rights to a large number of urban male workers and artisans. The consequences of the reform were still so uncertain that it was considered by Conservative Prime Minister Lord Derby as 'a leap in the dark'. Agitation in favour of the Reform Bill had been particularly intense in Manchester, and William Roberts, as a former Chartist, had taken part in it. He explained the reasons for his political involvement to Annie, to whom he had become attached, and who accompanied him everywhere: 'This dear old man was my first tutor in Radicalism, and I was an apt pupil', she recalled with emotion. Roberts described to her the miners' terrible working

[14] See CHALLINOR, Ray. *A Radical Lawyer in Victorian England: W. P. Roberts and the Struggle for Workers' Rights*. London: I. B. Tauris, 1990.

conditions, and explained why he fought for the 1842 law prohibiting women and children from working underground. Coming from a Whig family, Besant confessed that, until that point, she had only considered 'the poor' as 'folk to be educated, looked after, charitably dealt with, and always treated with most perfect courtesy'. Roberts helped her overcome this class prejudice, showing her that '"the poor" were the working-bees, the wealth producers, with a right to self-rule, not to looking after, with a right to justice, not to charity.' It was a lesson that Besant never forgot, and one that would lead her toward socialism.

Besant's time with the Roberts soon took a tragic turn. In September 1867, around thirty members of the Irish Republican Brotherhood, founded in 1859, were arrested in Manchester for having allegedly taken part in the escape of two of their leaders, during which a police officer was killed. Roberts offered to defend ten of them, alongside another Radical and former Chartist, Ernest Jones.

The trial began on 28 October, amidst extreme tension between the English and Irish working-class communities of Manchester. Even though the shooter had fled without being identified, five young men were accused of murdering the policeman. At the end of a trial that went on for several days, William Allen, Michael Larkin, Michael O'Brien, Thomas Maguire, and Edward O'Meagher Condon were found guilty and sentenced to death by hanging — the only possible sentence for murder according to Victorian law. Thanks to new testimony, two of them, Maguire and O'Meagher Condon, were acquitted, but the other three were publicly hanged on the morning of 23 November in front of Salford prison: they became the 'Manchester Martyrs' for those who supported their cause.

Besant attended the whole trial. She thus discovered a ritual at the centre of which she would find herself several times during her life, and which she would learn to use to her advantage during her struggles. The nineteen-year-old woman also proved to have unexpected physical courage and presence of mind, when the horse-drawn carriage bringing her to court, along with Mrs. Roberts and her daughters, got surrounded by a crowd of enraged Irishmen, with whom she managed to reason.

The injustice of these three young men's death sentence was one of Besant's first great indignations. She recalled with compassion the distress of the fiancée of William Allen, the youngest of the condemned, not yet twenty years old. She nevertheless overcame this purely emotional reaction to outline Britain's hypocrisy, as a country that would have hailed these men's action had they been young Italian nationalists, she said, but hanged them because they were Irish. In 1924, while she was fighting alongside Indian nationalists, Besant explained that her love for freedom dated back to that very moment, when the Manchester Martyrs were sentenced to death, writing in an article for *New India*: 'Then the flame of passionate love of liberty burst out in my heart and has never flickered since'[15]. Yet, a few weeks later, Besant surrendered her own freedom to marry a man whom she did not even love.

The Marriage Trap

Despite the death of her father and subsequent financial difficulties, young Annie Wood had lived an extremely sheltered life, between her mother and Ellen Marryat. By 1866, her days of playing with her mother's boarders at the vicarage in Harrow and of Marryat's tutoring were far behind her. Annie had an older brother, Harry, but he was a student and soon a young lawyer, and they hardly saw one another. She had no married sisters, cousins or close female friends who could have acquainted her with the facts of married life. Emily Wood prohibited her from reading novels, thinking any sentimental story improper. Besant recalls going to a few dances, but not frequently. Her mother, unbeknownst to Annie, had discouraged several young men from courting her daughter, under the pretext that she was too young. It was indeed a pretext, since she was over sixteen, at which age young ladies were supposed to come out in society, and enter the 'marriage market'. The way Annie was overprotected was unusual, even then, and reveals her mother's

[15] Quoted in KUMAR, Raj. *Annie Besant's Rise to Power in Indian Politics, 1914–1917*. New Delhi: Concept Publishing Co., 1981, p. 25.

possessive nature.

In the Victorian era, the ideal marriage already was one of love[16]. Arranged marriages were considered as a form of prostitution and, in Protestant Britain, as a sacrilege. This is the reason why so many Victorian melodramas began with a cruel and greedy father trying to force his daughter to marry a man she did not love. In fact, everything was done so that young upper or middle-class people would meet and choose one another in their own social environment, under very strict and ritualized conditions, in order to avoid mismatches. The engagement period often lasted quite a long time, allowing the young couple to get to know one another better, with moments of relative freedom, nevertheless excluding any physical contact apart from kissing. These engagements could be broken with no serious consequence to the young woman's reputation, as long as the reason was lack of love or personal incompatibility. It is important to recall all of this as, in this context, Annie was under no real obligation to marry Frank Besant.

Besant's maternal grandfather still lived in Albert Square, in Clapham, and she visited him regularly for Christmas and Easter. In the spring of 1866, Annie and her young aunt Minnie discovered a small 'mission church' in a poor Clapham neighbourhood. The term may sound surprising but, since the Religious Census of 1851, which revealed the extent of the working classes' de-christianization, the Anglican Church had undertaken the mission of recapturing the souls of the poor, often competing in that with other Protestant denominations[17]. Such a mission was perfect for young Annie Wood, who was looking for an occupation that could satisfy her aspiration for sacrifice. She and Minnie Morris brought back bunches of flowers from Harrow, with which they decorated the small church before Easter: she recalled that most of the local children had never even seen a garden. Young Rev. Frank Besant, a recent Cambridge graduate, was the deacon of this church.

---

[16] See the chapter 'Marriage' in THOMPSON, F. M. L. *The Rise of Respectable Society: A Social History of Victorian Britain, 1830–1900*. London: Fontana: 1988.

[17] See Chapter 2.

Frank Besant, born in 1840, came from a family of drapers in Portsmouth. Novelist and historian Walter Besant was one of his brothers. A brilliant student, Frank Besant had won a scholarship to study mathematics at King's College, London, then at Emmanuel College, Cambridge. Very religious, he was naturally drawn to the Anglican priesthood and was ordained in 1865, while pursuing a career as a mathematics teacher. Frank Besant was an austere young man, simultaneously shy and uncompromising, a contradiction that could bring him to fits of rage, as his young wife was to discover.

Annie Besant did not seem to remember much of their first meeting: Easter 1866 was above all else the moment of her first religious doubts. She did not think of marriage, nor love even, apart from her mystic love of Christ. Her mother, however, was much more pragmatic. She knew only too well the difficulties experienced by middle-class women who were not supported by husbands. Additionally, Annie could not rely on any income or inheritance that would allow her to support herself in the lifestyle she was accustomed to if, as more than ten percent of women in her social class, she did not marry. Emily Wood therefore saw in Frank Besant a perfectly suitable option.

The trap closed on Annie the following summer. The Morris family always stayed for a month at St Leonards. That year, without telling her daughter, Emily Wood invited the young clergyman to join them for a week. As she had hoped, the two young people spent much time together, walking and chatting. Yet Annie was taken completely by surprise when, just before catching a train back to London, Frank proposed. Naive and thrown into confusion, she feared that she had involuntarily encouraged him. Instead of following her instincts and refusing him immediately, she asked him for some time to think about it. Consequently, Frank Besant considered them to be engaged.

After returning from her vacation in Switzerland with the Robertses, Annie tried to break the engagement. Her mother dissuaded her from doing so, arguing her daughter had given her word to Frank Besant and that her honour was at stake, even though Annie's respectability surely would not have suffered from this split. Aware of her extreme religiosity, Emily Wood consoled her by extolling a lifetime of charitable devotion as the wife of a clergyman, who, furthermore, represented Christ, whom she loved so passionately. In her autobiography, Besant summarized those weeks: 'out of sheer weakness and fear of inflicting pain I drifted into an engagement with a man I did not pretend to love.' The date was set for a little over a year later. In the meantime, Annie lost a friend and confidante when her frail aunt Minnie died prematurely, shortly after that fateful summer.

Annie Wood rarely saw Frank Besant during their strange engagement, which she spent partly with the Robertses in Switzerland and Manchester. Repeating Emily Wood's arguments, Frank Besant, aware of his fiancée's reluctance, promised her a life dedicated to religion and self-sacrifice. Annie wrote him two essays, one on fasting and one on communion, the style and content of which were all but romantic.

A Traumatizing Discovery of Sexuality

The couple married on 21 December 1867, in St. Leonards, then left for a brief honeymoon in Paris. In her autobiography, Annie Besant revealed the trauma of her discovering sexuality, which she had not been prepared for:

> My ignorance of all that marriage meant was as profound as though I had been a child of four […]. My darling mother meant all that was happiest for me when she shielded me from all knowledge of sorrow and of sin, when she guarded me from the smallest idea of the marriage relation, keeping me ignorant as a baby till I left her home a wife.

There was no irony when she referred here to Emily Wood as her 'darling mother', considering her attitude with remarkable indulgence. She did not speak of any moral fault, just of the 'blunder' of having thus been maintained in total ignorance regarding the facts of life by a mother whom the reader could only perceive as both prudish and possessive, especially when Besant adds: 'That 'perfect innocence' may be very beautiful, but it is a perilous possession, and Eve should have the knowledge of good and of evil ere she wanders forth from the paradise of a mother's love.'

Her friend and confidante, journalist W. T. Stead, proved much more critical of Emily Wood when he wrote his character sketch of Besant in 1891: 'To the criminal wickedness of parents in this respect there seems sometimes to be literally no limit. A little elementary physiology would have stood her in better stead than "The Library of the Fathers".' It must be said that in 1885 Stead had led a courageous struggle to raise the age of sexual consent for young girls from thirteen to sixteen, mainly in order to curb child prostitution. Stead, who had posed as a client in order to demonstrate the extent of this type of prostitution, had spent a few months in jail, even though he had ended up victorious[18]. His fight had been as daring as that which Besant undertook in 1877 for access to information on birth control, which was also brought to court[19]. They were both among the very few who defied the powerful Victorian taboo of sexuality, and paid the price, despite their victories.

It is common today to consider Victorians as hypocrites when discussing their sexual prudishness, especially considering the extent of prostitution at the time. This vision is largely anachronistic, however, and summarily describes moral attitudes that were actually much more complex. Most Victorians sincerely believed in their ethics, even though they did not always manage to live up to the extremely demanding moral code that they imposed on themselves. Those moral values remained an ideal, however, even for those who could not achieve them, for personal or social reasons. Besant herself never really rejected those Victorian values, she only denounced their excesses and deviancies. Her mother's sincerity, who really thought she was doing the right thing in not giving her daughter any sort of sexual education, cannot be doubted, and probably explains Besant's indulgence. No more was there hypocrisy on Frank Besant's part, as he was probably as inexperienced as his young wife. After their separation,

---

[18] See ROBINSON, W. Sydney. *Muckraker: The Scandalous Life and Times of W. T. Stead: Britain's First Investigative Journalist*. London: Robson Press, 2012.

[19] See Chapter 3.

his own chastity, likely similar to that of Annie Besant, prevented them from getting a divorce, for which adultery was then the only possible legal justification.

In the 1893 version of her autobiography, Besant made more explicit reference to her wedding night: 'Many an unhappy marriage dates from its very beginning, from the terrible shock to a young girl's sensitive modesty and pride, her helpless bewilderment and fear.' It is clear that Frank Besant imposed his husbandly rights on her without any regard for her ignorance, with the same brutal impatience that would thereafter characterize their relationship. This explains why Besant would become one of the very first Victorian women to dare to allude to marital rape in clear terms. In 1878, in an essay titled *Marriage, As It Was, As It Is, and As It Should Be: A Plea for Reform*, Besant described in detail the past and present legal status of married women, and explained:

> A married woman loses control over her own body; it belongs to her owner, not to herself; no force, no violence, on the husband's part in conjugal relations is regarded as possible by the law; she may be suffering, ill, it matters not; force or constraint is recognised by the law as rape, [...] no rape can be committed by a husband on a wife; the consent given in marriage is held to cover the life [...].

Nevertheless, the reasons for the failure of Annie and Frank Besant's marriage went even deeper. In her autobiography, Besant acknowledges their incompatibility in temperament, but also her lack of interest in being a Victorian middle-class wife, an admission both courageous and subversive at the time.

Cheltenham: Loneliness and Boredom

In January of 1868, Frank Besant was appointed mathematics teacher at Cheltenham College, a private boy's school. Annie and he moved to Cheltenham, an elegant spa town in the Cotswolds, where they spent the first three years of their marriage. Socially isolated in this small town where she did not know anyone, the young Mrs. Besant only received visits from other teachers' wives. She barely took any pleasure in them, recalling in her autobiography those:

> [...] ladies visiting me who talked only of servants and babies — troubles of which I knew nothing — who were profoundly uninterested in everything that had formed my previous life, in theology, in politics, in questions of social reform, and who looked on me as 'strange' because I cared more for the great struggles outside than for the discussions of a housemaid's young man, or the amount of 'butter when dripping would have done perfectly well, my dear,' used by the cook [...].

Her humorous tone here hardly softened her ferocious criticism of the domestic role to which middle-class wives were reduced, but also of those 'ladies', willingly complicit to their own servitude.

It is surprising to observe that Besant discovered the demands of this role, especially that of maintaining a bourgeois household, only after her marriage. At just twenty years old, she had to impose herself on the servants who took shameless advantage of her inexperience. Such was the paradox of an education whose end goal was to charm potential husbands, but which hardly offered any preparation for the concrete demands of the 'job' of being a wife and mother. In 1787, in *Thoughts on the Education of Daughters*, Mary Wollstonecraft had already outlined this aberration: eighty years later, Besant was still a victim of it.

In her autobiography, Besant dissected the reasons why her marriage had failed. She told of her neglecting domestic chores, in order to return to her books and her writing as quickly as possible. Faced with her husband's demands that she conformed to a more traditional model, Besant proved herself to be fractious, rebellious even: 'in truth, I ought never to have married, for under the soft, loving, pliable girl there lay hidden, as much unknown to herself as to her surroundings, a woman of strong dominant will, strength that panted for expression and rebelled against restraint.' Her husband responded violently to this lack of obedience and respect to which he believed he was entitled, supported in that by the patriarchal Victorian society: 'he, with very high ideas of a husband's authority and a wife's submission, holding strongly to the "master-in-my-own-house theory"', Besant recalled. In reaction, she ended up erecting: 'a wall of ice round me within which I waged mental conflicts that nearly killed me.' Despite those hardships, Besant was aware of the significance of her new self-awareness. If Frank had shown himself to be patient and understanding, if he had given her sufficient space to express herself, it is possible that Besant would have been content as a clergyman's wife, spent between theological reflections and charitable works.

Her Children's births

The Besants shut themselves away in bitterness, but that did not keep Frank from imposing marital rights on his wife, a physical expression of the domination that he knew otherwise eluded him. Arthur Digby Besant was born on 16 January 1869. The pregnancy had been difficult, and the young couple could not afford a nurse. It took Besant several weeks to recover, but she said that she enjoyed taking care of Digby. She soon became pregnant again, and Mabel Emily was born on 28 August 1870. She was born prematurely, in all likelihood after Frank beat his pregnant wife, during an episode that was cited by Winterbotham, the family doctor, during the trial for Mabel's custody in 1878.

In the spring of 1871, the two children came down with whooping cough. Digby recovered, but Mabel, who was weaker, developed pneumonia. She hovered between life and death for several weeks, and her mother kept vigil beside her with no rest, only able to watch as her daughter suffocated during terrible coughing fits followed by convulsions. In desperation, she made the child inhale small doses of chloroform to calm her. This unconventional treatment allowed Mabel to rest and to overcome the illness, which nevertheless left her epileptic.

Besant, exhausted by these close births and by Mabel's illness, sank into a deep depression. Without any access to contraception, she lived in terror of becoming pregnant again. She tried to resist her husband's sexual advances, which only made him more violent, to the point that, when her depression was at its deepest, Besant considered killing herself with the remaining chloroform.

First Publications

Before this weariness consumed her, Annie Besant sought refuge in reading and in writing. Continuing the theological reflections from her adolescence, she set about writing biographies of the Black Letter Saints in 1868, those unsung martyrs whose names were printed in black in the Anglican calendar, as opposed to those whose names were written in red, and who were still commemorated. Besant assembled all of the religious history works available to her, and was satisfied enough in her compilation to submit it to Macmillan, who published Victorian thinkers as influential as Charles Kingsley or Matthew Arnold. They might have perceived it as naïve arrogance if Besant had not specified that her work could be included in their collection of religious books for children. Still, unsurprisingly, she did not receive any response from the publisher. A little while later, a religious congregation asked for the right to publish her Black Letter Saints' lives for free: she never saw her manuscript again and no trace of this work exists.

It is interesting to notice that Besant tried to be published very early on. Writing, as attested by the number of remarkable female Victorian novelists and essayists, was one of the rare acceptable paid occupations for middle-class women, even married ones, under the condition that they write about appropriate topics, of course. Besant kept that in mind, even though she crossed a limit set by her mother by throwing herself into fiction. She wrote a short story called 'Sunshine and Shade', which featured a young married couple who were the opposites of Annie and Frank Besant: in love, respectful of one another, and immersed in happiness — until a horse accident leaves the wife paralysed. With the unfailing support of her husband, she overcomes her despair, and they both turn their house into a nursing home for invalids.

That time, Besant proved herself judicious when she submitted this enlightening story to the *Family Herald*, a very respectable Victorian family weekly founded in 1843, self-described as 'Select Reading for Leisure Moments. Interesting to All — Offensive to None. Facts and Philosophy for Gentlemen. Hints and Entertainment for Ladies.' A few weeks later, Besant received an acceptance letter, accompanied by a cheque for thirty shillings[20]. Besant recalled the joy that she felt: 'It was the first money I had ever earned, and the pride of the earning was added to the pride of authorship.'

It would be wrong to see any greed in that reaction. Besant delighted, before anything else, in this fragment of autonomy: 'it was "my very own," I thought, and a delightful sense of independence came over me.' She even began to imagine herself as being rich 'and becoming quite a support of the household.' That a married woman should rejoice in financial independence and dream of replacing her husband as breadwinner went against all Victorian patriarchal patterns. Incidentally, the law protected society from what was then considered a dangerous deviancy, and Frank Besant used it to his advantage. Indeed, until the Married Women's Property Act 1870, a husband owned all of his wife's assets and earnings, acquired before or after their marriage. Besant only learned of this when Frank pocketed her cheque. In getting married, she had abdicated all legal existence in favour of her husband[21]. As a pathetic form of rebellion, the short story was published in the 2 May 1868 issue of the *Family Herald*, signed 'A. W.' (Annie Wood) instead of 'A. B.' (Annie Besant).

Frank Besant appropriated all that his wife was paid for the few other short stories published in the *Family Herald*, publications that were interrupted by her first pregnancy. Prophetically, the weekly meanwhile rejected the novel that she sent them, now lost, because it was 'too political.'

[20] About £100–120 in the mid-2010s. http://www.measuringworth.com/ukcompare/

[21] See Chapter 3.

Supporting Farm Labourers in Lincolnshire

In 1871, Rev. Frank Besant was finally offered a parish living thanks to William Wood, by then Lord Hatherley, from whom Annie Besant had taken upon herself to request assistance. Her husband saw this as a humiliation and bitterly reproached her for it. The parish living, which he nonetheless accepted, and where he would spend the rest of his life, was located in Sibsey, a small town with then about 800 inhabitants in the Fens. Annie Besant had finally become the wife of an Anglican priest, as she had naively dreamed. Ironically, she had by then once again fallen prey to religious doubts. To make up for this, she took her charitable deeds to heart, particularly when it came to the farm labourers, whom she found to be living in extreme poverty. In her autobiography, she described their cramped cottages, in which up to eleven people spanning four generations were crammed into a single room. Those cottages had leaking roofs that let in rain, because the farmers, who had to pay exorbitant rents to the great aristocratic landowners, did not look after the housing they provided to their farm hands, and paid them pittances.

In 1872, Methodist preacher Joseph Arch organized farm labourers into a vast union, the National Agricultural Labourers' Union, a first. He offered 'to elevate the social position of the farm labourers of the county by assisting them to increase their wages; to lessen the number of ordinary working hours; to improve their habitations; to provide them with gardens or allotments'[22]. Annie Besant immediately supported these demands, but the nearby farmers resisted by refusing work to anyone remotely involved with the union. During one of her visits to these poor people, Besant discovered, horrified, a destitute family in a tiny cottage where a dead child lay in the only bed, while the mother too was dying.

Recalling the lessons of Radical William Roberts, Besant wondered why farmers made these miserable labourers pay the price of their own difficulties, rather than turning against the often absentee aristocratic

[22] ARCH, Joseph. *The Story of his Life Told by Himself*. London: Hutchinson & Co., 1898, p. 87.

landowners, who demanded increasingly high rents for their land: 'They made common cause with their enemy, [...] instead of leaguing themselves with the laborers [*sic*], as forming together the true agricultural interest.' Besant observed this with anger and compassion, but also reflected on the situation: 'seeing all this, I learned some useful lessons, and the political education progressed.' The issue of land reform would return regularly to her, whether referring to Ireland or India, and she later worked alongside Joseph Arch himself.

Her political consciousness created a new contentious rift between Annie and Frank Besant: as a Tory, Frank naturally aligned with the landowners and their farmers. Annie Besant fled his increasing violence by visiting her mother in London for long stretches of time in 1872. Emily Wood had been ruined by an unscrupulous lawyer; she had lost her house in St Leonards and lived with her unmarried son Harry, who worked at a fairly modest level for the Royal Society of Arts. Humiliated by her dependence, the proud Emily Wood was in poor health. All the same, Annie Besant took advantage of her stays in London to attempt to resolve her religious questioning.

Losing her Christian Faith

In her autobiography, Annie Besant detailed the process that led her to lose her Christian faith. The reason is obvious in the 1885 version, written when she defined herself as an atheist and was fighting for secularism. Nevertheless, she revisited this long transition extensively when she revised her autobiography in 1893, four years after converting to Theosophy. This shows that her renewed faith in spirituality was not a return to the Anglican Christianity of her youth, nor to the dogmas that she had rejected after three long and painful years of theological reflection.

These pages in her autobiography reveal a process of 'deconversion'[23],

[23] See MACKAY, Carol Hanbery. 'Confounding or Amazing? The Multiple Deconversions of Annie Besant'. *Quest* 90.2, March–April 2002, pp. 50–6

which occurred several times in Besant's life. Her detractors, unfortunately often relied upon by her biographers, used this against her, arguing an instability or suggestibility in keeping with their often gender-biased prejudices. Yet, in both versions of her autobiography, both published shortly after a conversion — to socialism in 1885, and to Theosophy in 1893 — Besant retraced the logic of her decisions, which she considered long and difficult in coming, because, as an intellectual, she was always wary of her initial emotions and first attempted to overcome them.

The religious doubts that Besant had suppressed resurfaced at a moment of psychological exhaustion, during her daughter's long illness. Like so many before her, she wondered how a supposedly merciful God could accept such tortures, inflicted upon a toddler. Her despair was amplified by her marital difficulties, and by the hardships that she observed among the poor of Sibsey, whom she assisted during the typhoid epidemic of 1872.

For once acknowledging his helplessness, Frank Besant asked for assistance from another local Anglican clergyman, whose conventional consoling words made Annie Besant's doubts even stronger, despite the sympathy that she felt for him. She read the essays by Christian socialist F. D. Maurice that he recommended to her, as well as those of Robertson[24], a theologian who was just as dedicated to social action. Like her mother, she immersed herself into the writings of Stanley, the Dean of Westminster, but also into those of Liddon[25], an Anglo-Catholic priest whose lectures on the divinity of Christ had appeased more than one Victorian sceptic. All of them had managed to reconcile doubts and faith, sometimes by choosing the path of action, often at the cost of fragile theological compromises which hardly convinced Besant.

Still incapable of separating religion and spirituality, her rejection of the dogmatism and inconsistencies of the one led her to deny the very existence of the other, despite these words from her clergyman friend: 'Know Christ and judge religions by him; don't judge him by religions.' Besant therefore read Matthew Arnold, the great agnostic thinker, whose poem 'Dover Beach'

[24] Frederick William Robertson (1816–1853).

[25] Henry P. Liddon (1829–1890).

remains one of the most beautiful expressions of Victorian religious doubt:

> The Sea of Faith
> Was once, too, at the full, and round earth's shore
> Lay like the folds of a bright girdle furled.
> But now I only hear
> Its melancholy, long, withdrawing roar,
> Retreating, to the breath
> Of the night-wind, down the vast edges drear
> And naked shingles of the world.

Matthew Arnold composed this poem in 1851, during his honeymoon, and the last stanza calls to the consoling forces of earthly love: 'Ah, love, let us be true / To one another!' Besant, trapped in a loveless marriage, could find no such refuge, and sank even more deeply into depression.

Winterbotham, the family doctor, tried to distract her from her theological ruminations by lending her scientific works. The immediate consequences of this gesture surely exceeded his intentions, since Besant decided to adopt a scientific approach to all Christian dogmas, 'so that I should never again say "I believe" where I had not proved.' She thus studied eternal punishment, mercy, vicarious atonement and Biblical inspiration. Despite her attempts at scientific objectivity, Besant conceded in 1893 that her rejection of these dogmas was, above all else, ethical. She took advantage of her long stays in London to visit her mother to do theological research. In her autobiography, she explained with bitter irony:

> So it will easily be understood that my religious wretchedness only increased the unhappiness of home [...]. Surely it was a woman's business to attend to her husband's comforts and to see after her children, and not to break her heart over misery here and hell hereafter, and distract her brain with questions that had puzzled the greatest thinkers and still remained unsolved!

She lucidly concluded, in the context of her era: 'truly, women or men who get themselves concerned about the universe at large, would do well not to plunge hastily into marriage.'

Yet, religious tolerance reigned in Victorian London. All of the branches of Christianity were represented, down to the most marginal, alongside spiritualists, freethinkers and believers in all the main religions of the Empire. Preachers of all kinds filled not only churches, but also conference halls and their sermons and pamphlets circulated liberally[26]. London in 1872 lent itself admirably to Besant's quest.

Theism

Annie Besant went to listen to the sermons of Theist preacher Charles Voysey at St. George's Hall. Voysey had been excluded from the Anglican Church and had just founded a Theist church in London. He still believed in the existence and unity of an immanent and transcendent God, with whom a personal relationship was possible, but he rejected the doctrines and dogmas of the Church. Voysey's sermons gave Besant a glimmer of hope that she could continue believing in God: 'a gleam of light across the stormy sea of doubt and distress on which I had so long been tossing.' She wrote several poems during this moment of appeasement:

> Human speech has not broken
>   The stillness supernatural,
> Yet there ever is spoken
>   Through silence eternal,
> With growing distinctness
>   God's thought of Himself.

Besant became friends with the Voysey family, who suggested that she read the writings of Theist Francis Newman — brother of Catholic convert Cardinal Newman — especially his 1867 essay *On the Defective Morality of the New Testament*. Thanks to them, she also discovered the writings of Irish

[26] See SMITH, Warren S. *The London Heretics: 1870–1914*. London: Constable, 1967.

feminist Frances Power Cobbe, a Unitarian preacher who was involved in social struggles. Finally, she met freethinker Thomas Scott through them. At the same time, Besant began to become interested in Islam, Buddhism and Hinduism. Voysey even introduced her to the great orientalist John Muir. These readings and meetings led Besant to put the specificity of Christianity into perspective, and from there, to doubt Christ's divinity.

Besant's intellectual struggle with this last rampart against atheism was 'a sharp one', she said. However, aware of the implications for an Anglican clergyman's wife of abandoning the Christian faith, she gave herself one last chance. She managed to meet Edward Pusey at Oxford, whom she had previously admired, and with whom she had already been corresponding. The interview was a complete failure. Pusey proved himself patronizing: 'He treated me as a penitent going to confession, seeking the advice of a director, not as an enquirer struggling after truth', she recalled. Pusey was horrified by the doubts that this young woman dared to express regarding Christ's divinity, and could only tell her: 'You are blaspheming; the very thought is a terrible sin […]; you have read too much already. You must pray.' He rejected all scepticism, all questioning:

> 'It is not your duty to ascertain the truth,' he told me sternly. 'It is your duty to accept and to believe the truth as laid down by the Church; at your peril you reject it; the responsibility is not yours so long as you dutifully accept that which the Church has laid down for your acceptance.'

Besant, on the contrary, described herself as being 'hot, eager, passionate in my determination to know, resolute not to profess belief while belief was absent', and resolved not to partake in the slightest of 'that meek, chastened, submissive spirit to which he was accustomed in the penitents wont to seek his counsel as their spiritual guide.' Accordingly, he accused her of being 'full of intellectual pride', although Besant could take it as a compliment by then. When walking back to the Oxford train station, she concluded that: 'Out of such men were made the Inquisitors of the Middle Ages.' Yet, upon Pusey's death in September 1882, Besant, an atheist at that point, paid homage to the man (not to the theologian, though) in the secular weekly the *National Reformer*, admiring, she said, his sincerity, courage, refusal to compromise and integrity, setting aside their profound spiritual disagreement. These were qualities that Besant would constantly seek to develop and promote in herself.

Ultimatum and Separation

Annie Besant returned to Sibsey in the autumn of 1872. Believing in sincerity, she announced to Frank that she would no longer take communion from that day on, not even at the church where he presided, which she would leave just before the Eucharist. Contrary to some other Protestant denominations, Anglicans have retained the sacrament of the Eucharist, the symbol of Christ's divinity. Besant's refusal to take part in it therefore had a powerful symbolic impact. Encouraged by Thomas Scott, Besant wrote an essay called *On the Deity of Jesus of Nazareth*[27], which was published in the *Scott Series* in the spring of 1873, with a preface by Charles Voysey. The text was signed in a provocative manner: 'By the Wife of a Beneficed Clergyman.' Her brother-in-law, Walter Besant, easily saw through this, and sent the essay to her husband. At the same time, Besant compiled a collection of hymns for Voysey's Theist church, even though her husband had tried to forbid her from corresponding with him.

As summer drew to its close and Besant had already sought refuge with her brother in London, Frank, fearing for his reputation before anything else, gave an ultimatum to her: the Eucharist, or definitive separation. Annie Besant chose the second option and left her husband. She was twenty-five at the time, and this brave choice, dictated by the integrity and refusal to compromise that determined her entire path, automatically removed her from respectable Victorian society.

Divorce, difficult and onerous anyway, was impossible for them:

[27] 'By the Wife of a Beneficed Clergyman' [Annie Besant]. *On the Deity of Jesus of Nazareth. An Enquiry into the Nature of Jesus by an Examination of the Synoptic Gospels*. Edited and prefaced by Rev. Charles Voysey. London: T. Scott, 1873.

although the Divorce and Matrimonial Causes Act 1857 had made the procedure easier, adultery had to be established on the part of the wife or husband (the latter also had to commit abandonment, acts of cruelty, incest or bigamy), and no adultery had occurred in their case. On the advice of her brother, Harry Wood, who was aware of the marital abuse that she had endured, Besant negotiated a deed of separation with his help. She cited the recent Married Woman's Property Act 1870, which stipulated that wives were thereafter allowed to retain their own incomes, in order to free herself financially from her husband. However, there still remained the question of their children. Annie Besant referred to the Custody of Infants Act, amended in April 1873: it allowed the mother to demand visitation rights or custody for children under sixteen. She thus gained custody of Mabel, as well as a small child support payment of £110, approximately a quarter of Frank Besant's income. Digby, for his part, was to stay with his father, and his mother only had visitation rights for one month out of the year. Still legally married to Frank, up to his death in 1917, Annie Besant was obliged to keep her married name, but she modified the pronunciation, moving the stress from the second to the first syllable.

Until the end, Emily Wood, who feared shame above all else, tried to dissuade her daughter from legally separating from her husband. She knew only too well that Besant would forever after suffer the same fate as those middle-class Victorian women who, deprived of male support and victims of an education that only prepared them for marriage, had to face a near-total absence of prospects in a society that marginalized them. Besant's situation was even worse than Emily Wood's, since she was neither a widow, nor unmarried, but separated from her husband: 'the mere fact that a woman is young and alone justifies any coarseness of slander', she soon discovered. Yet, when she revised her autobiography in 1893, Besant had no regrets:

> Then I did not guess how cruel men and women could be, how venomous their tongues; now, knowing it, having faced slander and lived it down, I deliberately say that were the choice again before me I would choose as I chose then; I would rather go through it all again than live in 'Society' under the burden of an acted lie.

Her brother would only allow her to continue living with him if she promised to stop seeing her '"heretical friends" and keep quiet', an ultimatum that was sadly reminiscent of that set by Frank a few weeks earlier. Besant refused, of course: 'being freed from one bondage, nothing was further from my thoughts than to enter another.' Despite the legal assistance and the moral support that he had initially offered, Harry Wood closed his door to his sister.

Financial Difficulties

In 1872, Annie Besant had met Moncure D. Conway. Once he and his wife learned that she had separated from her husband, they invited her and Mabel into their home. With remarkable open-mindedness, they gave her permission to stay as long as she needed. Years later, she still recalled their 'kindness generously shown when I was poor and had but few friends.' She did not stay for long at the Conways', however, protective as she was of her dearly won independence, but their influence, help and friendship would be decisive in the next phase of her path.

Conway came from a family of Virginia plantation owners. In the 1850s, his discovery of Ralph Waldo Emerson's transcendentalism led him to fight for the abolition of slavery and to become a Unitarian preacher. He moved to London in 1863, in order to rally the British to the abolitionist cause, and never left. Even though he was a preacher at a Finsbury church, his faith turned to Theism, then toward a form of humanist freethinking. The Conways evolved in Radical and feminist circles, and their friends and correspondents included Charles Dickens, Thomas Carlyle, Robert Browning, and Charles Darwin.

Between the Voyseys, the Scotts and the Conways, Annie Besant found herself in a particularly stimulating intellectual and freethinking environment, where her intelligence, culture and curiosity were appreciated and soon put to use. She decided to move close to the Scotts, managing to rent 'a tiny house' on Gipsy Hill, in Norwood.

The child support that Frank paid her was too small to allow Besant and her daughter to live up to the demands of their middle-class rank; yet, such was the social price of giving up on those demands that she feared she would die of 'respectable starvation'. Frank had managed to retain all of the couple's moveable assets, except for a few of his wife's personal effects. Besant therefore had to furnish her home all over again. Both her situation and her pride kept her from asking her family for any financial assistance, so she decided to earn her living, and quickly realized both her naivety and lack of skills.

In a few weeks, Besant made her way through the few opportunities of paid work available to a young middle-class woman. She tried her hand at needlework, offered to 'ladies in reduced circumstances' out of their own homes. Clearly exploited, she only managed to earn a shilling a week, even less than if she had worked in a factory. The employment agencies to which she applied only found her similar occupations, while demanding payment for their unhelpful advice.

Besant therefore accepted a position as a governess, so as to save enough money to furnish her little London house. In many respects, she fit the profile. In 1848, the *Quarterly Review*, a respectable conservative periodical, described the ideal governess in its famous review of *Jane Eyre*[28] as 'our equal in birth, manners, and education, but our inferior in worldly wealth.' The governess had to impart the values and codes of the middle class, and pass on the superficial culture that she herself had acquired in the — generally unfulfilled — hope of getting married. To most Victorians, however, Besant was in a precarious financial situation of her own making, which went against respectability: by refusing to conform to her role as a wife, and by expressing religious doubts, it was felt she only had herself to blame for her difficulties.

Ironically, Besant was hired by an Anglican vicar, Mr. Woodward of Folkestone. The good man knew Besant's grandmother and her two maternal aunts, who were living in Folkestone, and he believed that her

[28] [RIGBY, Elizabeth.] '*Vanity Fair* and *Jane Eyre*'. *Quarterly Review* 84.167, December 1848, pp. 153–85.

spiritual crisis was just a phase, 'sent as trial by the Lord', he said. Besant was happy to teach his children, but: 'I became head cook as well as governess and nurse', she wrote, as the vicar found it pointless to replace the two servants who then left his employment. His wife being of poor health, he also trusted Besant with caring for his children when they came down with diphtheria, then scarlet fever. It was thus with relief that she returned to her little house in London in the spring of 1874. She hoped to live there with her mother, but fate had decided otherwise.

Her Mother's Death

Upon her arrival back in London, Annie Besant received a telegram from her brother saying that their mother was dying. Exhausted by concern and sorrow, Emily Wood no longer had the will to live, and her heart was giving out. Besant watched over her during weeks of suffering that Victorian medicine could not relieve. However, to the very end, Emily Wood tried to impose her views on her daughter. She thus demanded that Besant take communion with her during her last rites, preferring, she affirmed, not without pathos, damnation to never seeing her daughter in Heaven. Even though Besant was as rigid and stubborn as her mother, her adoration for her was as irrational as it was immense. While she had preferred the social disgrace of leaving her husband rather than taking communion, she nevertheless conceded to do so for her mother.

Besant then encountered a difficulty that foretold the struggles she would soon undertake for freethought. Because she made a point of mentioning her lack of faith in Christ's divinity to them, all of the clergymen to whom she spoke refused to include her in communion. In desperation, Besant decided to go see Arthur P. Stanley himself, the Dean of Westminster, whom her mother admired. Her intuition proved correct, for this great reformist and liberal theologian agreed to come in person to talk to Emily Wood, who was at death's door, but also to Besant. His attitude was quite different from Pusey's: far from being horrified, or even trying to bring Besant back to the faith, he contented himself with explaining to her why he would still give her communion. The humanist definition that he gave of his Christianity deeply marked Besant. It influenced her personal ethic, and, after 1889, her renewed spirituality. Significantly, she recounted Stanley's words in detail, not only in the 1893 version of her autobiography, but in the 1885 one already:

> He finally told me that conduct was far more important than theory, and that he regarded all as 'Christians' who recognised and tried to follow the moral law. On the question of the absolute Deity of Jesus he laid but little stress; Jesus was, 'in a special sense,' the 'Son of God,' but it was folly to jangle about words with only human meanings when dealing with the mysteries of divine existence [...]. The one important matter was the recognition of 'duty to God and man,' and all who were one in that recognition might rightfully join in an act of worship, the essence of which was not acceptance of dogma, but love of God and self-sacrifice for man. 'The Holy Communion,' he said, in his soft tones, 'was never meant to divide from each other hearts that are searching after the one true God; it was meant by its founder as a symbol of unity, not of strife.'

Stanley also assuaged Emily Wood's concerns for her daughter's soul. His words, as reported by her mother, considerably influenced Besant: 'remember that our God is the God of truth, and that therefore the honest search for truth can never be displeasing in his eyes.' Stanley had perfectly understood Besant's motivations, and had managed to justify them, not only in Emily Wood's eyes, but also in her own.

Her mother died two days after Besant brought her to their little house in Norwood, in May 1874. 'You have always been too religious', Emily Wood reproached her with tenderness, just before she died. She knew how much her daughter's exaltations and hardships were part of an intense spiritual quest, which was only just beginning. Emily Wood was buried in Kensal Green Cemetery, alongside her husband and little Alfie.

Besant's love for her mother was so strong that it is difficult to imagine the next phase in her intellectual and spiritual life had her mother not died prematurely. Emily Wood exercised a considerable amount of emotional control over her daughter, and she would doubtless have been quite critical of her stances. Emily Wood was surely the only person capable to make Besant compromise, as her insistence on making her take communion shows.

Pamphleteer for Thomas Scott

Annie Besant was devastated: despite Mabel's presence, she felt frightfully alone, and still had to face financial difficulties, to the point of regularly missing meals. The contemporary reader of her autobiography is astonished then to read that in spite of it all she had hired a servant, Mary. The first reason for this was due to social conventions, for a family could not claim to belong to the middle class without domestic help. Besant, whose respectability was at this point so fragile and yet indispensable to her social survival, could not allow herself to break this tacit social rule. The second reason was pragmatic: at a time when washing machines, vacuums or even efficient detergents did not exist, when heat came from coal fires, when stoves could never be allowed to go out, and when running water was limited to one or two cold taps, maintaining a house, even one as small as hers, was a full-time job, especially in a city as dirty and polluted as London[29]. Without Mary's precious and efficient help, whom she called 'the most thoughtful and most generous of comrades', Besant would never have been able to start her career as a pamphleteer, then as a lecturer, and she was grateful for it.

Thomas Scott asked her to write theological essays for his *Scott's Series*. Scott, of Catholic origins, had been a page at the court of French King Charles X. He had then used his personal fortune to travel, especially to North America, where he had spent several years among Native Americans. After losing his faith in 1856, Scott established himself in London, where his house became a freethinking salon. Scott financially supported Voysey's

[29] See FLANDERS, Judith. *The Victorian House: Domestic Life from Childbirth to Deathbed*. London: Harper Perennial, 2003.

Theist church and published his *Scott's Series* out of his own pocket from 1862, for 'love of Truth and desire to spread Freedom among men.' In line with Strauss and Renan, he wrote an *English Life of Jesus* in 1872, specifically meant for an English readership[30].

The few guineas[31] that Besant received for her writings were most welcome. Researching her essays allowed her to pursue her self-education, in a continuous and structured way, and confirmed her taste for studying, reflection, and writing. Very few research places were open to Victorian women, then excluded from most universities and their libraries. There was one notable exception, however, dating from 1857: the Reading Room of the British Museum. Its first handbook read: 'The reading room of the British Museum is open to men and women of any country, or shade of political or other opinions.' Users had to apply in writing to be issued a reader's ticket by the Principal Librarian, but in practice, access to the entire catalogue was granted to almost anyone, including women. As a result, the Reading Room became an important research and meeting place for them, and Besant joined a prestigious line of intellectual women, stretching from George Eliot before her to Virginia Woolf after, who all made the most out of this rare opportunity[32].

Besant spent entire days in the Reading Room, reading Spinoza, Charles Darwin, John Stuart Mill and Auguste Comte. Her essays, now signed under her own name, were serious indictments of the Church's dogmas. At this time, Besant still considered herself to be a Theist, but her writings revealed how close she was to taking a leap in the dark into atheism.

---

[30] WHEELER, J. M. 'Scott, Thomas (1808–1878)' (revised by H.C.G. Matthew), *Oxford Dictionary of National Biography*, Oxford University Press, 2004.

[31] A guinea was worth 21 shillings in the Victorian era. The gold coin had been withdrawn from circulation in 1816, but its name remained.

[32] See HOBERMAN, Ruth. 'Women in the British Museum Reading Room during the Late-Nineteenth and Early-Twentieth Centuries: From Quasi- to Counterpublic'. *Feminist Studies* 28.3, Autumn 2002, pp. 489–512.

2

Annie Besant's Struggles for Freethought and Secularism (1874–1890)[1]

Religious Context

In order to assess the issues at work in Annie Besant's rejection of Christianity and her struggles for freethought and secularism, it is essential to describe the religious context[2] in which she evolved. Today, it is difficult to understand the importance Christianity held in Victorian society, which extended well beyond individual faith. Christian values had a tremendous impact on the era, and they were expressly supported by the vast majority of the ruling classes. The Bible remained a primary reference, to the point of branding Victorian minds with an indelible imprint, including those of a large proportion of radical militants, trade unionists, and socialists.

There is no separation between Church and State in Great Britain. Since the Reform launched by Henry VIII in the early 1530s — with the exception of his daughter Mary's short reign and Cromwell's Puritan Interregnum in the seventeenth century — Anglicanism has been the established religion in England and Wales. Queen Victoria, like all sovereigns since Elizabeth I,

---

[1] See BESANT, Annie. *Autobiographical Sketches*. London: Freethought Publishing Co., 1885 (republished and annotated by MACKAY, Carol Hanbery, ed., Peterborough, Ont.: Broadview Press Ltd, 2009); *Annie Besant: An Autobiography*. London: T. Fisher Unwin, 1893; and *My Path to Atheism*. London: Freethought Publishing Co., 1885 (3rd ed.); as well as NETHERCOT, Arthur Hobart. *The First Five Lives of Annie Besant*. University of Chicago Press, 1960.

[2] See COSTE, Bénédicte, ed. *Believing in Victorian Times, Cahiers victoriens et édouardiens* 76. Montpellier: Presses Universitaires de la Méditerranée, October 2012.

was the Supreme Governor of the Church of England. The 'C of E' is headed by the Archbishop of Canterbury, appointed by the Sovereign, on the advice of the Prime Minister. From 1868 to 1882, the Archbishop of Canterbury was Archibald Tait.

The Archbishops of Canterbury and York, as well as around twenty other Bishops, have an automatic right to sit in the House of Lords, where these 'Lords Spiritual' also have the right to vote. Archibald Tait was very active in Parliament, and often used his legislative power. He slightly relaxed the demands of the Established Church, for instance supporting the Burial Laws Amendment Act 1880 that allowed non-Anglicans to be buried in a parish cemetery according to their own funeral rites — a reform which also pleased believers in other faiths as well as atheists.

Even though Anglicanism was defined, since Elizabeth I, as a *via media* between Calvinism and Catholicism, the Church of England always comprised different theological tendencies. In the Victorian era, three main movements emerged. In the 1830s, the High Church Movement, also known as the Oxford Movement, developed as part of the Anglo-Catholic revival led by John Henry Newman — who, for his part, ended up converting to Catholicism and becoming a Cardinal. This movement was later primarily represented by Edward Pusey, whom Besant had consulted at the height of her religious doubts. Besant, like her mother, was emotionally close to this High Church Movement, to the point that her friends and family had briefly feared that she would convert to Catholicism.

Emily Wood was more moderate than her daughter, however, appreciating above all the aesthetic choices of the High Church Movement. Thanks to her husband's influence, she was theologically more aligned to the Broad Church Movement, the liberal, latitudinarian branch of the C of E. It was a rather intellectual and relatively tolerant movement, and so generally favoured by Government institutions. Stanley, who agreed to give Emily Wood last rites and to take communion with atheist Besant, belonged to this movement.

Within the Victorian Anglican Church, these two branches struggled to coexist with the Low Church Movement, a more puritanical tendency, close to Calvinism. It was part of the Evangelical revival that had begun at the end of the eighteenth century, in reaction to the rationalist Deism that developed at the time of the American and French revolutions. Evangelicalism had a considerable influence during the first half of the nineteenth century. It declined from the 1850s, but continued despite the weakening of its purely theological component. Evangelical Victorians had to seek salvation, while recognizing the intrinsically corrupt nature of Man and accepting the redeeming sacrifice of Christ. Their mystical faith expressed itself in an emotional and individual relationship with God and with the Bible — more important to them than clergy, rituals and doctrines. This faith also had to be acted upon by making sacrifices for just causes. Evangelicals emphasized charity, social action and the need to lead by virtuous example. Under the guidance of William Wilberforce, they had been very active in the fight for the abolition of slavery in the British Empire, achieved in 1833. Archibald Tait, the Archbishop of Canterbury, who was of Scottish and Presbyterian origins, was close to Evangelicalism. He favoured philanthropy, and actively opposed the ritualism of the High Church Movement with the Public Worship Regulation Act 1874.

In his 1880 book *Duty*[3], moralist Samuel Smiles explored this Victorian value, which directly stemmed from Evangelicalism. Radical Calvinist Smiles had become famous with his 1859 essay *Self-Help*, followed in 1871 by *Character*, then, in 1875, by *Thrift* — his bibliography sounding like a catalogue of the Evangelical values that underpinned Victorian society. To Smiles: 'Life is of little value unless it be consecrated by duty', but he went beyond ethics to reach a spiritual, even mystical dimension:

> As the mind has become enlightened, and conscience shows its power, the responsibility of man increases. He submits himself to the influence of the Supreme Will, and acts in conformity with it — not by constraint, but cheerfully; and the law which holds him is that of Love. In the act of belief, implying knowledge and confidence, his humanity unfolds. He feels that by

[3] SMILES, Samuel. *Duty, with Illustrations of Courage, Patience & Endurance*. London: John Murray, 1880.

> his own free act, his faith in and his working in conformity to the purpose of a Divine Will, he is achieving good, and securing the highest good. [...]
>
> [Duty] does not follow the routine of worldly-wise morality. It does not advertise itself. It adopts a larger creed and a loftier code; which to be subject to and to obey, is to consider every human life, and every human action, in the light of an eternal obligation to the race. Our evil or our careless actions incur debts every day, that humanity, sooner or later, must discharge.

Smiles called for people to take refuge in work and action, and denounced the temptation of a contemplative life. He quoted Emanuel Swedenborg, then widely read in Britain, advocating 'not a life of retirement from the world, but of action in the world.'

It was these Evangelical values and principles that Ellen Marryat had imparted to Annie Besant. Although Besant ended up rejecting Christianity in 1874, she retained the Evangelical ethic of sacrifice. Walter E. Houghton explained in *The Victorian Frame of Mind* that the Evangelical Gospel of Work had come to the rescue of many a Victorian agnostic:

> Its ideals penetrated into the homes – and consciousness – of half-believers and outright agnostics. Most retained the ethical fervor of the childhood belief they had discarded. But it was not merely a matter of ingrained habits. [...] Intellectual radicalism produced a frightened clinging to conservative morals, especially at a time when agnosticism was under attack for its supposed tendency to destroy the moral life.

He continued by quoting agnostic George Eliot: 'The words God, Immortality, Duty: how inconceivable was the first, how unbelievable was the second, and yet how peremptory and absolute the third.'

Evangelicalism encompassed not only Low Church Anglicans but also a number of Non-Conformist or Dissenting Protestants. The term Dissenters had appeared in 1662 to designate the members of different Protestant denominations, especially Presbyterians, Baptists, Quakers and Congregationalists, who refused to join the Anglican Church when it was restored under Charles II. Methodists, led by John Wesley, also separated from the Anglican Church upon his death in 1791.

The Victorian Spiritual Crisis[4]

Annie Besant's spiritual crisis occurred in a context of religious questioning, when a number of Victorians had their faith shaken by the increasingly frequent debates regarding scientific discoveries, Biblical exegesis and comparative religious studies.

In the early Victorian era, to most people there was no contradiction between faith and science. Oxford and Cambridge universities were Anglican institutions, and half of their students became Anglican clergymen. So were their science lecturers, who taught 'natural theology', that is to say, God's work in the world, understandable through reason and experience, as opposed to 'revealed theology' from the Scriptures[5]. Nevertheless, from the 1830s, Victorians began to contemplate evolution and the laws of nature. Geologist Charles Lyell published *Principles of Geology* in 1833, in which he explained that landscapes had slowly been formed by natural processes that were still at work, especially erosion. He concluded that the Earth was much older than Genesis appeared to say. Another geologist, Robert Chambers, found great success in 1844 with his essay *Vestiges of the Natural History of Creation*. In it, he developed a theory of 'transmutation' to demonstrate that everything that exists derives from more ancient forms, including the solar system or Man. Chambers, however, still believed in divine intervention, which he called the First Cause, placing it at the origin of the whole process. For this reason, his theory was widely accepted, even at the highest levels, since Prince Albert read *Vestiges* aloud to Queen Victoria during one of her

[4] See TURNER, Frank M. *Contesting Cultural Authority. Essays in Victorian Intellectual Life*. Cambridge University Press, 1993; LARSEN, Timothy. *Crisis of Doubt: Honest Faith in Nineteenth-Century England*. Oxford University Press, 2006; and NASH, David. 'Reassessing the "Crisis of Faith" in the Victorian Age: Eclecticism and the Spirit of Moral Inquiry'. *Journal of Victorian Culture* 16.1, 2011, pp. 65–82.

[5] See CLAVIER, Paul. *Qu'est-ce que la théologie naturelle*. Paris: Librairie philosophique J. Vrin, 2004.

pregnancies. From then on, to most Victorians, the question no longer was 'do organisms evolve', but rather: 'how and why do they evolve?'

As a consequence, and contrary to popular belief, *On the Origin of Species*, published in 1859, was not a 'revelation': Charles Darwin, who was turned into a secular prophet, actually belonged to a broad movement. Darwin had defined his theory of evolution at the end of the 1830s, but he only decided to publish it after Alfred Russel Wallace, who had come to the same conclusions as him, sent his manuscript to him for review in 1858. Although *On the Origin of Species*, in which Darwin still refrained from speaking about Man, was much discussed, the essay was not as controversial as often described. In fact, for Darwin, the origin of species was not the same as the origin of life: he had not killed God, he had just displaced him, like Chambers before him. It was only in 1871, in *The Descent of Man*, that Darwin showed that Man belonged to the animal kingdom, and had evolved from apes. Even then, debates and caricatures masked the fairly general assent of a vast readership. Darwin himself, while of an extremely anxious nature, wrote: 'everybody is talking about it without being shocked', which he found 'proof of the increasing liberality of England'[6]. Far from being the scientific martyr that some would like him to be, Darwin was buried in Westminster Abbey upon his death in 1882, not far from Isaac Newton[7]. Only the most fundamentalist among Evangelicals still believed in a literal interpretation of Genesis, and they were a small minority. Other British Christians read Genesis as the symbolic narrative of a spiritual truth that was compatible with new scientific discoveries.

Besant had acquired a solid scientific culture during her spiritual crisis, and adopted what she considered as a scientific point of view: in the introduction of her 1878 collection of essays, *My Path to Atheism*, she explained that she had eventually stopped praying because she had come to

---

[6] Cited by DARWIN, Francis, ed. *The Life and Letters of Charles Darwin, Including an Autobiographical Chapter*. 3 vols. London: John Murray, 1887, vol. 3, pp. 133 and 138.

[7] Newton's research into alchemy and astrology are often forgotten by positivist historians. See RIVIÈRE, Jean. 'La Face cachée de Newton: antitrinitarien et alchimiste', in DESCHAMPS, Yannick and Suzy HALIMI, ed. *Orthodoxie et hérésie dans les îles britanniques. Revue française de civilisation britannique* 18.1, Spring 2013, pp. 73–9.

the conclusion that prayer had no scientific validity. She had immediately found the theory of evolution convincing and, she said, 'Darwin had done much towards freeing me from my old bonds.'

Meanwhile, David Strauss's *Das Leben Jesu*, translated in 1846 by George Eliot as *The Life of Jesus*, had launched a new form of Biblical exegesis, which benefited from the development of better organized historical, paleographical and archaeological research. After Strauss, historian John Robert Seeley's *Ecce Homo* (1866), in its turn, underlined the differences between Jesus, the 'historical' man, founder of an institution, the Church, and the 'Biblical' Christ. *La Vie de Jésus* by Ernest Renan also was translated into English as *The Life of Jesus*, shortly after its publication in 1863. Besant read Renan during her spiritual crisis, but she was not convinced by his arguments. She much preferred her friend Thomas Scott's *English Life of Jesus* (1872), which she thought was 'as useful a book on this subject as could be put into the hands of an inquirer.'

Victorian anthropological works, such as *Primitive Culture* by Edward Tylor, published in 1867, began to consider religion in a detached manner, as a social and cultural phenomenon. Tylor developed the idea of a universal cultural evolution, similar to Auguste Comte's Positivism, well known to Victorians in general and to Besant in particular. One of Tylor's disciples was James Frazer, who published *The Golden Bough: A Study in Comparative Religion* in 1890, a very influential comparative study of myths and religions. Before him, the works of German philologist and orientalist Friedrich Max Müller, who had been a professor at Oxford since 1854, had brought the similarities between the Bible and the great sacred texts of other civilizations to light. Müller worked to make these sacred texts known to the general public: their translations were published by Oxford university between 1879 and 1910 in fifty volumes as *The Sacred Books of the East*, which included texts from Hinduism, Buddhism, Taoism, Confucianism, Zoroastrianism, Jainism and Islam. Müller thus contributed to putting Biblical scriptures into perspective, which planted seeds of doubt in some Victorian minds. In *My Path to Atheism*, Besant wrote that, as early as 1872–1873, she had put 'some efforts to understand the creeds of other nations, to investigate Mahommedanism, Buddhism and Hinduism, all led in the same direction, until I concluded that inspiration belonged to all people alike, and there could be no necessity of atonement, and no eternal hell prepared for the unbeliever in Christianity.' Interestingly, in 1878, that is over a decade before her conversion to Theosophy, she concluded: 'there appeared no *raison d'être* for the Incarnation. Besides, there were so many incarnations, and the Buddhist absorption seemed a grander idea.'

This intellectual questioning, to which Besant contributed with her essays and lectures, was compounded by what Victorians perceived with concern as a de-Christianization of the working class. This phenomenon had been revealed by the Religious Census of 1851. Anglican and Dissenting clergymen were asked how many worshippers had attended services on Palm Sunday. Rabbis had to do the same the Saturday before in their synagogues. The other religions, especially Islam, whose believers were thought to be very few, were unfortunately not included in the census.

Victorians were fascinated by statistics, in which they placed hope of supposedly objective and rational reforms. The *Report on Religious Worship*, published in 1853, after two years of compilation and analysis, therefore caused a huge stir. It was written, with great attention paid to synthesis and style, by Horace Mann, a brilliant twenty-eight-year-old civil servant. It revealed a powerful link between social class and the importance of religion and faith. While his figures claimed to be objective, Mann's conclusions were hardly so. He lauded the Dissenting middle classes, whose rate of religious practice was proportionately higher than the rest of the population: Dissenters, who made twenty per cent of the population, represented forty-three per cent of worshippers, and Mann believed them to be sincere Christians, given the disadvantages that still existed for those not belonging to the Established Church. Anglicans, on the other hand, only made fifty-two per cent of worshippers. Mann underlined the social and moral influence of the rising middle classes who had obtained the right to vote in 1832. According to him, the upper classes and the aristocracy, the large majority of whom were Anglicans, had begun to practice regularly again mostly for the sake of decorum, emulating the behaviour of the influential new middle classes.

Meanwhile, the working classes seemed to have deserted churches in large industrial cities. Horace Mann noted: 'a sadly formidable proportion of the English people are habitual neglecters of the public ordinances of religion.' The Victorian middle classes were horrified to learn that only sixty per cent of the total population had attended Palm Sunday services in 1851, and that the vast majority of the absent forty per cent were from the working class. While the most sincere among Christians feared for their souls, the middle and upper classes also dreaded losing a means of social control, with dangerous ideologies or so-called debauchery filling this religious void.

Besant had therefore grown up in a missionary-like religious atmosphere. Archibald Tait's predecessor John Sumner had started a vast campaign to build Anglican churches, especially in the working-class neighbourhoods that had previously been neglected. It was in one of these mission churches in Clapham that Besant had met her husband. The Anglican Church thus managed to remain the primary religious denomination of the country, resisting the competition from Dissenters, especially Methodists, who were very active amongst the poor: the Salvation Army was founded in 1865 by a Methodist preacher, William Booth and his wife Catherine, in the East End of London. Nevertheless, even though no other official religious census was organized before 2001, most social observers agreed that decline in religious practice continued among Victorians[8]. Historian Hugh McLeod estimated that only twenty-seven per cent of Victorians still regularly went to church in the 1890s[9].

However, religious practice should not be equated with ethics and spirituality. Minimal practice did not automatically mean that moral values,

---

[8] Two unofficial religious censuses were later conducted by newspapers: The *British Weekly* in 1886, whose results were published as *The Religious Census of London: Reprinted from the* British Weekly. London: Hodder and Stoughton, 1888; and the *Daily News* in 1902–1903, published as MUDIE-SMITH, Richard, ed. *The Religious Life of London*. London: Hodder and Stoughton, 1904.

[9] McLEOD, Hugh. *The Religious Crisis of the 1860s*. Oxford University Press, 2007, p. 172.

founded on the Victorian vision of Christianity, had lost their influence. These values, especially Evangelical ones, continued to weigh on society as a whole: openly, through institutions and laws, but also more insidiously, in choices, behaviours, tastes, taboos and tacit codes. Besant had to contend with this value system just as much as with religion in her struggles for freethought and secularism.

Positivist historians often made a strong case for the spiritual crises leading to atheism – or at least agnosticism – among a number of Victorian thinkers, such as Harriet Martineau, George Eliot and Matthew Arnold, as well as of the painful doubts of many others. While Victorians were effectively confused and concerned by what they perceived as religion losing ground, and endlessly discussed the issue, those who totally abandoned their Christian faith, like Besant, remained a small minority, and did not represent a well-established trend. Frank Turner and Timothy Larsen also demonstrated that, contrary to the Positivist vision, several Victorian agnostics often experienced a 're-conversion' toward Christianity, sometimes Catholicism or, like Besant, toward an alternative form of spirituality.

Theist

At the end of Chapter 1, we left Annie Besant in the spring of 1874 in London, living — or, better, surviving — by her pen, thanks to her theological essays, published by her friend, freethinker Thomas Scott. In order to write them, she conducted more and more specific research in theology and philosophy, mostly in the Reading Room of the British Museum. At the time, Besant defined herself as a Theist. What exactly did she mean?

Theism — from the Greek *theos*, for god — defines any belief or doctrine that affirms the existence of God and His influence in the universe. According to religious Theism, the relationship between God and mankind needs intermediaries, provided through religion. According to philosophical Theism, God directly rules over the universe, but has no material substance: He transcends His purely physical work. It was with this philosophical branch of Theism that Besant aligned herself after losing her faith in Christ's divinity. She dated this turning point back to Thomas Scott's publication of her 1873 essay *On the Deity of Jesus of Nazareth*, with a preface by Charles Voysey: 'I place this essay as the starting-point of my travels outside the Christian pale', she wrote in *My Path to Atheism.*

Besant's friendship with Charles Voysey was hardly surprising, for their spiritual evolutions were very similar. In 1861, Voysey, the humble Anglican curate of St. Mark's church in Whitechapel, London, had been exiled to the small village of Healaugh, in North Yorkshire, for having dared to preach a sermon refuting the dogma of eternal punishment — one of the first dogmas against which Besant had rebelled. Three years later, still in Yorkshire, Voysey gave a sermon in which he questioned literal interpretations of the Bible, and he collected this and similar sermons under the title *The Sling and the Stone*[10]. In these texts, Voysey rejected original sin as a moral impossibility, and so the usefulness of Jesus' sacrifice. He refuted the conclusions of the First Council of Nicea in 325 on Jesus' divinity, even speaking of their idolatry. According to him, believing that God could have bidden the sufferings endured by Jesus was blasphemous. In any case, the Bible, a compilation of translations of original texts, that had been lost and rewritten well after the reported events, he said, could not be taken as a revelation. This could only happen in one's heart, he concluded, in a mystical fashion. Besant, in *My Path to Atheism*, affirmed, not without provocation, that any serious study of the Bible, like that which she had undertaken, could only lead to 'heresy'.

The Anglican Church once again dismissed Voysey from his curacy, but offered to allow him to retain his small annual income of £100, as well as access to his twenty acres of land, if he withdrew *The Sling and the Stone* from sale. Voysey, though he had to provide for his wife, their eight children and his sick, elderly mother, refused to recant, demonstrating the same integrity as Besant. *The Sling and the Stone* was incompatible with the Thirty-Nine Articles defining Anglican doctrine and in 1869, William

[10] VOYSEY, Charles. *The Sling and the Stone*. London: Williams and Norgate, 1865.

Thomson, the Archbishop of York therefore excluded Voysey from the Anglican Church.

Voysey appealed this decision before the Judicial Committee of the Privy Council. He had no hope of winning this heresy trial, but he wanted to take advantage of it to broadcast his theological views — a tactic which Besant would use several times to promote her own struggles. Voysey was right: the trial caused quite a stir and was widely reported in the press. He conducted his own defence before the Archbishop of York, revisiting the main points of *The Sling and the Stone*, while reaffirming his absolute sincerity and the strength of his convictions. He accused the Anglican Church of causing the Catholic revival by clinging to dogmas that were becoming less and less morally acceptable to Victorians. His plea was published by the *Daily Telegraph* on 2 December 1869, and then more widely circulated in the form of a pamphlet. Even though Voysey lost his trial, he received so much publicity that *The Sling and the Stone*, to which he went on adding new texts, sold more than a million copies before 1871. Voysey's lecture tour, which took place just after the trial, was an immense success, and the money he collected allowed him, with Thomas Scott's help, to found a Theist Church in St. George's Hall in London, where Besant met him in 1872.

In *My Path to Atheism*, Besant recalled having followed Voysey's heresy trial, which, she said, had reminded her of her doubts caused by her comparative study of the Synoptic Gospels in 1866, meaning that she had reflected on them again even before the spiritual shock caused by her daughter's illness. It is also obvious that Besant, at that point still the wife of an Anglican clergyman, perfectly knew who Voysey was when she went to hear him in St. George's Hall for the first time.

Toward Atheism

In the preface of *My Path to Atheism*, Annie Besant described the painful process of de-conversion she endured. Losing her faith in Christianity and then in God, was not a brutal counter-revelation, but a slow intellectual deconstruction, conducted rationally after the emotional shock of her first doubts. The style she used in evoking this process is nevertheless imbued with lyricism:

> The path from Christianity to Atheism is a long one, and its first steps are very rough and very painful; the feet tread on the ruins of the broken faith, and the sharp edges cut into the bleeding flesh; but further on the path grows smoother, [...] and in the distance we see the promise of the autumn, the harvest that shall be reaped for the feeding of man.

Thomas Scott was one of the essential figures on this path. In 1885, the third edition of *My Path to Atheism* was dedicated to him, with this vibrant homage:

> To Thomas Scott, whose name is honored [*sic*] and revered wherever Freethought has spread; whose wide heart and generous kindness welcome all forms of thought, provided the thought be earnest and honest; who knows no orthodoxy save that of honesty, and no religion save that of goodness; to whom I owe most grateful thanks, as one of the earliest of my Freethought friends, and as the first who aided me in my need; — To him I dedicate these pages, knowing that, although we often differ in our thought, we are one in our desire for truth.

This dedication reveals much of Besant's personality: not only what became her reason to live and her motto — her quest for truth —, but also her great loyalty to her friends, despite the disagreements that arose over the course of her own evolution. It is interesting to note that even though the Voyseys had taken her and Mabel in after her separation from Frank Besant, it was Thomas Scott, the one who published her essays, whom she considered to be the first to have come to her aid.

The theological essays that Besant wrote for the *Scott Series* were important steps in her *Path to Atheism*. She compiled them in this 1878 book, with the same intellectual honesty evident in her autobiographies:

'I have thought it more useful — as marking the gradual growth of thought — to reprint them as they were originally published, so as not to allow the later development to mould the earlier forms.' In a sad irony, it is because Besant felt no embarrassment in recalling all the steps in the evolution of her thinking, that her detractors, even to this day, accused her of inconsistency. Yet, none of her de-conversions and re-conversions were sudden, irrational or purely emotional. Besant so distrusted her emotions and intuitions that she repressed them until she considered them to be justified by long, rational research and reflection. In *On the Nature and the Existence of God*, she redeemed the intellect: 'The "serpent intellect" — as the Bishop of Peterborough calls it — has twined itself firmly round the tree of knowledge, and in that type [...] with the older faiths we reverence it as the symbol of life.'

In publishing Besant's works, Thomas Scott gave her the possibility to conduct her reflection and research in the best possible conditions, given her sex and her precarious social situation. Not only did he help her to come to theological conclusions that were considered very marginal and subversive, but also to express and circulate them, and to make a small living by her thought and her pen. In her autobiography, Besant speaks of the pleasure of leading an intellectual life, and of 'the joy of freedom, the joy of speaking out frankly and honestly each thought.' This freedom of speech, still rare amongst Victorian women restrained by the requirement of respectability, became one of Besant's great causes.

Her 1873 essay on the divinity of Jesus, provocatively signed 'by the Wife of a Beneficed Clergyman', with a preface by Voysey, was completed with a comparative study of the Gospels in which Besant finally explored the doubts that she had suppressed in 1866. In 1874, Scott published Besant's critique of natural theology in *Natural Religion versus Revealed Religion*, followed by another essay, *On the Atonement*, on vicarious atonement of sin, then by *On Eternal Torture*, on eternal punishment. These had been Besant's first theological questionings. They were followed by *On Inspiration* and *On the Religious Education of Children*, also published in 1874. The next year, she dared to come out in favour of lethal injection for patients suffering from incurable and painful illnesses in *Euthanasia*; then she cast doubt on the usefulness of the clergy with *On the Meditation and Salvation of Ecclesiastical Christianity*.

The summer of 1874 marked a new phase in Besant's evolution. In July, when looking for Auguste Comte's works in the bookstore of freethinker Edward Truelove, she saw on the counter the *National Reformer*, the weekly published by the National Secular Society (NSS), founded in 1866 by Charles Bradlaugh. She bought it to read in the omnibus back home. With a sense of humour that too many biographers deny her, Besant described in her autobiography the horrified look of the gentleman seated across from her, once he realized that this young woman in mourning[11] was browsing through an atheist periodical. Besant was impressed by Bradlaugh's restraint in his articles and responses to his ideological adversaries. In fact, due to 'the stupid, ignorant reflection of other people's prejudices', she admitted, she had not followed Mrs. Voysey's advice encouraging her to attend Bradlaugh's lectures, although he had supported Voysey during his heresy trial.

Besant read two of Bradlaugh's essays, *Plea for Atheism* and *Is There a God?*, which, along with her analysis of Auguste Comte, led her to the ultimate question of the existence of God: 'every step we take onwards towards a more reasonable faith and a surer light of Truth leads us nearer and nearer to the problem of problems, "What is That which men call God?"' She therefore began to write *On the Nature and the Existence of God*, from which the above quote was taken. She justified it by the need to find the basis of all morality: 'Is the mainspring of our actions to be the idea of duty to God, or a sense of the necessity of bringing our being into harmony with the laws of the universe?' She asked Thomas Scott for his permission to write this essay. He gave it to her, with these words that she recorded in her autobiography: 'Ah, little lady, you are facing, then, that problem at last? I thought it must come. Write away.' Besant also wrote *On Prayer* in 1875, and *Constructive Rationalism* in 1876 for Thomas Scott. Her last essay for

[11] For her mother.

the Scott Series was a short biography of Giordano Bruno[12], published in 1877. In the meantime, she had joined the National Secular Society.

Besant went to the Hall of Science of the NSS, one Sunday in August 1874, to pick up her membership card from Bradlaugh himself as President of the Society — even though he had been described to her, she recalled, as 'an ignorant demagogue'. First, she attended his lecture, the subject of which strangely foreshadowed her later spiritual evolution, as it focused on the similarities between Christ and Krishna. Besant had already read about this subject, which allowed her to evaluate the quality of Bradlaugh's erudition and argumentation, for he was also an excellent orator. He recognized her name when handing her card to her, and invited her to visit him a few days later to have a longer discussion about atheism. Besant wrote emotionally in her 1893 autobiography that: 'From that first meeting in the Hall of Science dated a friendship that lasted unbroken till Death severed the earthly bond, and that to me stretches through Death's gateway and links us together still.'

Atheist or Agnostic?

Annie Besant made Charles Bradlaugh read the manuscript of *On the Nature and the Existence of God* when she visited him in his tiny apartment off Commercial Road, cluttered with books. She had been cautious in her essay, saying in the introduction that: 'the very object of the present paper is to provoke discussion on this point.' Bradlaugh's verdict was, however, irrevocable: 'You have thought yourself into atheism without knowing it.'

Even though, in her essay, Besant had written: 'the term "atheist" is often flung unjustly at any thinker who ventures to criticize the popular and traditional idea of God', she used it henceforward to define her philosophical position, which she also called 'materialist'. It was a courageous and subversive decision, for, as she explained in her essay: '[the term atheist]

[12] Giordano Bruno (1548–1600). The errant monk, philosopher and scientist was burned at the stake by the Roman Inquisition, and became a martyr for free thought, despite his interest in Hermeticism, divinatory arts, and metempsychosis.

carries with it, at present, so much popular prejudice, that it prevents all possibility of candid and free discussion.' That she adopted it seems all the more ironical as a close reading of this text and of others, shows that Besant was in fact agnostic.

In *On the Nature and the Existence of God*, the question that Besant asked was nuanced: 'is there a God at all in the sense in which the word is generally used? [...] is there any idea of God, worthy to be called an idea, which is attainable in the present state of our faculties?' Her conclusion was the exact definition of agnosticism, as formulated in 1869 by Thomas Huxley, a biologist and staunch supporter of Charles Darwin. Like him, Besant only admitted that Man could not know God and that nothing could therefore be said about Him — at least for the time being:

> It seems to me that to deny His existence is to overstep the boundaries of our thought-power almost as much as to try and define it. We pretend to know the Unknown if we declare Him to be the Unknowable. Unknowable to us at present, yes! Unknowable for ever, in other possible stages of existence? — We have reached a region into which we cannot penetrate; here all human faculties fail us; we bow our heads on 'the threshold of the unknown.'

Besant was influenced by the Positivism of Auguste Comte — of whom she was then writing a short biography — when she used as an argument her very Victorian belief in Progress:

> There is another fact, an historical one, still on the destructive side, which appears to me to be of the gravest importance, and that is the gradual attenuation of the idea of God before the growing light of true knowledge. [...] As civilisation advances, the deities lessen in number, the divine powers become concentrated more and more in one Being [...].The next step forward was to separate the physical from the moral [...]; as the kingdom of science extends, so the kingdom of miraculous interference gradually disappears.

She did not put Western civilization at the apex of what she considered as progress toward atheism, however. Instead, to refute the argument of a universal religious instinct, she recalled: 'what are we to say of the immense number of philosophical Buddhists and Brahmins, for whose comfort or moral guidance the idea of a God or a hereafter is felt to be quite unnecessary?'

Besides, Besant rejected pure materialism, as well as the dualism of mind and matter: 'Matter is, in its constituent elements, the same as spirit; existence is one, however manifold in its phenomena; life is one, however multiform in its evolution.' Besant preferred to speak of 'substance' over 'matter', and even, in a Neoplatonic way, of 'essence'. Her lack of distinction between matter and mind, without primacy of one over the other, led her to reject the definition of Theists who believed that God was purely spiritual, and brought her toward a form of vitalism. In fact, what Besant refuted most ardently was the anthropomorphic idea of God:

> Thus we identify substance with the all-comprehending and vivifying force of nature, and in so doing we simply reduce to a physical impossibility the existence of the Being described by the orthodox as a God possessing the attributes of personality.

Earlier in the text, Besant had already written:

> [...] a Deity cannot be conceived of as apart from the universe, pre-existent to the universe, post-existent to the universe; [...] the Worker and the Work are inextricably interwoven, and in some sense eternally and indissolubly combined.

Her conclusion was inspired by the 1858 Bampton Lectures[13], *The Limits of Religious Thought*, by theologian Henry Mansel, whom she quoted several times. Mansel applied a form of metaphysical agnosticism, similar to Kant's, to Christian theology. Like Mansel, Besant went beyond mere philosophical

---

[13] A prestigious series of annual or biennial lectures held in Oxford on Christian theological topics, first offered in 1780 due to a bequest by John Bampton.

materialism to develop a neo-Pantheism, with near-mystical accents:

> There is only one kind of prayer which is reasonable, and that is the deep, silent, adoration of the greatness and beauty and order around us, as revealed in the realms of non-rational life and in Humanity; as we bow our heads before the laws of the universe and mould our lives into obedience to their voice, we find a strong, calm peace steal over our hearts, a perfect trust in the ultimate triumph of the right, a quiet determination to 'make our lives sublime.' […]. Study Nature's laws, conform to them, work in harmony with them, and work becomes a prayer and a thanksgiving, an adoration of the universal wisdom, and a true obedience to the universal law.

Eager to prove the uselessness of an exterior and personal God, Besant included morality in 'Nature's laws', drawing on the utilitarianism detailed by John Stuart Mill, whom she had studied too:

> […] just as physical laws are discovered by the observation of natural phenomena, so must moral laws be discovered by the observation of social phenomena. That which increases the general happiness is right; that which tends to destroy the general happiness is wrong. Utility is the test of morality. […] When we admit that God is beyond our knowing, morality becomes at once necessarily grounded on utility, or the natural adaptation of certain feelings and actions to promote the general welfare of society.

Unable to say anything about God, it was religion that Besant rejected in her conclusion, calling for a form of secularism linked to her utilitarian conception of moral progress:

> […] never will real and steady progress be secured until men acquiesce in this beneficent law of their nature, which draws a stern circle of the limits of Religious Thought and bids them concentrate their attention on the work they have to do in this world, instead of being for ever peering into and brooding over the world beyond the grave.

These are the profound reasons why Besant devoted fifteen years of her life to the National Secular Society. It was a commitment, both to herself and to mankind, a secular form of sacrifice:

> We cannot serve God in any real sense; we are awed before the Unknown, but we cannot serve it. For the Mighty, for the Incomprehensible, what can we do? But we can serve man ay, and he needs our service; service of brain and hand, service untiring and unceasing, service through life and unto death.

In 1893, Besant revisited this term 'atheist' that she had adopted in 1874: 'I called myself Atheist, and rightly so, for I was without God, and my horizon was bounded by life on earth.' She explained that it remained precious to her, because: 'Atheists are the vanguard of the army of Freethought,' and that, in any case, her main struggles within the National Secular Society had always been for 'the elevation of humanity.' Freethought and humanism were the main reasons of her total commitment to the secularist cause.

The National Secular Society[14]

What exactly was the National Secular Society that Annie Besant joined in the summer of 1874[15]? The term secularism was still rather new, having been coined by George Jacob Holyoake at the beginning of the 1850s. Holyoake, a working-class man from Birmingham, was involved in the co-operative socialist movement launched by Robert Owen in the 1820s. Since the end of the eighteenth century, anticlericalism — sometimes even atheism — was a traditional feature of the working-class communities of the North and the Midlands that the Evangelical revival or Methodism had, as yet, not reached. Their anti-religious feelings were strongly politicized, especially

[14] The National Secular Society exists to this day. It still campaigns for the separation of the Anglican Church from the State, but also for a form of inclusive Secularism, protecting practising members of different religions as much as atheists. See http://www.secularism.co.uk/about.html

[15] See the chapter 'The Secularists', in SMITH, Warren S. *The London Heretics 1870–1914*. London: Constable, 1967.

their rejection of a politically and socially conservative Established Church that defended the *status quo* at their expense. During a lecture that Holyoake gave in Cheltenham in 1842, he said, in answer to a clergyman, that obviously religion would have no place in the socialist communities imagined by Owenites. His candour led him to be sent to jail for six months for blasphemy. Upon his release, Holyoake, in defiance, returned to Cheltenham and repeated the words that had led to his condemnation, this time without legal consequences. Despite this victory for freedom of speech, Holyoake was not at ease with atheism. He therefore defined a new concept, secularism, in 1851:

> Secularism relates to the present existence of man, and to action, the issues of which can be tested by the experience of this life — having for its objects the development of the physical, moral, and intellectual nature of man to the highest perceivable point, as the immediate duty of society; inculcating the practical sufficiency of natural morality apart from Atheism, Theism, or Christianity; engaging its adherents in the promotion of human improvement by material means, and making these agreements the ground of common unity for all who would regulate life by reason and ennoble it by service.[16]

Holyoake, who had launched a freethinking periodical in 1845, the *Reasoner*, founded the London Secular Society in 1853. Harriet Martineau, as a social thinker specializing in Auguste Comte, understood the usefulness of the term secularism right away. This is interesting, for what Besant called her atheism was in fact very close to Harriet Martineau's definition of secularism[17]. In an 1853 letter quoted by Holyoake in his *Principles of Secularism*, Martineau wrote:

---

[16] HOLYOAKE, George Jacob. *The Principles of Secularism*. London: Austin & Co., 1871 (3rd ed.).

[17] See BOUCHER-RIVALAIN, Odile. 'Harriet Martineau (1802–1876), from Unitarianism to Agnosticism', in COSTE, Bénédicte, ed. *Believing in Victorian Times: Cahiers victoriens et édouardiens* 76. Montpellier: Presses Universitaires de la Méditerrannée, October 2012.

> The adoption of the term Secularism is justified by its including a large number of persons who are not Atheists, and uniting them for action which has Secularism for its object, and not Atheism.

Despite a degree of misunderstanding with Holyoake, who remained more moderate, Charles Bradlaugh retained the word secular when he founded the National Secular Society in 1866, absorbing the LSS that he had presided since 1858, and for which the *National Reformer* became the official voice. Incidentally, the NSS motto was, humbly: 'We Search for Truth'. In its 14 June 1874 issue, the *National Reformer* published the four great principles of the National Secular Society, which were the same as those defined by Holyoake. Besant explains that she had consulted them before joining in August 1874, and accepted them fully:

> (1) This Association declares that the Promotion of Human Improvement and Happiness is the highest duty.
> (2) That the theological teachings of the world have been, and are, most powerfully obstructive of human improvement and happiness [...].
> (3) That [...] every individual of the human family ought to be well placed and instructed, and all who are of a suitable age ought to be usefully employed for their own good and the general good.
> (4) That human improvement and happiness cannot be effectually promoted without civil and religious liberty; and that, therefore, it is the duty of every individual — a duty to be practically recognised by every member of this Association — to actively attack all barriers to equal freedom of thought and utterance for all, upon political and theological subjects.

Under Bradlaugh's energetic presidency, the NSS developed quickly, attracting a number of skilled workers, artisans and clerks at the beginning of the 1870s. Its debates and lectures took place in its London Hall of Science, built in 1868 for an audience of up to 1200. The NSS also held secular marriage ceremonies, baptisms and funerals there, and published an Almanac in which the Saints were replaced by great historical freethinkers, such as Shelley, Thomas Paine and Benjamin Franklin.

Charles Bradlaugh[18]

Given Charles Bradlaugh's importance in Annie Besant's life and intellectual development, it is appropriate to describe his personality.

Like Besant, Bradlaugh was a Londoner. He was born in the East End in 1833, the eldest of a family with seven children. His father, a lawyer's clerk, could only offer his son a limited education, and Charles left elementary school at eleven to work first as an errand boy, then as a helper to a coal merchant. Meanwhile, young Bradlaugh taught Sunday School at the Church of St. Peter's in Hackney. His first religious doubts appeared in circumstances remarkably similar to those that caused Besant's. While he was preparing for his Sunday School lesson, in 1849, Bradlaugh discovered inconsistencies between the Thirty-Nine Articles and the Gospels, as well as between the Gospels themselves. Incidentally, in 1850, he wrote about this topic in his first theological essay, which remained in manuscript form: *Examination of the Four Gospels According to Matthew, Mark, Luke, and John*[19]. Bradlaugh shared his doubts with the local vicar, Rev. J. G. Parker, who consequently forbade him from teaching Sunday School. Bradlaugh then set about reading and listening to contemporary freethinkers, to the point when his parents ended up kicking him out of the family home, although he had not turned seventeen yet.

His trials only reinforced his religious scepticism, and he was taken in by Elizabeth Sharples Carlile, a women's rights campaigner. She was the common-law widow of Richard Carlile, a Radical, freethinking printer and pamphleteer, who had been jailed several times for his publications,

[18] See ROYLE, Edward. 'Bradlaugh, Charles (1833–1891)', in *Oxford Dictionary of National Biography*. Oxford University Press, 2004; BRADLAUGH, Charles. *The Autobiography of Mr Bradlaugh. A Page in His Life*. London: Austin, 1873; and BRADLAUGH-BONNER, Hypatia. *Charles Bradlaugh: A Record of His Life and Work by His Daughter With an Account of His Parliamentary Struggle, Politics and Teachings by John M. Robertson, M.P.* 2 vols. London: T. Fisher Unwin, 1895.

[19] Quoted by LARSEN, Timothy. 'The Bible and Belief in Victorian Britain', in COSTE, Bénédicte, ed. *Believing in Victorian Times: Cahiers victoriens et édouardiens* 76. Montpellier: Presses Universitaires de la Méditerrannée, October 2012, pp. 11–26.

especially those by Thomas Paine. Her friends took the young Bradlaugh under their wing, as the Voyseys and the Scotts would do later on with Besant, and helped him pursue his self-education. A brilliant young man, he gave his first lecture in 1850, at the age of seventeen, on the ambitious subject of *The Past, Present, and Future of Theology*.

Bradlaugh's public stance soon led him to lose his job. Without any money, he had no other option than to enrol in the army in that same year of 1850, but he joined his regiment with the works of Euclid and Hebrew and Arabic dictionaries in his luggage. He was posted in Ireland, in the wake of the Great Famine, in charge of protecting the bailiffs who evicted the poorest from their homes. Bradlaugh developed a profound attachment to Ireland, another similarity between him and Besant. When she wrote in her autobiography about the trial of the Manchester Martyrs, which she had attended with lawyer William Roberts in the autumn of 1867, she added:

> I have found, with a keen sense of pleasure, that Mr. Bradlaugh and myself were in 1867 to some extent co-workers, although we knew not of each other's existence, and although he was doing much, and I only giving such poor sympathy as a young girl might, who was only just awakening to the duty of political work.

In October 1867, Bradlaugh had published a vibrant plea for the Irish cause in the *National Reformer*, which Besant quoted at length in her 1885 autobiography, when she did not yet know that she would use very similar arguments against the British administration in India several years later:

> Where is our boasted English freedom when you cross to Kingstown pier? Where has it been for near two years? The Habeas Corpus Act suspended, the gaols crowded, the steamers searched, spies listening at shebeen shops for sedition, and the end of it a Fenian panic in England. Oh, before it be too late, before more blood shall stain the pages of our present history, before we exasperate and arouse bitter animosities, let us try and do justice to our sister land. Abolish once and for all the land laws, which in their iniquitous operation have ruined her peasantry. Sweep away the leech-like Church

> which has sucked her vitality, and has given her back no word even of comfort in her degradation. Turn her barracks into flax mills, encourage a spirit of independence in her citizens, restore to her people the protection of the law, so that they may speak without fear of arrest, and beg them to plainly and boldly state their grievances. [...] let us honestly legislate, not for the punishment of the discontented, but to remove the causes of the discontent. It is not the Fenians who have depopulated Ireland's strength and increased her misery. It is not the Fenians who have evicted tenants by the score. It is not the Fenians who have checked cultivation. Those who have caused the wrong at least should frame the remedy.

Bradlaugh also gave a speech defending the three young Irishmen sentenced to death in Manchester the following month, that was also published in the *National Reformer*. This text was remarkable in its legal argumentation, contesting the validity of the accusations brought against them, for Bradlaugh was a lawyer by then. A small inheritance, left by his great-aunt, had allowed him to release himself from the army. Returning to London in 1853, he found employment as an errand boy for a law firm, where he learned Law on the job, and was soon promoted to a clerk. This also allowed him to marry in 1855.

For different reasons, this union proved to be as disastrous as Annie and Frank Besant's. Bradlaugh had fallen passionately in love with Hypatia, the aptly-named[20] daughter of Elizabeth Sharples Carlile when he lived with her, but the young girl did not reciprocate his feelings. He therefore married Sussanah Lamb Hooper, a young woman from a freethinking family from Sussex, with whom he had three children: Alice, born in 1856, Hypatia, born in 1858, and Charles, born in 1859. Sussanah Bradlaugh soon sank into alcoholism, made worse by the death of their son in 1870. The couple separated that year, and Bradlaugh's wife, who had gone insane, went back to live with her parents. She died in 1877, at the age of forty-six. Sussanah Bradlaugh's illness made divorce impossible, even though her husband had a long affair with Mina de Brimont-Brissac (née Shepperd) from 1870, a

[20] Hypatia (370–415): female mathematician, astronomer and Neoplatonic philosopher from Alexandria, stoned to death by Christians.

Republican married to a French Viscount, whom he even entrusted with Alice and Hypatia's education in Paris, from 1871. Bradlaugh's daughters came back to their father in 1877, thereafter sharing his ideals and his struggles.

Bradlaugh used his knowledge of the Law to defend the poor, just like William Roberts. To protect the reputation of the lawyers with whom he worked, he adopted the pen-name Iconoclast to sign his secularist articles and pamphlets, published first in the *Reasoner*, then in the short-lived *Investigator* he launched in 1858, and finally in the *National Reformer*, of which he became assistant editor in 1860, then bought in 1861. Bradlaugh's oratory and rhetorical talent earned him a solid reputation as a lecturer and large audiences, which explains his election as President of the London Secular Society in 1858. He soon toured all of Great Britain, then the United States, where he was so successful that he was introduced to Grant's Vice President, Henry Wilson.

Bradlaugh also joined or supported various Radical movements, including the executive committee of the Reform League, founded in 1865 to obtain universal male suffrage in Britain and secret ballot. He also fought for land reform, especially in Ireland, and expressed neo-Malthusian and feminist positions. Between 1868 and 1874, he ran (unsuccessfully) three times as a Radical, in Northampton. Finally, Bradlaugh supported the European republican and democratic liberation movements of the era, through which he met Mazzini and Garibaldi. In 1871, his presence in Paris during the Commune led him to be briefly jailed in Calais. Two years later, he went to Spain to support the Republicans against the Carlists.

Her Friendship with Bradlaugh

Annie Besant published her first autobiography in 1885, when her socialist involvement had irreversibly separated her from Bradlaugh. However, she never stopped paying homage to him. This homage was even more moving in the 1893 version, written after Bradlaugh's death in 1891, but also after the even deeper ideological schism between them, caused by Besant's conversion to Theosophy in 1889. Her homage remained that of a friend, but also of a student, for Bradlaugh had been her intellectual mentor when she had first started as a pamphleteer and lecturer for the NSS:

> [...] how great is my debt to him I can never tell. Some of his wise phrases have ever remained in my memory. 'You should never say you have an opinion on a subject until you have tried to study the strongest things said against the view to which you are inclined.' 'You must not think you know a subject until you are acquainted with all that the best minds have said about it.' 'No steady work can be done in public unless the worker study at home far more than he talks outside.' 'Be your own harshest judge, listen to your own speech and criticise it; read abuse of yourself and see what grains of truth are in it.' 'Do not waste time by reading opinions that are mere echoes of your own; read opinions you disagree with, and you will catch aspects of truth you do not readily see.' Through our long comradeship he was my sternest as well as gentlest critic [...]. He saved me from the superficiality that my 'fatal facility' of speech might so easily have induced; and when I began to taste the intoxication of easily won applause, his criticism of weak points, his challenge of weak arguments, his trained judgment, were of priceless service to me, and what of value there is in my work is very largely due to his influence, which at once stimulated and restrained.

Such friendship, between a man and a woman separated from their spouses, fighting for freethought and, soon, for access to information on birth control, did not fail to create scandal. Rumours were leisurely spread by their religious and political adversaries, in order to discredit their stances, in a society where loss of respectability amounted to social death. That many of their contemporaries believed these rumours is undeniable, since the moral context lent itself to them. It is, however, strange that some of Besant's later biographers also believed them to be true, especially Anne Taylor[21]. It is appropriate to remember that, apart from a few remarks from George Bernard Shaw more than forty years later, there is no primary source

[21] TAYLOR, Anne. *Annie Besant: A Biography*. Oxford University Press, 1992.

supporting the idea of a romantic relationship between Besant and anyone else after 1873, including Charles Bradlaugh, socialist Edward Aveling and journalist W. T. Stead. To interpret the fondness or admiration that she expressed for her male friends in her letters as any proof of romantic feelings would be misleading, as Victorians tended to pour their hearts out in writing. Though sexuality was a powerful taboo, emotions were effectively expressed without our contemporary fear of ridicule or vulnerability.

Besant and Bradlaugh repeatedly denied being lovers in their respective writings. Admittedly, they might have tried to avoid a scandal that would only have harmed the already difficult struggles that they had undertaken, but W. T. Stead gave a decisive argument in the biographical sketch of Besant that he wrote in 1891:

> [...] never, in all the prolonged litigations in which Mrs. Besant has been engaged, has there ever been any imputation cast upon her personal character. For whatever breach of conjugal contract there was she has not to answer. And since the separation, although she has been tracked by detectives, enveloped in a cloud of scandal, and made the mark for every reckless calumniator, no human being has ever ventured to stand up in public and attempt to substantiate a single accusation against the character of Mrs. Besant.

The detectives to whom Stead referred were hired by Frank Besant in the vain hope of discovering flagrant proof of adultery on the part of his wife, so that he could gain custody of their daughter in 1878.

Anne Taylor heavily relied on Hypatia Bradlaugh's 1895 biography of her father[22], in which she hardly spared Besant, of whose influence over her father she appeared to have been somewhat jealous. Taylor quoted her biography: 'They were mutually attracted; and a friendship sprang up between them of so close a nature that had both been free it would undoubtedly have ended in marriage', and made much of the words 'so close' to prove that Bradlaugh and Besant were lovers. Nevertheless, Taylor

[22] BRADLAUGH-BONNER, Hypatia. *Charles Bradlaugh: A Record of His Life and Work by His Daughter with an Account of His Parliamentary Struggle, Politics and Teachings by John M. Robertson, M.P. 2 vols.* London: T. Fisher Unwin, 1895.

did not quote the end of the paragraph, in which Hypatia Bradlaugh added: 'In their common labours, in the risks and responsibilities jointly undertaken, their friendship grew and strengthened and the insult and calumny heaped upon them only served to cement the bond.' Theodore Besterman, one of Besant's first biographers, who had worked with her in the Theosophical Society, also explained that she and Bradlaugh would perhaps have married, but that 'neither of them had the wish to indulge in an intrigue which would moreover in their position have been fatal to both. They remained devoted friends and colleagues'[23].

Hypatia Bradlaugh's conclusion undoubtedly sprang from Besant and her father's companionship, something that Besant recalled with a nostalgia that expressed all of the happiness she had experienced in an intellectual relationship that was so different from her husband's attempts at dominating her:

> [...] for many years he was wont to come to my house in the morning, after the hours always set aside by him for receiving poor men who wanted advice on legal and other matters, [...] bringing his books and papers, he would sit writing, hour after hour, I equally busy with my own work, now and then, perhaps, exchanging a word, breaking off just for lunch and dinner, and working on again in the evening till about ten o'clock — he always went early to bed when at home — he would take himself off again to his lodgings, about three-quarters of a mile away. Sometimes he would play cards for an hour, euchre being our favourite game.

Whether or not Besant remained chaste after separating from her husband would be of very little importance in itself, if it were not for the hypotheses constructed by some of her biographers. Nethercot even turned amateur psychoanalyst when he described Besant as romantically transfixed by all of the great male figures who came into her life, in an attempt to explain her intellectual evolution only as an incestuous quest for her dead father. Nethercot even dared to suggest a homoerotic attraction

---

[23] BESTERMAN, Theodore. *Mrs. Annie Besant: A Modern Prophet*. London: Kegan Paul, 1934, p. 106.

Besant would have felt for Madame Blavatsky, when he had to justify her conversion to Theosophy.

It is best to leave the last word on this subject to Besant, for, beyond trivial facts, it remains that, in her 1885 autobiography, she defined her friendship with Bradlaugh as an egalitarian ideal and a model to follow:

> It will be a good thing for the world when a friendship between a man and a woman no longer means protective condescension on one side and helpless dependence on the other, but when they meet on equal ground of intellectual sympathy, discussing, criticising, studying, and so aiding the evolution of stronger and clearer thought-ability in each.

Writer for the *National Reformer* [24]

A few days after their first long conversation about *On the Nature and the Existence of God*, Charles Bradlaugh, impressed by Annie Besant's intelligence and culture, asked her to join the staff of the *National Reformer*, then edited by Charles Watts. According to David Nash, the London-based *National Reformer* was 'a sober paper which claimed the moral high ground populated by politically and morally minded Liberalism', which, besides news items, 'carried articles of a self-consciously intellectual nature.' Aimed at the self-improving members of the lower middle class and skilled workers, the weekly was already the most influential Victorian freethinking periodical. Besant gladly accepted the small weekly wage of one guinea, that gave her the financial independence and freedom she longed for. In exchange, she committed to writing articles and reviews for up to five books a week, which allowed her to go on self-educating in theology, philosophy, sociology, economics and science.

Bradlaugh soon entrusted Besant with a column, which she titled 'Daybreak'. Her autobiography shows how attached she was to this metaphor

---

[24] See NASH, David S. 'Unfettered Investigation: The Secularist Press and the Creation of Audience in Victorian England'. *Victorian Periodicals Review*, 28.2, 1995, pp. 123–35.

of light as a symbol of her quest for truth. She signed her first articles 'Ajax', her '*nom de guerre*'[25], referring to the statue *Ajax Crying for Light*, on display in the central hall of the Crystal Palace, rebuilt in Sydenham after the Great Exhibition of 1851. The statue was inspired by the *Iliad* and the prayer to Zeus made by Ajax during the Trojan War, in order to find the body of Patroclus: 'If our fate be death, Give light, and let us die!'

Besant explained that the *National Reformer* was considered so radical and subversive that Thomas Scott's publications, though dedicated to freethought, could suffer from association with this weekly if she signed her articles with her real name. Her change of allegiance was symbolized by the fact that she reversed her decision a few months later, publishing her last essays for Scott anonymously, but signing her *National Reformer* articles with her real name.

Besant's very first column was published in the issue of 30 August 1874. In it, she announced:

> The series of papers, of which this is the first, will weekly point out these signs of the coming day; whether they betoken freedom of thought or freedom of action, they are dear to us as signals of that coming reign of Liberty, when men shall dare to think for themselves in theology, and to act for themselves in politics.

She devoted the rest of her first 'Daybreak' to ridicule the theological stances of Christopher Wordsworth, Bishop of Lincoln, ironically asserting that: 'Few help forward as he does the cause of Freethought; few allies, such as he, have we in the enemy's ranks. This inestimable prelate must be a thorn in the side of Mother Church; he will not be quiet.' She then proceeded to list the Bishop's clumsy, even absurd sayings. It was nevertheless a personal attack, as Frank Besant's vicarage was part of Wordsworth's diocese, and Wordsworth had taken up his vicar's cause against her during the couple's separation.

Even though Besant did not hesitate to use her column to express

[25] The French expression used by Besant.

personal resentment, she also tackled such issues as cremation, secular education and spiritualism — revealing herself to be quite sceptic about the latter. Along with these secularist subjects, Besant commented on political and social current events: she thus wrote about Joseph Arch's National Agricultural Labourers' Union, and the need of a land reform.

Bradlaugh's departure for an American tour in autumn allowed Besant to assert herself and to take on more subjects. This was how she was entrusted with the review of the long inaugural speech given by scientist John Tyndall before the British Association for the Advancement of Science, founded in 1831, of which he had just been elected President. In this address, the highly respected Tyndall supported Darwin's theory of evolution, and concluded that religious sentiment should not be 'permitted to intrude on the region of *knowledge*, over which it holds no command'[26]. He therefore proclaimed the authority of science over religion, which constituted a complete reversal of the Victorian value system. That the task of summarizing and elucidating Tyndall's arguments in the *National Reformer* was entrusted to Besant shows how quickly the young woman had been able to gain the confidence and respect of the long-term members of the NSS. When Bradlaugh returned from his tour sooner than expected to run in the Northampton by-election, Besant was promoted to political correspondent for the *National Reformer*, in addition to her regular work for the weekly.

Historian Louise Raw defined Besant as a 'journalist'[27]. This categorization is reductive, however, and reverses Besant's priorities. The *National Reformer*, like other periodicals that she wrote for or that she launched, was only a means to an end, in that case the struggle for freethought and secularism, not an end in itself. Besant dedicated at least as much time and energy to the other great Victorian means of spreading ideas: public lecturing, in which she soon excelled.

---

[26] TYNDALL, John. *Address Delivered Before the British Association Assembled at Belfast, With Additions*. London: Longmans, Green & Co., 1874.

[27] RAW, Louise. *Striking a Light: The Bryant and May Matchwomen and their Place in History*. London: Continuum, 2009.

Public Lecturer

At a time before radio, cinema, television, and the internet, public lectures were enormously successful. Some of the best orators were veritable stars, and they drew large audiences no matter their subject. As such, thousands of people hurried to each of Charles Bradlaugh's lectures in the London Hall of Science, and during his British and American tours.

In the spring of 1873, while Annie Besant was still in Sibsey, 'queer as it may seem', she wrote in her autobiography, she decided to see how it felt to preach in a church. Even though it still seemed inconceivable to her she would one day stand on a platform, she had a hunch about her oratory gifts, and wanted to test them. Under the pretext of playing the organ in her husband's small church, she shut herself inside and climbed the pulpit, where she improvised a sermon on Biblical inspiration. In doing so, she discovered two things: first, her ease of improvisation that Bradlaugh would teach her to distrust; and second, the power of her own voice:

> I shall never forget the feeling of power and of delight which came upon me as my voice rolled down the aisles, and the passion in me broke into balanced sentences, and never paused for rhythmical expression, while I felt that all I wanted was to see the church full of upturned faces, instead of the emptiness of the silent pews. [...] I knew of a verity that the gift of speech was mine, and that if ever — and it seemed then so impossible — if ever the chance came to me of public work, that at least this power of melodious utterance should win hearing for any message I had to bring.

It was rare for Besant to forgo humility in her autobiography, but here she expressed a sense of pride, justified by the numerous accounts from people who attended her lectures. Thus, in his *Memoirs*, trade-unionist Tom Mann recalled:

> The first time I heard Mrs. Besant was in Birmingham, about 1875. The only women speakers I had heard before this were of mediocre quality. Mrs. Besant transfixed me; her superb control of voice, her whole-souled devotion to the

> cause she was advocating, her love of the down-trodden, and her appeal on behalf of a sound education for all children, created such an impression upon me, that I quietly, but firmly, resolved that I would ascertain more correctly the why and wherefore of her creed.[28]

Sydney Ansell Gimson, who presided over the Leicester Secular Society from 1883 until his death in 1938, wrote in his 'Random Recollections' of it:

> I am sure it is safe to say that [Besant's] were the most eloquent lectures we ever heard from our platform. One could hear a lecture from her and disagree with every word of it and yet sit entranced by the music of her voice and words and beauty of her phrasing and her imagery.[29]

Besant also expressed pride as a woman, for women still were an extreme minority among public speakers. Victorians held a poor opinion of those who dared to venture into the public eye, 'exhibiting themselves' in front of an audience. As such, a female lecturer was hardly considered better than an actress, especially if she discussed seditious subjects. The National Secular Society had, however, already proven its open-mindedness and its feminism by offering its platform to Harriet Law[30]. Born into a very pious Baptist family, Law had lost her faith while trying to convert London secularists, including Holyoake himself. Defeated by their arguments, she thereafter lent her missionary skills to the service of the NSS and to socialism. She was a lecturer for the London Secular Society from 1859, and began her own journal, the *Secular Chronicle*, before becoming the

[28] MANN, Tom. *Memoirs*. London: Labour Publishing Co., 1923, p. 8.

[29] Quoted by NASH, David. 'Reassessing the "Crisis of Faith" in the Victorian Age: Eclecticism and the Spirit of Moral Inquiry'. *Journal of Victorian Culture* 16.1, 2011, p. 75.

[30] See ROYLE, Edward. 'Harriet Teresa Law (1831–1897): Feminist, Secularist, Radical', in BELLAMY Joyce M. and John SAVILLE, eds. *Dictionary of Labour Biographies* Vol. 5. London: Macmillan, 1979; TAYLOR, Barbara. *Eve and the New Jerusalem: Socialism and Feminism in the Nineteenth Century*. London: Virago, 1983; and SCHWARTZ, Laura. *Infidel Feminists: Secularism, Religion and Women's Emancipation in England, 1830–1914*. Manchester University Press, 2013.

only woman to sit on the Executive Committee of the First International. Despite Eleanor Marx's admiration, Law sank into obscurity, because the end of her career was eclipsed by Besant's immense public success.

Besant gave her first lecture on 25 August 1874. In her autobiography, she admitted to having spoken in public only twice since her experience in the little Sibsey church: during an informal debate at a garden party, where her ease reassured her, then during a discussion about opening museums on Sundays, organized by the Liberal Social Union, from which her atheism shortly after had excluded her. That time, she stood alone on the floor of the Co-operative Institute, on Oxford Street, to give a speech on *The Political Status of Women*[31], a topic that she had chosen herself. After being introduced to the audience by Bradlaugh, Besant discovered stage fright, which she compared to how one feels at the dentist:

> When a visit to the dentist is made, and one stands on the steps outside, desiring to run away [...], then the world seems dark and life is as a huge blunder. But all such feelings are poor and weak when compared with the sinking of the heart, and the trembling of the knees, which, seize upon the unhappy lecturer as he advances towards his first audience, and as before his eyes rises a ghastly vision of a tongue-tied would-be speaker facing rows of listening faces, listening to silence.
>
> All this miserable feeling, however, disappeared the moment I rose to my feet and looked at the faces before me. No tremor of nervousness touched me from the first word to the last.

Besant then experienced complete harmony with her audience, which she described in her autobiography as a near-mystical form of ecstasy. She admitted to a certain feeling of intoxication, but she respected this extraordinary power, using it exclusively to promote the causes in which she sincerely believed:

> [...] none can know, save they who have felt it, what joy there is in the full

[31] Published under the title *On the Political Status of Women. Lecture of August 25, 1874: Co-operative Hall, Castle Street*. London: Charles Watts, 1874.

> rush of language that moves and sways; to feel a crowd respond to the lightest touch; to see the faces brighten or darken at your bidding; to know that the sources of human emotion and human passion gush forth at the word of the speaker as the stream from the riven rock; to feel that the thought which thrills through a thousand hearers has its impulse from you, and throbs back to you the fuller from a thousand heart-beats. Is there any emotional joy in life more brilliant than this, fuller of passionate triumph, and of the very essence of intellectual delight?

She had believed herself to be of delicate health, but she discovered that her lecturing acted 'as a tonic', making her little by little 'strong and vigorous.'

The *National Reformer* declared her first lecture a 'success.' There was doubtlessly a favourable bias toward their colleague, but Moncure D. Conway shared their opinion, and asked Besant to speak on *The True Basis of Morality*, in September 1874, in his Camden Town church. There again, she was successful, and she was invited by a Unitarian preacher to repeat the lecture.

Even though they were openly polemical, Besant's public lectures, like her articles, were nonetheless very argumentative, with multiple precise references, found during research in the Reading Room of the British Museum, or in the private libraries of her freethinking friends. Many of her lectures were thereafter published in pamphlet form.

Captivated by her oratory talent, Bradlaugh decided to entrust Besant with regular lectures in the Hall of Science. Hypatia Bradlaugh recalled having heard her father exclaim, at the end of Besant's first lecture, that it was 'probably the best speech by a woman' that he had ever heard. Harriet Law's reaction to Bradlaugh's statement remains unknown.

The Path of Total Commitment

In January 1875, Annie Besant decided 'after much thought and self-analysis' to 'give myself wholly to propagandist work, as a Freethinker and a Social Reformer, and to use my tongue as well as my pen in the struggle.'

This is when she gave up the pen-name 'Ajax', signing papers with her own from then on, no matter what her estranged husband — whose name she had to use — might think. He tried to prevent some of her texts from being published in September of that year, but in vain, for Annie Besant responded with a complaint against him, on the grounds that he was trying to keep her from earning a living. The NSS decided not to conceal any part of her marital situation, so as not to leave themselves open to rumours that could be worse than the truth. Besant accepted the risks of her stances, but also, she outlined, the intellectual responsibility that she felt vis-à-vis her readers and listeners, whom she hoped to influence and convince.

Besant constructed a public image, which included a carefully considered black dress for her lectures, understated but close-fitting, whose austerity was tempered by a high collar trimmed with white pearls — which highlighted the face of the charming young brunette Besant was then: photographic portraits of her in this outfit were distributed as postcards by the NSS. For the rest of her public life, she showed the same care in her appearance, and made her clothing into symbolic messages of her struggles, the most powerful of course being the white sari that she adopted in India twenty years later.

In February 1875, Besant began the largely itinerant life that would be hers until the end. It is difficult today to understand the courage of such a choice for a Victorian middle-class woman. Besant did not hesitate to put her respectability, but also her physical integrity in peril to defend freethought, and, later, socialism, Theosophy, and India.

Her first lecture tour was an uncompromising initiation. Besant travelled alone, in the middle of winter, through the north of England and all the way to Aberdeen, in Scotland. In her autobiography, she recalled her terror, alone in a third-class compartment on a night train to Glasgow, with a man who was surely drunk and, soon, overly friendly. She only owed her safety to an unscheduled stop that allowed her to alert the conductor through the window. Upon her arrival in Glasgow, a city where she knew no one, her feeling of isolation and vulnerability was such that she only had one wish: 'to sit down and cry', she said, but she pulled herself together quickly.

In large cities, Besant stayed in 'temperance hotels', which she deemed safer for a single woman, although 'I rarely went to a temperance hotel in which water was liberally used for other purposes than that of drinking', she recalled with humour. In the smallest communities, like the mining villages of Yorkshire, she had no other choice than to stay with members of the local NSS branch, with whom she shared meals, and occasionally rides to the next village. She would discuss politics with the miners whose forthright opinions she admired, and who, like her, had no civil rights at the time.

The pace of this tour, like many others to follow, was exhausting: Besant gave up to twelve lectures per week, sometimes in very risky situations. While mining communities welcomed her warmly, she regularly encountered hostile crowds elsewhere. In June 1875, people threw stones at her at Darwen, Lancashire. The windows in halls where she spoke were regularly broken, and in September 1876, she barely escaped a lynching in Hoyland, Yorkshire. Her adversaries' anger was fanned by violent campaigns in the local press, organized against her by the clergy, who did not hesitate to spread unfounded rumours about her morality, intentionally equating free thought with free love. These confrontations nevertheless had the consequence of considerably increasing her fame. While her first tour was a financial failure, the following ones went on to earn money for the NSS. Outbursts of violence became rarer, she explained, as attitudes evolved. Incidentally, she paid homage to Harriet Law's courage, as she had met with violence even worse than what Besant experienced at the beginning of her lecturing career.

Besant took advantage of her lectures to pursue her intellectual development, and chose to discuss topics that required research and reflection on her part. Thus, during the autumn of 1875, she gave a series of six lectures on the French Revolution in the Hall of Science. She had prepared for them by researching the books by Louis Blanc, Michelet and Lamartine that Bradlaugh owned, and which she read in French.

Besant's unfailing commitment led to her being elected one of the five vice-presidents of the National Secular Society as early as 1875. As such, her main struggle for the next fifteen years became equality of civil rights for atheists.

Struggle for the Atheists' Civil Rights[32]

Until the end of the 1820s, Anglicanism was the only officially recognized religion. The Sovereign was its Supreme Governor, and any subject belonging to another religious denomination was considered a potential traitor to the Crown. After Oliver Cromwell's Puritan Interregnum, several laws limiting the rights of non-Anglicans were passed under the reign of Charles II. In 1661, the Corporation Act thus required that anyone elected to a local council or nominated to a Government position must take communion according to the Anglican rite. In 1673, the first Test Act also required anybody occupying an official, civil or military position to swear an oath of allegiance, as well as a declaration refuting the dogma of transubstantiation, which immediately excluded Catholics[33]. This law did not apply to the Members of Parliament (MPs), nor to the Lords, but it was completed in 1678 by a second Test Act, which imposed a similar oath upon them.

These religious discriminations were gradually lifted during the Victorian era. Protestant Dissenters were emancipated in 1828 with the repeal of the Test and Corporation Acts. This opened the door to the Great Reform of 1832, which gave the right to vote and to sit in Parliament to middle-class men — the majority of whom were Dissenters. Catholics were

[32] See ARNSTEIN, Walter. *The Bradlaugh Case: A Study in Late Victorian Opinion and Politics*. Oxford University Press, 1965.

[33] This Roman Catholic doctrine takes the name of transubstantiation from the Council of Trent (1551), when it was officially proclaimed by the Catholic Church, thus taking position against the Protestant doctrine of consubstantiation: 'The doctrine of the real substantial presence of the body and blood of Christ together with the bread and wine in the Eucharist, as distinguished from transubstantiation in which the whole substance of these elements is held to be changed into the body and blood of Christ.' (*Oxford English Dictionary*).

likewise emancipated in 1829.

The Jews' emancipation took longer, even though Britain was one of the least anti-Semitic among European nations. In 1837, Moses Haim Montefiore was elected Sheriff of London, and knighted by Queen Victoria in that same year. In 1841, Isaac Lyon Goldsmid was bestowed the title of Baronet, and thus became the first English Jewish aristocrat, joined in 1846 by Montefiore[34]. However, neither of them were allowed to sit in the House of Lords.

There had been converted Jews sitting in Parliament since Samson Gideon in 1770. Benjamin Disraeli, who had converted to Christianity in his youth after a quarrel between his father and their synagogue authorities, had been a Conservative MP since 1837. However, Lionel de Rothschild, also elected that year, had not been allowed to sit, having refused to swear the Christian oath of allegiance. A Jewish Emancipation Bill was approved in the House of Commons, but rejected by the Lords. What Jewish MPs had to go through in the following years heralded the difficult struggle faced by Bradlaugh, with Besant at his side. In 1851, Sir David Salomons was elected as an MP. He decided to swear the oath, omitting the phrases relating to Christianity. Salomons was forcefully removed from the House of Commons by a sergeant-at-arms, and sentenced to a heavy fine of £500 — a fate that awaited Bradlaugh. Still, the support that Salomons then received was so clear, that in 1855, he was elected to the honorific but prestigious position of Lord Mayor of the City of London. In the meantime, Lionel de Rothschild had been returned to Parliament in 1852 but excluded again, and the Lords once again decided against Jewish emancipation in 1853.

The Jews Relief Act was eventually passed in 1858, and Lionel de Rothschild became the first Jewish MP allowed to sit, after swearing an oath of allegiance which no longer included the exclusively Christian segments, saying 'so help me, Jehovah' instead. David Salomons followed suit in 1859. The House of Lords, this Conservative stronghold, resisted a while longer,

[34] See HALIMI, Suzy. 'Sir Moses Montefiore (1784–1785), défenseur de la loi', in DESCHAMPS, Yannick and Suzy HALIMI, ed. *Orthodoxie et hérésie dans les îles britanniques, Revue française de civilisation britannique* 18.1, Spring 2013, pp. 151–60.

but in 1884, Victoria conferred the hereditary title of Baron upon Nathan Mayer Rothschild, the son of Lionel de Rothschild, which allowed him to take a seat in the House of Lords.

Meanwhile, religious discrimination toward non-Anglicans, imposed by Oxford and Cambridge universities, was increasingly criticized. Until 1854, it was impossible for a non-Anglican to study at Oxford. Although it was possible to do so at Cambridge, non-Anglicans could not be granted degrees. It was not until 1871 that the Universities Tests Act finally allowed non-Anglicans, whether they be Catholics, Dissenters or 'non-Christians' to study, to pursue post-degree research and to teach at Oxford and Cambridge. This discrimination was abolished thanks to Numa Edward Hartog, a brilliant Jewish student at the University of London who had wished to continue his studies at Cambridge[35].

However, Protestants, whether Anglicans or not, Catholics, and the majority of Victorian Jews were united by the same faith in God. Atheists, accused of materialism, amorality, and subversive political ideas, met with even more challenging difficulties in getting their civil rights recognized. Bradlaugh led this long fight, with the unswerving support of Besant.

The first step consisted of Bradlaugh getting elected to the House of Commons. Since 1867, property-based male suffrage had been extended to urban skilled workers, artisans, and clerks who occupied lodgings of their own. After 1868, Bradlaugh chose to run as a Radical in a constituency in Northampton, an industrial city in the Midlands, with around 75,000 inhabitants. Though Bradlaugh did not conceal his atheism, his primary motivations remained political: he was a republican and a Radical, who sincerely believed that it was possible to improve the poor's condition, and to assert their rights by parliamentary reform. Although Bradlaugh lost his first attempt at election in 1868, John Stuart Mill paid homage to his campaign in his *Autobiography*, published in 1873, as quoted by Besant in

[35] The Bill received Royal Assent on 16 June 1871. Unfortunately Hartog died from smallpox three days later, on 19 June, before he could benefit from the Universities Test Act. See ALDERMAN, Geoffrey, 'Hartog, Numa Edward (1846–1871)', in *Oxford Dictionary of National Biography* (online ed.), Oxford University Press, 2004.

her own:

> 'He had the support of the working classes [...]. Men of this sort, who, while sharing the democratic feeling of the working classes, judge political questions for themselves, and have the courage to assert their individual convictions against popular opposition, were needed, as it seemed to me, in Parliament; and I did not think that Mr. Bradlaugh's anti-religious opinions (even though he had been intemperate in the expression of them) ought to exclude him.'

Besant accompanied Bradlaugh to Northampton in September 1874 as political correspondent for the *National Reformer*, to report on what was by then his third attempt, following his second defeat in February of that same year. Besant, who claimed to know nothing of politics, experienced a true baptism by fire, discovering the intrigues, alliances, treasons, and even the demagogy and violence that surrounded such elections. Meanwhile, however, she also discovered the British parliamentary system that she, like Bradlaugh, would always respect and admire, in spite of its faults.

The Radicals depended on the support of the Liberals and their electoral machine; yet the Liberals were so opposed to Bradlaugh's candidacy that they refused any alliance, and nominated a candidate of their own against him. This split the Radical vote and led to the victory of the Tory candidate. Despite this, the campaign against Bradlaugh, who, along with Besant, had been accused of immorality, was so violent that riots broke out against his supporters, and even against the Liberal candidate, and Bradlaugh was forced to flee. Order was only re-established in Northampton when the army was called.

In 1880, after six years in power, Benjamin Disraeli's Conservative Government was so unpopular that the Liberals were predicted to win the General Election by a landslide. Bradlaugh ran again, this time with the support of Liberal Party, in the same Northampton constituency. As in 1874, Besant was charged with reporting his campaign in the *National Reformer*. It is important to remember that, as a woman, she had almost no civil rights herself: she could not even attend the vote count at the Northampton Town Hall, as women were barred from the counting room. She lamented this, for

Bradlaugh, this time, won the seat. His victory was only the beginning of an exhausting battle, albeit one Bradlaugh seemed to have sincerely believed he would not have to fight.

Since 1866, the oath of allegiance that MPs had to swear to sit in the Commons excluded any reference to a particular religion, but still referred to God. This oath was also monarchist, since the MPs owed their allegiance to Queen Victoria, which could only displease a republican like Bradlaugh. When he entered the House of Commons for the first time, in May 1880, Bradlaugh asked to affirm instead of swearing the oath. This was not unreasonable, for, since 1869, it was possible to affirm in court cases and, as a lawyer, Bradlaugh had often used this right. He made his case, but Henry Brand, the Speaker of the House of Commons was hesitant. He called for a parliamentary commission, who ruled against Bradlaugh with eight votes to seven. Bradlaugh therefore made a difficult decision, which proved that his motivations were mainly political, in the noblest sense, for he hoped to be able to vote for land reform in Ireland and to protect the rights of labourers and small farmers there: at the risk of losing the confidence of the most intransigent of his secularist friends, he decided to swear the oath.

He was surely not the first atheist to do so, but his atheism was publicly known and declared. Moreover, Bradlaugh could not refrain from writing a provocative letter to the *Times*, in which he said: 'so much the worse for those who force me to repeat those words, which I have scores of times declared are to me sounds conveying no clear and definite meaning.' Even though he added: 'I regard myself as bound not by the letter of its words, but by the spirit which the affirmation would have conveyed had I been permitted to use it,' his letter triggered such a scandal that the Speaker refused to allow Bradlaugh to swear the oath, since it did not mean anything to him. Bradlaugh, after a noteworthy speech, which he considered to be his maiden speech in the House, refused to leave the Commons. He was seized by a sergeant-at-arms and imprisoned in the Clock Tower[36] of the Houses of Parliament.

Besant, who reported on these events in detail in the *National Reformer*,

[36] Commonly called Big Ben, after the name of its bell.

then entered the scene, ending her article with these words: 'As this paper goes to press, I go to Westminster to receive [Bradlaugh's] directions as to the conduct of the struggle with the nation into which the House of Commons has so recklessly plunged.' She used all of her propagandist talent to rally the greatest possible number of people to Bradlaugh's cause, including distributing a leaflet called *Law Makers and Law Breakers* in the street, in which she concluded:

> Let the people speak [...]. No time must be lost. While we remain idle, a representative of the people is illegally held in prison. Northampton is insulted, and in this great constituency every constituency is threatened. On freedom of election depends our liberty; on freedom of conscience depends our progress. Tory squires and lordlings have defied the people and measured their strength against the masses. Let the masses speak.

Bradlaugh was released the following day and welcomed in Westminster Hall by a crowd of several thousand people, led by Besant. The demonstration of support that followed, a few days later, was the biggest that Trafalgar Square had ever seen.

In July 1880, the Liberal Prime Minister William Gladstone, though very religious, gave Bradlaugh the right to affirm and to sit in the House of Commons[37]. However, the law had not been amended to that effect, and one Henry Clarke made a complaint, accusing Bradlaugh of sitting illegally. Clarke turned out to be the puppet of a Conservative MP, Charles Newdegate, who had already opposed Jewish emancipation in 1858. Because he was too busy, Bradlaugh sent Besant in his stead to the International Freethought Conference, which took place in Brussels in August. Besant's secularist fight then took on an international dimension, which would thereafter be the case for all of her struggles.

In March 1881, the Court of Appeal ruled against Bradlaugh, and sentenced him to a fine of £500 for each of his votes in Parliament: as

[37] See ARNSTEIN, Walter L. 'Gladstone and the Bradlaugh Case', in *Victorian Studies* 5.4, Indiana University Press, June 1962, pp. 254–69.

Bradlaugh had voted over two hundred times, he was potentially ruined. The legal struggle went on for three years, until his successful appeal in the House of Lords.

Despite this threat of bankruptcy, Bradlaugh immediately ran for his own seat again, and Besant worked ceaselessly at his side during this new campaign, that openly focused on civil rights for atheists. Besant even wrote an atheist and republican *English Marseillaise* for the occasion. Bradlaugh won his by-election, but nothing was settled.

His only hope rested with a Bill officially stating the right to affirm, the Parliamentary Oaths Bill, proposed by the other Northampton MP, Liberal Henry Labouchere, an agnostic, even though he referred to himself — with a mix of humour and caution — as 'the Christian member for Northampton.' The Bill was rejected, and in August 1881, Bradlaugh decided that he would swear the oath, no matter what. Fifteen thousand people gathered in Trafalgar Square to hear him speak, along with Besant, before marching to Parliament. Besant managed to get past the police barrier and to fight her way through the crowd into Westminster Hall, where hundreds of supporters were waiting to learn of Bradlaugh's fate. The Speaker again denied him the right to swear the oath, and four clerks seized Bradlaugh to drag him outside, not an easy task, as he was a very strong man.

When the crowd in Westminster Hall and around Parliament realized what had happened, there came a cry of anger and a spontaneous movement toward the doors separating the Hall from the rest of Parliament. As in Manchester in 1867, Besant revealed her physical courage: she threw herself between the crowd and the police guarding the doors of Parliament, managing to subdue the situation with her powers of persuasion. Her desire to avoid any violence that could discredit a just cause, and her distrust of poorly-controlled crowds would guide her in all of her later political struggles, especially the socialist ones, and later in India. However, when she learned exactly what had happened in the House of Commons, she used such sharp words that, the next day, an MP asked Gladstone during Prime Minister's Questions what he intended to do to prevent a riot incited by Besant.

Bradlaugh was re-elected three times by his Northampton constituents, in 1882, 1884 and 1885, each time with a larger margin. In February 1882, no fewer than 240,000 people signed a petition supporting him, at a time when such a petition meant a considerable amount of work gathering support, giving speeches and spreading information, to which Besant greatly contributed. The circulation of the *National Reformer* and the demand for secularist texts increased so much that the NSS was obliged to move its printing press to a more spacious location on Fleet Street, the historical centre of the British national press. Besant, being one of the NSS's most prolific propagandists, saw her notoriety grow just as much.

The Government Bill on the right to affirm was rejected by merely three votes, in 1883, despite a stirring speech of support from Gladstone himself. The situation only cleared up in 1886, with the election of a new Speaker of the House of Commons, Arthur Wellesley Peel, who at last allowed Bradlaugh to swear the oath in spite of his atheism. His reasons mostly were political, based on Bradlaugh's reassuring stance against socialism by then. In 1888, Bradlaugh managed to pass the bill allowing the right to affirm. Though still monarchist, the affirmation replaced God with 'the Law': 'I [...] do solemnly, sincerely and truly declare and affirm that I will be faithful and bear true allegiance to Her Majesty Queen Victoria, her heirs and successors, according to Law.' Bradlaugh's joy at this victory was marred by the sudden death of his daughter, Alice, in December that year.

Finally allowed to sit in the House of Commons, Bradlaugh proved a very active MP, working on questions as diverse as customs fees, pensions and vaccination. Bradlaugh also made the most of the Radical honorary title 'MP for India' he inherited from Henry Fawcett, through his defence of the rights of the Indian population under the Raj[38]. However, exhausted by his long fight, as well as a blasphemy trial that would take too long to detail even though Besant was involved in it, Bradlaugh died in January 1891, at the early age of fifty-seven.

---

[38] See NASH, David. 'Charles Bradlaugh, India and the Many Chameleon Destinations of Republicanism', in NASH David and Antony TAYLOR, eds. *Republicanism in Victorian Society*. Stroud: Sutton, 2000, pp. 106–24.

While Annie Besant never withdrew her friendship, gratitude and respect toward Charles Bradlaugh, her own political and spiritual evolution already had irredeemably parted them from 1885 onwards. Before that, however, they had to lead another victorious fight, this time initiated by Besant, for access to information on birth control, which fell within Besant's broader struggles for women's rights.

3

Annie Besant's Fights for Women's Rights (1874–1933)[1]

Annie Besant's feminist[2] fights tend to remain unknown or underestimated, because she incorporated them into larger struggles, for freethought[3], socialism, Theosophy or Indian nationalism. Besant believed that discrimination against women derived from systems that had to be completely reformed. Furthermore, duc to her proclaimed atheism and her stances on birth control, she was marginalized by most Victorian feminists, who were generally very keen on respectability. Yet Besant regularly lent her pen and her oratorical talent directly to the service of those Victorian women who were discriminated against by the Law, who had no access to information on birth control, or to whom universities refused to grant degrees. She also helped Indian women who had fallen victim to various antiquated traditions; and, of course, she demanded the right to vote for women, in Britain as well as in India. It is therefore appropriate to recall

[1] See BESANT, Annie: *Autobiographical Sketches*. London: Freethought Publishing Co., 1885 (republished and annotated by MACKAY, Carole Hanbery, ed. Peterborough, Ont.: Broadview Press Ltd, 2009); *Annie Besant: An Autobiography*. London: T. Fisher Unwin, 1893; NETHERCOT, Arthur Hobart. *The First Five Lives of Annie Besant*. University of Chicago Press, 1960, and *The Last Four Lives of Annie Besant*. University of Chicago Press, 1963.

[2] According to the *Oxford English Dictionary*, the term 'feminism' was first used with this contemporary meaning in 1895: 'advocacy of equality of the sexes and the establishment of the political, social, and economic rights of the female sex; the movement associated with this.'

[3] See SCHWARTZ, Laura. *Infidel Feminism: Secularism, Religion and Women's Emancipation, England 1830–1914*. Manchester University Press, 2013.

Besant's struggles for women's rights — and to study her writings on the topic — in order to assess their extent and influence.

Denouncing Victorian Women's Inferior Status[4]

First of all, Annie Besant embodied the fight for women's rights through her own rejection of the moral, religious and legal constraints that held sway over Victorian women, whose status improved only slowly, from the second half of the nineteenth century. Besant called for reforms from her very first public lecture, *The Political Status of Women*, given in 1874 and immediately published as a pamphlet. Her arguments against the social, civil and legal discrimination imposed on women were inspired by her personal experience, but also by John Stuart Mill's essay *The Subjection of Women*, co-written with his wife Harriet Taylor and published in 1869. In this first lecture, Besant went beyond her particular situation:

> If the man to whom her lot falls [...] is unkind, she will be unhappy; but, unless she be an exceptional character, she will not think of resistance. But women *are* now beginning to think of resistance; a deep, low, murmuring is going on, suppressed as yet, but daily growing in intensity; and such a murmur has always been the herald of revolt.

Shifting to the second person plural 'we' in this very militant text, Besant directly addressed the men who held power and abused it:

> We don't agree with some of your views; we don't like some of your laws; we object to some of your theories for us. You do not really represent *us* at all; what you represent is your own interests, which, in many cases, touch ours.

[4] See BROWN, Richard. *Sex, Work and Politics: Women in Britain, 1830–1945*. CreateSpace, 2014; GLEADLE, Kathryn. *British Women in the Nineteenth Century*. Basingstoke: Palgrave Macmillan, 2001; and STEINBACH, Susie. *Women in England 1760–1914: A Social History*. London: Weidenfeld and Nicolson, 2004.

And she warned: 'We will win the right of representation in Parliament, and when we have won that *these laws will be altered*.' What were the laws against which Besant rebelled?

After carrying out an impressive amount of legal research, she detailed her findings in 1878 in *Marriage, As It Was, As It Is, and As It Should Be: A Plea for Reform*. It must be recalled that, in getting married, Victorian women abdicated any legal existence: husband and wife were one person in law, but this 'person' was exclusively represented by the husband, in what was called the system of *coverture*. The wife lost everything, including rights to her own body, since her husband could legally confine her or subject her to marital sex — 'a particular aspect of wife abuse which until October 1991 in England was legally non-existent'[5]. He could also take anyone to court who offered his wife refuge without his consent.

For most of the Victorian era, wives had the same legal status as underage children, criminals or mentally disabled persons. Before 1882, a married woman could not sue anyone; only her husband was allowed to do so, on her behalf, for it involved an infringement on, or damage to, his 'property'. This status also held some disadvantages for husbands, who were considered legally responsible for their wives' misbehaviours and debts, even if they were separated. Besant underlined this in 1878, wondering: 'It is hard to see what advantage society gains by this curious fashion of reckoning married women as children or lunatics.' Wives' status also was very similar to that of servants, including male ones, who, incidentally, had to wait almost as long for the right to vote, because their employers were supposed to represent them legally.

'Marriage, to a man, is regarded as a kind of lucrative business', Besant asserted in 1878. She explained that, until 1870, all of married woman's property and earnings belonged to her husband, and she could not even inherit it back at his death. In 1878, Besant commented on the exceptions to this with a sense of irony and class awareness: 'So cruel, as regards property,

---

[5] PAINTER, Kate. 'Wife Rape in the United Kingdom'. Paper presented at the American Society of Criminology 50th Anniversary Meeting, November 20–23 1991, San Francisco, p. 1. http://www.crim.cam.ac.uk/people/visitors/kate_painter/wiferape.pdf

was felt to be the action of the common law, that the wealthy devised means to escape from it, and women of property were protected on their marriage by "marriage settlements", whereby they were contracted out of the law.' However, as she explained, even in that case, the wife lost access to her assets, which were placed under the supervision of her husband, who also received any interests and rents from them.

The Divorce and Matrimonial Causes Act 1857 allowed deserted women to keep their personal incomes, however; and the very few divorced women to regain the same property rights as unmarried ones. In 1874, Besant underlined that, according to the 1861 census, no fewer than three and a half million women worked in Britain, one million of whom were married — a social reality which went against the ideal of separate spheres on which the law was based — yet, it was only with the Married Woman's Property Act 1870 that married women could keep their earnings, but they still could not sign contracts nor make a will. Furthermore, the law only applied to women who married after 1870. The same was true of the Married Woman's Property Act 1882, which allowed them to keep what they owned before marriage.

While the Divorce and Matrimonial Causes Act 1857 facilitated divorce procedures, the moral double standard was written into the law: a husband could seek divorce by reason of adultery, but a wife could only seek it if her husband's adultery was made worse by desertion, acts of cruelty, incest or bigamy. Divorce by mutual consent remained impossible: this explains why Annie was only legally separated from Frank Besant, not divorced. In 1874, she asked men, provocatively: 'Do you acknowledge that you make home-life so dull, so wearisome, that you dare not open the cage-door, lest the captive should escape?'

Underage children were the property of the husband until 1839, when the law allowed women, separated from their husbands but deemed 'innocent', to obtain custody of their children under seven, and under sixteen from 1873. Besant is considered the first woman to use this latter amendment in order to gain custody of Mabel until she came of age — not suspecting then the extent of Frank Besant's bitterness and the legal battle ahead. Although the Infants Custody Act 1886 declared, for the first time, that legal decisions had to be made in the child's best interests, their father remained the sole legal guardian of underage children in all cases, until the end of the Victorian era.

According to Besant, these laws accounted for the growing proportion of common-law marriages among the urban working class, as she explained in 1878:

> Looking at a woman's position both as wife and mother, it is impossible not to recognise the fact that marriage is a direct disadvantage to her. In an unlegalised union the woman retains possession of all her natural rights; she is mistress of her own actions, of her body, of her property; she is able to legally defend herself against attack; all the Courts are open to protect her; she forfeits none of her rights as an Englishwoman; she keeps intact her liberty and her independence; she has no master; she owes obedience to the laws alone.

Even though Besant never advocated free love, she refuted the argument of immorality that was too easily levelled against cohabiting working-class couples, blaming instead the law-makers and their bourgeois vision of women and marriage.

Besant used her position as a pamphleteer and lecturer for the National Secular Society to continue denouncing the Victorian status of women. She established a link between secularism and feminism, believing that the patriarchy of Victorian society was rooted in and justified by traditional Christian faith[6]. She worked to demonstrate this in *God's Views on Marriage, As Revealed in the Old Testament* (1881), and in *Woman's Position According to the Bible* (1885). In the latter, she observed that 'whether in marriage or in other relation woman is in the Bible regarded as man's property — a mere chattel.' She leaned heavily on St. Paul's view in his Fifth Epistle to the Ephesians, verses 22–24:

---

[6] See BLYTH, Caroline. 'Unhappy Anniversary: Women, Marriage and the Biblical Law in the Writings of Annie Besant', in CALVERT-KOYZIS, Nancy & Heather E. WEIR, eds. *Strangely Familiar: Protofeminist Interpretations of Patriarchal Biblical Texts.* Williston, Vt.: Society of Biblical Lit, 2009, pp. 121–37.

> Wives, submit yourselves unto your own husbands, as unto the Lord.
> For the husband is the head of the wife, even as Christ is the head of the church: and he is the saviour of the body.
> Therefore as the church is subject unto Christ, so let the wives be to their own husbands in every thing.

In 1878, Besant could only observe: 'the Rights of Man have become an accepted doctrine, but, unfortunately, they are only rights of *man,* in the exclusive sense of the word.' In 1874, she had defined the Rights of Man as 'natural', not transcendent; anticipating the arguments from those who based their belief in feminine inferiority on women's nature, Besant replied:

> If this natural mental inferiority of woman be a fact, one cannot but wonder how nature has managed to make so many mistakes. Mary Somerville[7], Mrs Lewis (better known as George Eliot), Frances Power Cobbe[8], Harriet Martineau, were made, I suppose, as nature was asleep.

In 1885, Besant concluded *Woman's Position according to the Bible* with these optimistic lines, inspired by Mary Wollstonecraft, who had predicted in 1792 in *A Vindication of the Rights of Woman* that 'woman will be either the friend or slave of man'[9]:

> The chains bound around her by the Bible are being broken by Freethought and soon she shall walk upright and unfettered in the sunshine, the friend, the helper, the lover, but nevermore the slave, of man.

Besant dwelt on this ideal of gender equality, especially within marriage, in *The Marriage Question* (1875), one of the greatest successes of the Sunday morning lectures organized in the Hall of Science. She revisited this theme

---

[7] Mary Somerville (1780–1872): Scottish scientist and mathematician.

[8] Frances Power Cobbe (1822–1904): Irish writer, social reformer, and women's suffrage campaigner.

[9] WOLLSTONECRAFT, Mary. *A Vindication of the Rights of Woman.* London: Penguin Books, 2004 (1792), p. 34.

in 1878 with *Marriage, As It Was, As It Is, and As It Should Be: A Plea for Reform*, imagining marriage as a partnership:

> In short, marriage ought no more to affect a woman's position than it does a man's, and should carry with it no kind of legal disability; [...] marriage should be regarded as a contract between equals, and not as a bond between master and servant. [...] dependence is touching in the infant because of its helplessness; it is revolting in the grown man or woman because with maturity of power should come dignity of self-support.

Besant believed that marriage ought to be founded on bonds of friendship and respect. No doubt recalling her own marriage, she justified this ideal, not without some naivety:

> Perfect equality would, under this system, be found in the home, and mutual respect and deference would replace the alternate coaxing and commandment now too often seen. Equal rights would abolish both tyranny and rebellion [...] — till then the truest love, the truest sympathy, the truest happiness in it, will be the exception rather than the rule.

In *A Vindication of the Rights of Woman*, Mary Wollstonecraft had explained: 'I do not wish [women] to have power over men; but over themselves'[10]. Besant's feminism was just as much a call to resistance, even to rebellion if necessary, but with an eye to equality rather than revolution. A victim of a value system ironically founded on an idealization of women, Besant was wary of erecting a new pedestal for them, and of belittling men; rather, she meant to address their complacency and the abuses to which society drove them. She therefore shifted the ideal toward the couple: 'Equal rights would abolish both tyranny and rebellion; there would be more courtesy in the husband, more straightforwardness in the wife.'

[10] Ibid. p. 70.

Denouncing Prostitution

Annie Besant publicly denounced prostitution, that scourge of Victorian society[11], at a time when a respectable woman was not even supposed to know about such things, much less to speak about them in public — an opinion incidentally shared by some male members of the National Secular Society. Besant spoke against prostitution all the same, especially in an article published in the 4 June 1876 issue of the *National Reformer*, 'The Legalisation of Female Slavery in England', in which she called men to their responsibilities:

> When men of the world angrily object to women touching such a subject, they should remember that if they really respected the modesty and purity of women no such subject would be in existence, and that to those who gain nothing by the perpetuation of prostitution their loud indignation looks very much like the angry dread of a slave-owner who fears that the abolitionist preacher may possibly, sooner or later, deprive him of the services of his human property. I assert that the Secular party, as a whole, has a duty [...] of asserting the sacredness of the individual liberty of women as well as of men, the inalienable rights of each over his or her own person.

In this article, she referred to the Contagious Diseases Acts of 1864, 1866 and 1869 — 'contagious diseases' being a euphemism for sexually transmitted ones — and paid homage to Josephine Butler, founder of the Society for the Repeal of the Contagious Diseases Acts[12]. These laws, passed in order to protect soldiers' health, allowed the Police to arrest any prostitute suspected of having contracted a sexually transmitted disease (STD), to have her examined and forcibly hospitalized if she had, with, Besant underlined, no more respect for her person than her clients would show her. These laws implied that prostitution was a necessary evil, and

[11] See WALKOWITZ, Judith. *Prostitution and Victorian Society: Women, Class, and the State.* Cambridge University Press, 1980.

[12] These laws were repealed in 1886 — though not in the colonies — but re-enacted during the First World War.

that 'the unfortunate women [be] sacrificed to the "necessities of men"', she denounced. If the real goal had been to fight STDs, the clients would also have been examined, which was not the case. Besant took a stand against such moral discrimination. The Victorian double standard meant that prostitutes were considered as 'fallen women', lost to society anyway.

Some middle- and upper-class women, in a gesture of feminine solidarity, had thrown themselves into a 'crusade', as Besant un-ironically defined it, against these laws and for the abolition of prostitution — hence Besant's reference to slavery in the title of her article, written at the same time as Josephine Butler's book, *The New Abolitionists*[13], was published.

It would be wrong, however, to believe that Besant was prudish. She condemned the celibacy imposed on soldiers just as much, and said so clearly in her article, returning to her ideal of marriage:

> [The Secularist] does not despise human passion, or pretend that he has no body; on the contrary, reverencing nature, he regards physical union as perfecting the union of heart and mind, and sees in the complete unity of marriage the possibility of a far higher and nobler humanity than either man or woman can attain in a state of celibacy. [...] By prostitution I mean simply and solely physical union sold by one sex and bought by the other, with no love, no respect, no reverence on either side.

Besant therefore demanded that the laws regarding divorce be relaxed, in order to account for cases of sexual incompatibility:

> Much secret immorality is caused by making the marriage tie so unfairly stringent as it is to-day; people who are physically and mentally antagonistic to each other are bound together for life, instead of being able to gain a divorce without dishonor [*sic*], and to be set free, to find in a more congenial union the happiness they have failed to find with each other. Reasonable facility of divorce would tend to morality, and would strengthen the bond of union between those who really loved, who would then feel that their true unity lay in themselves

[13] BUTLER, Josephine E. *The New Abolitionists: a Narrative of a Year's Work*. London: Dyer Brothers, 1876.

more than in the marriage ceremony, and was a willing, ever renewed mutual dedication instead of a hard compulsion.

Even more daring, Besant tackled the powerful Victorian taboos of birth control and feminine sexuality.

Struggle for Freedom of Speech on Birth Control: The Knowlton Trial (1877)[14]

Anglican clergyman Thomas Robert Malthus published his famous *Essay on the Principle of Population* in 1798[15]. In it, he asserted that 'The power of population is indefinitely greater than the power in the earth to produce subsistence for man', and concluded that it was necessary to limit the number of births, so that population would not exhaust its food resources. He added an ethical dimension, warning pessimistically, that 'the actual population kept equal to the means of subsistence, by misery and vice', and arguing that bringing children into the world without the certainty of being able to feed them was immoral. However, all Malthus proposed to that effect was chastity, which he called 'moral restraint', and delayed marriages.

The social reformers who promoted Malthus' population theory, but who advocated 'preventive checks', i.e. contraception, were known as 'neo-Malthusians'. Even though the term was only coined at the end of the 1880s, Charles Bradlaugh had become an early advocate of this neo-Malthusianism, in an 1861 essay entitled *Jesus, Shelley and Malthus.* Nevertheless, Malthusianism — and even more neo-Malthusianism —

[14] See CHANDRASEKHAR, Sripati. *'A Dirty, Filthy Book': The Writings of Charles Knowlton and Annie Besant on Reproductive Physiology and Birth Control and an Account of the Bradlaugh-Besant Trial.* University of California Press, 1981; and MANVELL, Roger. *The Trial of Annie Besant and Charles Bradlaugh.* London: Pemberton, 1976.

[15] See MALTHUS, Thomas Robert. *An Essay on the Principle of Population and Other Writings.* London: Penguin Classics, 2015 (1798); and LANGER, William L. 'The Origins of the Birth Control Movement in England in the Early Nineteenth century'. *Journal of Interdisciplinary History* 5.4, Spring 1975, pp. 669–86.

remained a delicate topic for the Victorians, as it had to do with sexuality.

In the summer of 1875, during a lecture in Leicester, Besant had to respond to the attacks of an audience member, who accused her, along with Bradlaugh, of defending *The Elements of Social Science*, an essay by George Drysdale, a young freethinking doctor[16], published in 1854 by Edward Truelove. The book, with which Besant was not familiar, promoted free love. Deeply wounded by what she considered slander, she discovered that in 1861 Bradlaugh had written a review of the book, whose neo-Malthusianism he had favourably underlined, while he had neglected to comment on Drysdale's arguments against feminine chastity. Besant and Bradlaugh's enemies seized upon this, and spread rumours about the nature of their relationship. Besant used the biography of Auguste Comte that she had written that year to defend herself, commenting on the relationship between Comte and Clotilde de Vaux in these terms: 'Those who are too base themselves to believe in a true and noble friendship between a man and a woman will alone try to cast any slur on the frank and loyal love which bound together these two great souls.' Yet, Besant's respectability was compromised, as was Bradlaugh's honour, which could affect the credibility of their causes and the effectiveness of their struggles. In spite of it all, less than two years later, Besant dared to confront the most powerful of Victorian taboos.

In December 1876, Henry Cook, a Bristol bookseller, was indicted by local magistrates because he sold a book entitled *The Fruits of Philosophy, or the Private Companion of Young Married Couples*, first published anonymously in 1832[17]. The author was an American freethinking doctor named Charles Knowlton, who addressed married couples, giving practical advice to limit their fertility. The work had been published in Britain for several years by Charles Watts, the NSS printer, and a close friend of Bradlaugh's. Since Bradlaugh was away from London at the time, Watts

---

[16] DRYSDALE, George. *The Elements of Social Science; or, Physical, Sexual, and Natural Religion. An Exposition of the True Cause and Only Cure of the Three Primary Social Evils: Poverty, Prostitution, and Celibacy*. London: E. Truelove, 1854.

[17] [KNOWLTON, Charles] *The Fruits of Philosophy, or the Private Companion of Young Married Couples. By a Physician*. New York: self-published, 1832.

turned to Besant for advice. Neither were aware that Henry Cook had added illustrations of a dubious nature to boost sales.

After reading the original version of *The Fruits of Philosophy*, Besant declared that it was possible to defend it against the Obscene Publications Act 1857[18]. Also known as Lord Campbell's Act, it was 'intended to apply exclusively to works written for the single purpose of corrupting the morals of youth and of a nature calculated to shock the common feelings of decency in any well-regulated mind', as explained by the Lord Chief Justice. This exempted scientific works, especially medical ones, from the law. Besant was therefore reasonably confident she would win the case. However, discovering the illustrations added to the original essay upon his arrival in Bristol, Watts ordered *The Fruits of Philosophy* to be withdrawn from circulation. He refused to testify in favour of Henry Cook, who was sentenced to two years' hard labour. Watts himself was arrested soon after, in London.

Bradlaugh, supported by Watts' wife, was prepared to compromise to clear Watts' name, and advised him to plead guilty. Besant, for her part, refused to give up, for two reasons: the principle of freedom of speech, as supported by the NSS, but also the content of the original essay. She saw in the methods of birth control promoted by Knowlton a means for working-class women to escape the horror of repeated pregnancies that brought misery to so many poor families. Bradlaugh ended up coming around to her position, at the cost of his friendship with Watts, from whom he withdrew the printing of the *National Reformer* and of all NSS publications.

Bradlaugh and Besant therefore founded the Freethought Publishing Company in equal partnership. In a gesture of calculated provocation, Besant decided to republish *The Fruits of Philosophy* in order to instigate a trial. At the time, trials were frequently sought by social reformers, as a means to generate publicity around a cause, but also because British Law largely relies on jurisprudence. A victory therefore could redefine the censorship imposed by the Obscene Publications Act. Besant and Bradlaugh

---

[18] See ROBERTS, M. J. D. 'Morals, Art, and the Law: The Passing of the Obscene Publications Act, 1857'. *Victorian Studies* 28.4, Summer 1985, pp. 609–29.

nevertheless removed the illustrations that had been added by Henry Cook, and replaced the too-explicit subtitle with the very Malthusian one: 'An Essay on the Population Question'. They wrote a preface, with a reminder that the book had been published legally in Britain for forty years. They also explained that their struggle involved freedom of speech:

> We republish this pamphlet, honestly believing that on all questions affecting the happiness of the people, whether they be theological, political or social, fullest right of free discussion ought to be maintained at all hazards. [...] since progress can only be made through discussion, and no discussion is possible where differing opinions are suppressed, we claim the right to publish all opinions, so that the public, enabled to see all sides of a question, may have the materials for forming a sound judgment.

Despite these precautions, the cause which Besant had embraced was extremely daring. Up to that point, very few essays on birth control had been published in Britain, and their authors, such as Francis Place, Richard Carlile, and Robert Dale Owen, were all secularists, often inspired by Jeremy Bentham's utilitarianism. Such was the taboo surrounding the issue that some of Besant's freethinking allies refused to support her in this struggle, including Moncure Conway and Harriet Law. George Holyoake assured her in a letter that if she persisted in republishing Knowlton's essay, she would be 'ruined as a lady'. He then left the NSS to found the competing British Secular Union. With this coming from a secularist, it is easy to imagine how the most conservative reacted. Besant accepted the possible consequences of this fight, recalling in her autobiography that she asked herself: 'Did it matter that my reputation should be ruined, if its ruin helped to bring remedy to this otherwise hopeless wretchedness of thousands?'

In March 1877, Besant and Bradlaugh decided to speed things up by distributing copies of *The Fruits of Philosophy* to the magistrates of the City of London and to the Police. They were arrested on 6 April, and formally accused of 'corrupting the morals of youth' and of inciting to 'indecent, obscene, unnatural and immoral practices.' The trial was set for June before the High Court of Justice, presided over by the Lord Chief Justice in person, second in the British legal hierarchy, after the Lord Chancellor.

Despite the invectives hurled against them by the press, Besant and Bradlaugh took advantage of their notoriety to sell over 100,000 copies of their reprint of Knowlton's treatise, including 500 during the first twenty minutes of the first day of sales. This earned them £2000, a very large but welcome amount of money, considering the cost of a Victorian trial. Meanwhile, Besant and Bradlaugh built their defence case, attempting to find witnesses who would testify in their favour. This proved difficult. The suffragist Millicent Garrett Fawcett refused to do so, so as not to tarnish the cause of women's vote; but Alice Vickery, the first woman who passed the examination of the Pharmaceutical Society of Great Britain accepted. Besant and Bradlaugh wrote to Charles Darwin, incidentally a father of ten. Besant recalled that 'he disagreed with preventive checks to population on the ground that over-multiplication was useful, since it caused a struggle for existence in which only the strongest and the ablest survived', but Darwin also revealed his conservative moral values in a letter to Bradlaugh, dated 6 June 1877:

> I believe that any such [contraceptive] practices would in time lead to unsound women & would destroy chastity, on which the family bond depends; & the weakening of this bond would be the greatest of all possible evils to mankind.

Garibaldi, however, Bradlaugh's old friend, wrote from Italy to ask that his name be added to the support committee, which also included the French economist and politician Yves Guyot and law professor Émile Acollas, one of the founders of the League of Peace and Freedom in 1867.

The courtroom was packed during the three-day trial, which most national and local papers reported at length[19]. Besant, after being allowed, like Bradlaugh, to affirm instead of taking the Christian oath on the Bible, took to the stand to defend Knowlton's book. In a factual manner, she described living conditions in overpopulated slums, and dared to touch

---

[19] See BANKS, J. A. and Olive. 'The Bradlaugh-Besant Trial and the English Newspapers'. *Population Studies* 8. 1, July 1954, pp. 22–34.

on the question of post-natal infanticide[20]. In doing so, she was the very first British woman to express herself officially and in public on the subject of birth control. It is easy to judge of Besant's oratory talent when even *The Times* praised it in their 'Law Report'[21], although they were strongly opposed to her views.

After an hour and a half of deliberation, the all-men jury handed down a most ambiguous verdict: 'We are unanimously of opinion that the book in question is calculated to deprave public morals, but at the same time we entirely exonerate the defendants from any corrupt motives in publishing it.' All the same, the Lord Chief Justice declared Besant and Bradlaugh guilty, and fined them £100 each. Besant responded by publishing a series of subversive articles, under the collective title *Is the Bible Indictable?*, in which she selected Biblical verses that, she said, could be considered as obscene under English Law. The Court of Appeal eventually annulled the incoherent verdict a few months later.

In July 1877, fortified by what was, nevertheless, only a half-success, Besant revived the Malthusian League[22], which Bradlaugh had founded fifteen years earlier but subsequently neglected. Besant was named secretary of the League, while the presidency was entrusted to Dr Charles R. Drysdale, brother of George Drysdale, who had supported Besant and Bradlaugh during the trial. The League, which soon gathered over 1000 members, focused on abolishing censorship of public debate on birth control, as well as spreading awareness of the subject. To achieve this goal, and because she rightly believed that Knowlton's book was scientifically outdated, Besant wrote an essay entitled *The Law of Population: Its Consequences, and Its Bearing upon Human Conduct and Morals*, sold at the small price of six pence. The success of this little book demonstrated

[20] For an excellent analysis of Besant's rhetorical strategy, see BRANDSER KALSEM, Kristin. 'Law, Literature, and Libel: Victorian Censorship of "Dirty, Filthy" Books on Birth Control'. *William and Mary Journal of Women and the Law* 10.3, 2004, pp. 533–68.

[21] [WALTER, Arthur], 'Law Report: High Court of Justice, June 21. Queen's Bench Division. The Queen v. Bradlaugh and Another'. *The Times*. 22 June 1877.

[22] See LEDBETTER, Rosanna. *A History of the Malthusian League 1877–1927*. Ohio State University Press, 1976.

the need for such information: it sold 175,000 thousand copies before 1891. Besant's influence then became international, as *The Law of Population* was translated into Swedish, Danish, French, German, Italian and Dutch. The following year, inspired by Besant's fight, Aletta Jacobs, the first Dutch female medical doctor, opened in the Netherlands what was undoubtedly the first clinic dedicated to birth control in the world

Besant came out as clearly neo-Malthusian in *The Law of Population.* In it, she denounced both the celibacy and delayed marriages recommended by Malthus as unnatural and harmful to health. Moreover, her book was explicitly meant for women, the physiological descriptions and practical advice only pertained to them, for, she said: 'The complete ignorance of their own bodies, which is supposed to be a necessary part of "female modesty" makes necessary a preliminary word on the mechanism of the womb and the process of fertilization.' Besant did not hesitate to explain, over four detailed pages, how to use some 'preventive checks' without a male partner's knowledge:

> [...] the most reliable checks are those which close the passage into the womb. Of these there are three useful kinds; the soluble pessary, the India-rubber pessary, and the sponge. [...] and they have the enormous advantage of being entirely in the hands of the woman and of being absolutely unobstrusive.

Besant's advice to her female readers evolved over the course of the essay's republications, as scientific discoveries followed one another, and contraceptive techniques improved. She nevertheless drew a clear distinction between contraception and abortive practices, defined as a crime by Victorian Law — a fact Besant used as an argument in favour of contraception: 'surely the prevention of conception is far better than the procuring of abortion.' Nevertheless, Besant admitted abortion could be acceptable when the mother's life was at stake.

Beyond health concerns, Besant also hoped that having fewer children would leave women time and energy to foster their intellect and so develop beyond what she described in 1879, in *The Social Aspects of Malthusianism,* as 'the radically false notion of "woman's sphere".' Finally, while eugenics, as defined by Francis Galton in 1883, gained traction among neo-Malthusians, influencing even George Bernard Shaw, Besant distanced herself from the concept. Leaning on utilitarian philosophy, she believed instead in the importance of environment, and of nurture with respect to nature, which also justified her later social struggles.

In 1891, newly converted to Theosophy, Besant changed her mind on chastity, and published *Theosophy and the Law of Population*. While she still said that the number of births should be limited to avoid overpopulation and poverty, she nevertheless criticized neo-Malthusianism as too materialist, promoting practical contraceptive techniques only. In this 1891 text, Besant recommended mastering sexual instincts, and a form of asceticism that drew her closer to Malthus' original thought[23], even though she was mostly inspired by Eastern spirituality by then. Besant therefore withdrew *The Law of Population* from circulation.

Her most critical biographers, especially Annc Taylor, made a great deal out of this reversal. Most failed to mention that — out of sheer pragmatism — Besant partly returned to her original opinion a few years later, although she went on believing in the necessity of moral restraint. She was the guest of honour of the Malthusian League at the dinner organized to celebrate the League's fiftieth anniversary in July 1927, presided over by John Maynard Keynes. In her speech, Besant rejoiced in the League's work and that the House of Lords had just approved the implementation of clinics in poor neighbourhoods, where married women could obtain information on birth control. She also remarked with satisfaction that the birth rate, which had been thirty-six per thousand in Great Britain in 1877, had been reduced by half in fifty years. The following September, Besant wrote in the *Theosophist*, recalling the Knowlton trial: 'When I closed my address to the jury with the words: "History will say to us, 'Well done,' whatever your verdict may be," I did not expect them to be realised during my lifetime'[24].

[23] See TERRIER, Marie. 'Le Néomalthusianisme d'Annie Besant (1877–1891) et la volonté d'"améliorer la race humaine"', in PRUM, Michel, ed. *Racialisation dans l'aire anglophone*. Paris: l'Harmattan, 2012, pp. 51–68.

[24] 'On the Watch-Tower: A Jubilee Function'. *Theosophist*, September 1927, pp. 650–1.

Losing Custody of Her Daughter

Annie Besant's struggle for freedom of speech on birth control had one consequence that she had not even imagined. The publicity surrounding the Knowlton trial encouraged Frank Besant to demand custody of their daughter Mabel, then seven years old. He had already attempted to in vain in 1875, by refusing to return Mabel at the end of her annual visit. This time, Frank Besant was advised by the Bishop of Lincoln himself. While the Custody of Infants Act 1873 allowed a woman who had separated from her husband to obtain custody rights for children under sixteen, it specified that it had to be in 'the benefit of the infant'. Frank Besant hoped to invoke this in the trial that he brought against his wife in 1878. However, beyond the scandalous opinions that his wife held regarding birth control, Frank Besant did not manage to provide evidence of immoral conduct on her part, especially of an adulterous relationship with Bradlaugh. He therefore used another precedent: that of Shelley, who in 1818 had been denied custody of his children after the death of his first wife, due to his publicly declared atheism — for Frank Besant had just learned that the headmistress of Mabel's school had been instructed to excuse her from religious instruction.

The trial took place in May 1878. As during the Knowlton trial, Annie Besant conducted her own defence. Frank, for his part, did not even attend. His lawyers declared that a young girl raised by an atheist and neo-Malthusian mother would be 'outcast in this life and damned in the next'. Despite lack of evidence, they insinuated that Annie Besant and Charles Bradlaugh's relationship was of a sexual nature. George Jessel, the Master of the Rolls, third in the legal hierarchy, sided with them. Extremely vindictive, he claimed, speaking of Annie Besant, that 'no "modest woman" will associate with one who spreads among her sex the knowledge which will enable her sisters to limit their families', thereby insulting all the women who had come to support her during the trial, including Alice and Hypatia Bradlaugh. His verdict was scathing: he withdrew custody of Mabel from Annie Besant, a ruling that was maintained during the appeal in April 1879.

It appeared Frank was motivated more by resentment than fatherly love, for he immediately sent Mabel away to a boarding school, as he had done with her older brother Digby, of whom he had always had custody. The visits allowed to Annie Besant were so heart-rending that she ended up relinquishing them. Her children did not hold it against her: in 1890, Digby made the decision to return to her, thus defying his father, who from then on refused any contact with him; Mabel visited her mother secretly when she was eighteen, and returned to living with her, also cutting off all ties with her father.

The trial, which Annie Besant had not chosen to instigate this time, was again widely reported in the press, especially her plea, and her case had consequences that affected all Victorian women. Even though Besant lost custody of Mabel, some of her arguments resonated with the public, and rapidly led to a legal reform of married women's rights regarding their children. Besant had indeed denounced the legal aberration that contradicted what Victorian marriage claimed to defend: 'if you are legally your husband's wife you can have no legal claim to your children; if legally you are your husband's mistress, then your rights as mother are secure.'

The legal knowledge and poise that Besant displayed during her two trials encouraged the Association to Promote Women's Knowledge of the Law in their own struggle. After denouncing the discriminations against women in the practice of the Law, the Association fought for them to be able to study at the London's Inns of Courts, and to take the bar exam. Despite the example set by Besant, it was not until 1919 that the Sex Disqualification Act allowed women to become lawyers. Maud Crofts, Carrie Morrison, Mary Pickup and Mary Sykes were the first British women granted a Law degree, in 1922.

After the trial that stripped her of the custody of her daughter, Besant sank into a deep depression. She briefly considered forcing entry into the Inns of Courts to take the bar exam and better defend herself, but renounced in the face of the powerful ban against women entering professions. However, this led Besant to her next struggle: that of women's access to higher education.

Struggle to Take a University Science Degree[25]

Annie Besant was, on the whole, self-taught, but only because she hardly had a choice in the matter. Making higher education available to women had been the first cause adopted by Victorian feminists, even before that of the vote. Most of them were middle-class because, while the Industrial Revolution had created job opportunities for working-class women — though poorly paid and hardly fulfilling — the great socio-economic changes of the era had worked against the emancipation of upper- and middle-class women. They were the main victims of the ideal of separate spheres, which assigned them to the domestic one of home and the family, while the public sphere theoretically remained men's exclusive domain. Since upper- and middle-class women's only 'profession' had to be marriage and motherhood, higher education was considered unnecessary for them and even dangerous for the social and moral stability of the nation. Besant knew only too well the faults of a moral ideal that not only excluded the vast majority of working-class women, but also a number of penniless middle-class ones — the unmarried, widowed, abandoned or, like her, separated — who also had to provide for themselves. With very little manual training, apart from needlework, becoming governesses was often their only recourse, as was briefly the case for Besant.

It is therefore unsurprising that the first demands for women's higher education should come from these same governesses. In 1843, they founded the Governesses' Benevolent Institution, a friendly society that also strove to improve their status. They understood that only by turning their occupation into a recognized profession would they no longer be considered as mere domestic help. Consequently, they demanded their training to be truly organized and sanctioned by official examinations. They found in Christian socialist F. D. Maurice an influential ally. He taught history and theology at King's College, London, and, in 1847, he convinced

[25] See GOZARD, Manon. *Annie Besant's Emblematic Struggle to Obtain a University Degree in London in the Mid-1880s*. Master I dissertation (n.p.), University of Paris-Sorbonne, Paris 4, 2012.

a number of his colleagues to organize courses and exams with him for young women going into teaching: Queen's College, London was founded to accommodate these classes the following year. In its turn, London University founded Bedford College for Women in 1849, which offered the same training as Queen's College, without the requirement of belonging to the Anglican Church.

These first higher education institutions open to women were an undeniable progress, but gender equality was far from achieved in Victorian universities. Oxford and Cambridge remained bastions of Anglican patriarchy, and only half-opened their doors to late-Victorian women. When Cambridge allowed women to attend courses — only with a chaperon and the lecturer's permission — Girton College, Cambridge, was established in 1869 by women's rights activist Emily Davies and painter and campaigner Barbara Leigh Bodichon, as a hall of residence for female students. Such was also the case for Lady Margaret Hall and Somerville College, founded in 1878 at Oxford. While the female students at Oxford and Cambridge gained the right to take exams fairly soon thereafter, no degree was awarded to them until the 1920s if they passed, and they had to wait until after the Second World War to win complete equality with male students. Oxford and Cambridge were outpaced by their Scottish counterparts, wherein female students earned the same rights and degrees as male students as early as 1892. In this context, London University proved revolutionary when they decided, in January 1878, to admit women equally with men, according to the principle of co-education, after a series of reforms spread out over a decade. Besant was one of the very first female students to benefit from this egalitarian education, but she soon unwillingly revealed its limits.

To enrol at London University, prospective students had to take five entrance exams, including one in mathematics and at least one in science, no matter what degree they intended to pursue. Enrolling for her entrance exams just after the painful loss of custody of her daughter, Besant recalled in her autobiography: 'I found it the very greatest relief to turn to algebra, geometry, and physics, and forget the harassing legal struggles in wrestling with formulae and problems.' Beyond this personal reason, Besant was also perfectly aware that earning a Bachelor of Science (BSc.) degree would lend more legitimacy to her scientific statements. Thus she explained, humbly, in her autobiography:

> [...] so I resolved to fill up the gaps in my scientific education, and to amuse myself by reading up for some examinations; I thought it would serve as an absorbing form of recreation from my other work, and would at the same time, by making my knowledge exact, render me more useful as a speaker on behalf of the causes to which my life was given.

She chose to be tutored by Edward Aveling, a Doctor of Science of London University, who taught comparative anatomy at the London Hospital in Whitechapel. Aveling joined the National Secular Society at the same time, and began to fight for secularism alongside his students: Besant, but also Hypatia and Alice Bradlaugh — which soon cost him his teaching position at the hospital.

In July 1879, Charles Bradlaugh was proud to announce in the *National Reformer*: 'Our readers will be pleased to learn that Mrs Annie Besant is now an undergraduate of London University, having successfully passed her matriculation examination.' Besant enrolled in as many courses as possible at the different institutions accredited by the London University, which still contented itself with organizing exams and awarding degrees. Besant chose a number of experimental science classes, without doubt hoping to put her as yet theoretical scientific knowledge into practice. She studied sound, light, and heat, as well as electricity and magnetism at Birkbeck Institute. She also took courses in acoustics, biology, animal physiology, botany, and mathematics at several other institutions. This demonstrates Besant's vast scientific curiosity, but also her sincerity, for such serious studies went beyond making a symbolic point. Moreover, she had chosen to join the extreme minority of Victorian women who studied science: there were only three women out of the thirty-seven students in her animal physiology class, for instance.

Besant proved an excellent student. The *National Reformer* adopted a habit of reporting her exam results, along those of other female students, in an openly feminist perspective. Besant took up the pen herself, in her 'Daybreak' editorial of 9 July 1882, to rejoice that 'in the awards made by UCL, it is gratifying to notice that where the women students have competed with the men, the women have taken a large proportion of the prizes.' The *National Reformer* announced that Besant came out of her first year having passed chemistry, mathematics, theoretical mechanics, electricity and magnetism, botany, biology, animal physiology, acoustics, and the study of light. She took a First Class in most and Honours in animal physiology. Yet, these exams were quite demanding: the botany one included no fewer than five topics: principal characteristics of the natural order of the vegetable kingdom, histology, morphology, physiology of vegetables, and systemic botany. After a six-hour written exam, followed by just as long a practical one, Besant earned yet another First Class ranking, the only First Class ranking of that year in botany.

However, in 1882–1883, during the third and final year of Besant's degree, the university authorities became increasingly obstructive in their attitudes towards her. Already in the summer of 1881, the Birkbeck Institute had intentionally omitted her name from the list of students who had passed their exams, and her certificates were sent to her instead of being handed during the official ceremony. When she took umbrage, the Institute responded that it relied on donors, who might no longer finance them if they learned that she was studying there. Besant, furious at their hypocrisy, related the whole story in the *National Reformer*.

In the autumn of 1882, as she recalled, with some bitterness, in her autobiography: 'When I asked permission to go to the botanical gardens in Regent's Park the curator refused it, on the ground that his daughters studied there', for he feared that they would be tainted by Besant's reputation. Besant, who needed to go to botanical gardens for her botany class, therefore turned to Joseph Dalton Hooker, director of Kew Botanical Gardens, who was agnostic and close to Darwin. Yet, even he only gave her permission to study there early in the morning, before it was open to the public. Rosa Morrisson, the Lady Superintendent of the University, to whom Besant registered a complaint in the spring of 1883, responded evasively that there were still 'some prejudices against you', and refused to expound upon them. Given Hooker's freethinking stance, it is obvious that these prejudices had nothing to do with Besant's atheism, but with her respectability as a woman. In fact, in a private letter quoted by Manon Gozard, Rosa Morrisson speaks of 'a trial in which Mrs. Besant had been engaged', referring to the 1877 Knowlton trial.

In May 1883, the University Council confirmed Besant's exclusion — as well as Alice Bradlaugh's, only because of their association — but they refused to justify their decision. Aveling therefore launched a petition among the university lecturers, demanding a general assembly, which took place on 18 July 1883. More than one hundred people attended, both students and lecturers, including Thomas Huxley, who had signed Aveling's petition. However, even he approved of the resolution confirming Besant's and Alice Bradlaugh's exclusion, a resolution that was, once again, not officially justified. It is clear that London University feared that Besant's notoriety would tarnish its reputation if she was awarded a degree, and as this touched on the taboo of sexuality, it could not be explained. In 1912, Professor Pollock wrote an unpublished letter to Hypatia Bradlaugh, quoted by Manon Gozard, in which he explained:

> I was one of a small minority who voted against the unjust decision — as we strongly felt it to be — to exclude [them] partly because of a merely surmised danger that Mrs Besant might start a propaganda of her opinions among the students, but chiefly for fear that these opinions might be obnoxious to the public as to drive away students from any lectures which Mrs Besant was known to attend, and thereby lose fees to the College.

Even more than Besant's atheism, which was tolerated in this secular university where Huxley and Hooker taught, it was surely her fight, as a woman, for women, against the Victorian taboo of sexuality, that cost her her degree.

There is a sad irony here, for Besant had not enrolled at London University in an openly feminist gesture. It must be noted, incidentally, that the other female students, fearing association with their classmate's notoriety, did not defend her when she was expelled. Most of them were middle- and upper-middle-class medical doctors', teachers', lawyers' and clergymen's daughters, who just wanted to make sure they would find a respectable occupation if they did not marry. They shared neither Besant's ambition, nor her feminism. In addition, despite the equal opportunities proclaimed by London University, female students still suffered discriminations, such as separate study rooms and dining halls, being required to sit at the back of amphitheatres, and they were excluded from the Debating Society and the Chemistry and Physics Clubs. Worse, they were not allowed to sit on the students' councils. However, the concern over propriety was such among the majority of these young women that very few of them complained. Besant's presence among them had only embarrassed, even worried them. Only Alice Bradlaugh, who ended up being collateral damage in Besant's exclusion, stirred up a bit of compassion and she received a few letters of support.

Besant stopped trying for a BSc. when she realized that her chemistry teacher had unjustly failed her, even though she had received a First Class ranking in this subject during her first year. Anyway, by then, she had joined the socialist cause: so this was more a matter of priorities to her than really giving up on a struggle.

After being dismissed from the London Hospital, Edward Aveling organized adult classes in the even more aptly named Hall of Science of the NSS. In 1883, no fewer than thirteen weekly science and Latin classes were offered there over thirty weeks, under the Science and Art Department at South Kensington, as well as London University matriculation classes. Besant had taken advanced certificates and qualified as a science teacher in eight different topics. From 1880, she taught some of these classes, soon joined by Alice and Hypatia Bradlaugh, who also took teaching certificates. Over eight years, Besant taught weekly science classes to up to thirty working or lower-middle-class young men and women. She taught elementary animal physiology, advanced chemistry, acoustics, light and heat, electricity and magnetism, and published textbooks. Her students' results stand as proof that Besant must have been an excellent science teacher: in June 1881, the *National Reformer* proudly announced that two of her fourteen students in elementary animal physiology had received a First Class ranking in South Kensington examination; the following year, no fewer than eight of her nine students in acoustics, and light and heat received this same ranking.

Besant barely expanded upon her disappointment of having been barred from taking a BSc. in her autobiography, so much would her socialist struggles soon monopolize her attention, but it is worth noting that at the end of her life, she always proudly used the honorific title of Doctor that Benares Hindu University awarded her in December 1921.

Struggle for Women's Vote

Annie Besant started as a militant reformer within the National Secular Society in the mid-1870s, just when the campaign for women's civil rights intensified[26]. She supported it actively, not only by being an influential lecturer and pamphleteer, but also by taking advantage of the fact that women's political rights slowly increased to take part in public life.

Victorian philanthropy was much developed, for the State was still comparatively little involved in social welfare. Upper and middle women's charitable deeds were socially and morally encouraged, as they were considered an extension of the feminine sphere, and went alongside the ideal of service and sacrifice imposed on women. Incidentally, Besant had hoped to make herself as useful as possible in this traditional domain as a clergyman's wife, as demonstrated by her work on behalf of labourers at Sibsey. However, the most committed of female Victorian philanthropists soon realized that their influence was limited by their social and political status. Besant experienced this when she understood that the labourers' condition could not truly improve without a land reform, which she could not really promote, due to her lack of civil rights. The first specific demands

[26] See BROWN, Richard. *Sex, Work and Politics: Women in Britain, 1780–1945.* CreateSpace, 2014.

for reforming women's political status therefore frequently came from Victorian women actively involved in charity. For this reason, the first civil rights granted to women were in fields deemed to be 'feminine' and already part of their usual philanthropic action: social work and education[27].

However, even in these sectors, reform came about slowly and hesitantly. The Poor Law Amendment Act 1834 provided for locally-elected Boards of Guardians. Due to a property-based electoral system, widowed or unmarried female ratepayers had the right to vote for the Boards. Victorian law-makers obviously considered this to be an error for, the following year, the Municipal Corporation Act, that reorganized urban local government, explicitly excluded women from any vote at the local level, including for the Boards of Guardians. This right was not returned to women until 1869, when the Municipal Franchise Act explained that 'words importing the masculine gender [...] shall be held to include females for all purposes connected with [...] the right to vote' for county councillors. However, as the vote was property-based, this was interpreted in 1872 as excluding married women, who still had no legal identity separate from their husbands'. This decision also applied to the Elementary Education Act 1870, that made elementary education available to all, and created locally-elected School Boards: female ratepayers once again were granted the same property-based right to vote as men, as well as the right to run for the Boards, but not ratepayers' wives. Nevertheless, most of the great Victorian female figures of the fight for women's rights began their public lives by running for these Boards: Emmeline Pankurst was elected Poor Law Guardian in Manchester in 1894, and so was Charlotte Despard, in Lambeth, London that same year — but Besant outpaced them by a few years.

In 1876, in her *National Reformer* editorial 'Daybreak', she rejoiced at the election of four women to the London School Board. In 1888, she ran for the School Board herself, for the working-class constituency of Tower Hamlets, in the East End. A third of its population lived in poverty, many of whom being Jewish families who had fled pogroms. In her manifesto,

[27] See HOLLIS, Patricia. *Ladies Elect: Women in English Local Government, 1865–1914.* Oxford University Press, 1987.

Besant asserted:

> […] women are wanted on the Board and there are too few women candidates. Women have proved themselves useful, especially in connection with administrative details whenever they have been elected to offices of public trust and, as a woman, I ask you to elect me.

Her manifesto was not feminist only: Besant also hoped to promote secularism in elementary schools then largely controlled by the Anglican Church. In her election platform, she also said that 'education should be for all classes alike, so that it may break class divisions and lay a basis for real equality.' Given the elitism of the British education system, this was a minority view, to say the least. Besant wanted to promote working-class children's education, at a time when elementary schools had been made available to all since 1870, but were still neither compulsory, nor free. Besant's manifesto also included the idea of free school meals. Anticipating what is now called 'fair trade', Besant demanded that only the companies that scrupulously respected the law as concerned wages and working conditions be allowed to become providers for State elementary schools. Finally, she paid homage to teachers: 'teaching is arduous and exhausting work, and those engaged in it should always be treated with consideration and sympathy'.

With the help of fellow socialist Herbert Burrows, Besant led an intensive electoral campaign in the vast, densely populated borough of Tower Hamlets, which she knew quite well. She addressed many meetings there, outdoors and in rented halls, at all hours of the day and sometimes late at night. Despite the local Anglican clergy's and the Conservative candidates' virulent campaign against her, Besant won her seat with flying colours in November 1888.

Besant worked relentlessly on the School Board to fulfil her electoral promises during the two years that she served[28]. She had to face a Conservative majority of thirty-two members out of fifty-five, sixteen of

[28] See Chapter 4.

whom were Anglican clergymen. She reported her work on the Board in the *National Reformer* — at the same time as Whitechapel, a district of Tower Hamlets, made headlines because of 'Jack the Ripper', who killed and mutilated five young women there in 1888. In her articles, Besant ceaselessly denounced the absenteeism of children forced to work at odd jobs for a pittance, and the hunger that tormented those who still reached their school desks.

In June 1890, *Reynolds's Newspaper* used Besant as an example when the House of Lords killed the bill introduced to remove the disqualification of women to sit on City Councils, concluding that 'some of these stupid Tories are afraid that able women who are now taking part in public life will put them to shame, as Mrs. Besant has, for instance, on the London School Board'[29]. However, despite the seriousness with which locally elected women such as Besant conducted their public work, and their sincere social and political involvement, such civil rights granted to Victorian women should not be overestimated. The reason why they had obtained them in the first place was because they fitted in the traditional feminine sphere. The Municipal Franchise Act 1869 had granted not only the right to vote to female ratepayers, but also to stand in council elections, but an 1880 court ruling, which set a precedent, withdrew the latter. Lord Justice Fry, who presided over the Court of Appeal, justified his decision thus: 'a woman is absolutely disqualified by nature from being elected.' History repeated itself with the County Council Act 1888, which reorganized local government once again, and created the London County Council (LCC): a court ruling refused women the right to sit on the LCC almost immediately. Incidentally, Besant ran for the School Board by default, as she had hoped to be elected to the LCC. It was only with the Local Government Act 1894 that women ratepayers were no longer denied the right to stand as well as to vote — and a long struggle awaited the British suffragists who demanded women's right to vote for Parliament.

---

[29] 'By a special contributor', 'From the Radical Benches: The Peers and Women'. *Reynolds's Newspaper*, 15 June 1890, p. 5.

Supporting the Suffragettes

The Victorian electoral system was not founded on the democratic principle of 'one man, one vote', but on the possession of property. Electoral reforms in 1832, 1867 and 1884 only lowered the property requirements, thus extending the right to vote, first to middle-class men, and then to a large part of working-class ones. However little democratic this property-based voting system was, it should not have discriminated against property-owning widows and single women who should, in all logic, have had the right to vote. It was therefore only by virtue of their sex that women had been explicitly excluded from the electorate for the first time by the Great Reform Act 1832. For this reason, Women's Suffrage Committees were founded in London and Manchester during the debates that led to the Second Reform Act 1867. Petitions were launched throughout Britain, and brought to John Stuart Mill, then a Liberal MP. Mill tried to amend the Bill so that it read 'persons' instead of 'men', but his amendment was rejected by 194 votes against seventy-three.

Such was the state of affairs when Besant gave her lecture on *The Political Status of Women* in 1874. Greatly inspired by Mill, who had died the previous year, this lecture reads like a call for complete equality of civil rights between men and women. Besant took a stand against so-called women's intellectual inferiority, believing that their social environment was the only reason for the under-use of their abilities: 'Tie up a man's hands, and then sneer that he has no aptitude for writing; or chain his feet, and show his natural incapacity for walking.' To those who believed that 'Women are sufficiently represented as it is', Besant responded, using Mill's term 'subjection': 'By whom? *by those whose interests lie in keeping them in subjection*'[30]. She therefore demanded: 'Let womanhood, as such, cease to be a disqualification [...]. Let the discussion on qualifications follow.' At the time, however, civil equality between men and women did not mean universal suffrage. Besant herself spoke of the property-based electoral system, but so as to take up one of the American revolutionaries'

[30] Original emphasis.

arguments, 'no taxation without representation', here with reference to widows and unmarried Victorian women: 'Taxation and representation run side by side, and if you will not allow us to be represented, you have no right to tax us.'

Nevertheless, when the Representation of the People Act 1884 extended the right to vote to the agricultural labourers left out of the 1867 reform, women were again explicitly excluded. Prime Minister William Gladstone rejected an amendment to that effect, on the pretext that the Lords could refuse to pass the Bill because of it. Gladstone, a Liberal, also feared that women would mostly vote Conservative, an unfounded but then widespread prejudice.

The women's suffrage movement suffered as a consequence of this failure, and remained divided on its objectives, and on how best to obtain them. Millicent Garrett Fawcett founded the National Union of Women's Suffrage Societies (NUWSS) in 1897, which remained moderate and law-abiding. She believed in parliamentary action, and was close to the Liberal Party. Fawcett thought that the militancy of the suffragettes[31] of the Women's Social and Political Union (WSPU), founded in 1903 by Emmeline Pankhurst and her daughter Christabel, was detrimental to the cause. Fawcett did not even ask for married women's right to vote. In 1890, Besant, for her part, gave a lecture entitled *Women in the State, the Labour Market and the Family*, in which she came out in favour of married women's right to vote, a fairly radical position at the time.

Both the NUWSS and the WSPU agreed on demanding for women the same rights as men. Only the Women's Freedom League (WFL), close to socialist groups and launched in 1907 by Teresa Billington-Greig, Charlotte Despard, and a group of dissident women from the WSPU, demanded universal suffrage. The WFL favoured passive resistance and civil disobedience over the militancy of the suffragettes. It was also one of the very few women's right movement to side with pacifists during the First

[31] The term coined in 1906 by the *Daily Mail* was meant as patronising, but it was appropriated by the militant members of the WSPU to differentiate themselves from the more moderate NUWSS 'suffragists'.

World War.

Even though Besant lived India for most of the year as of 1895, she was directly involved with the militant suffragist movement of the 1910s. The years before the war were so politically and socially tense in Britain that they were recalled as 'The Great Unrest', and the suffragettes greatly contributed to this. Besant marched in the Women's Coronation Procession, an immense parade of some 40,000 women organized on 17 June 1911, just before King George V's coronation. In addition to demanding women's right to vote, this over four-mile long procession was meant as a counterbalance to the official coronation ceremonies, dominated by men, and to women's institutional invisibility. It was structured in forty-five sections, representing as many contributions from women to British society. That evening, Besant addressed a crowd of 10,000 gathered at the Royal Albert Hall. She concluded her speech, simply entitled *Votes for Women*, with a call for universal brotherhood, which was greatly applauded:

> Do you think we are here tonight to support a woman's movement? It is not a woman's movement, it is a human movement. Men and women cannot be separated into two distinct classes. There is but one humanity.

When visiting England in 1912, Besant once again took up the struggle alongside the suffragettes. In March, the third Conciliation Bill on women's right to vote had been rejected, due to lack of support from the Liberal Prime Minister Herbert Asquith. Since 1909, the jailed suffragettes systematically went on hunger strikes, and were consequently force fed with tubes pushed down their throats or through their nostrils, a form of torture from which some died. On 18 November 1910, the suffragettes' demonstration on Parliament Square, after the rejection of the first Conciliation Bill, had led to such an outburst of Police brutality and even sexual abuse, that the WSPU remembered it as 'Black Friday'. The rejection of the third Bill in March 1912 led to further violent protest, especially as the suffragettes had by then officially adopted militant tactics, which aimed at property not people, but included sabotage, destruction of public and private property, arson and, from 1914, bombings. Christabel Pankhurst coordinated the operations from Paris, where she had taken refuge, while her mother, Emmeline Pankhurst, was regularly jailed and on hunger strike.

Besant defended the suffragettes and their actions in a letter published in *The Times* on 12 March 1912, entitled 'A Plea for Militant Policy'. In it, she told readers that only the right to vote would allow women to improve their status, and the economic conditions of those among them who worked. With a rare disillusioned irony, Besant concluded that 'violence is the recognized way of England of granting political reform.' She condemned Police repression, as well as the legal system's severity toward suffragettes, exclaiming, no doubt with painful personal memories: 'Why you do not punish wife-beaters as heavily as that!'

Besant replaced Emmeline Pankhurst, still in jail, on the platform of the large gathering organized by the WSPU in the Royal Albert Hall in April 1912. The success was such that the sum £10,500 was collected that evening, and that Emmeline Pankhurst was released shortly thereafter. In a second letter to *The Times*, published in October, after she had returned to India, Besant, hovering between humour and threat, once again defended the suffragettes' actions, explaining that it was better to break windows than heads. She also congratulated Emmeline Pankhurst for a speech she had recently given. The following year, in 1913, Besant visited Pankhurst at the convalescent home where she had gone to recover from her latest hunger strike.

Besant did not participate in the end of the struggle for women's vote, for she was unable to leave India during the whole of the First World War, and she was increasingly involved in the Indian nationalist movement. At the beginning of the war, the WSPU militants agreed to a truce with the Government and lent their forces to the war effort. In February 1918, the Representation of the People Act introduced universal suffrage for men, while women over the age of thirty who were householders, the wives of householders, or occupiers of property with an annual rent of five pounds obtained a property-based right to vote for Parliament, which was also granted to female university graduates. Then the Parliament (Qualification of Women) Act 1918, passed in November of that year, granted women over the age of twenty-one the right to stand for election as an MP. Universal suffrage, which did not put an end to all legal discriminations between men and women, was eventually granted by Stanley Baldwin's Conservative Government, with the Representation of the People (Equal Franchise) Act 1928[32]. Besant, then over eighty years old, was invited to join in the celebrations in London that followed the passing of the Bill.

Theosophy and Feminism[33]

Annie Besant joined the Theosophical Society in 1889, and became its president in 1907. As Joy Dixon showed, the multifaceted spiritual revival of the end of the Victorian era was largely brought about by women seeking a spirituality that did not belittle or discriminate against them, and that coincided with the moral and social — even socialist — causes they supported. Like Besant, many of them looked outside of the patriarchy of traditional Christianity towards Eastern philosophies, from which Theosophy was largely inspired. The Women's Coronation Procession, for instance, had been organized by Kate Harvey, who was both a member of the Women's Freedom League and a Theosophist.

Besant's conversion to Theosophy, in the spring of 1889, was widely commented upon, and helped to spread awareness of the Theosophical Society, not only in the general British public, but also among women's rights militants who knew of Besant's struggles for the cause. The Theosophical Society's prime object was to bring in 'Universal Brotherhood of Humanity, without distinction of race, creed, sex, caste or colour.' For this reason, this form of spirituality attracted many Victorian and Edwardian

[32] See SMITH, Harold L. *The British Women's Suffrage Campaign, 1866–1928*. London: Longman, 2009 (2nd ed.); and WINDERGERDEN, Sophia A. *the Women's Suffrage Movement in Britain, 1866–1928*. London: Palgrave, 2003.

[33] See DIXON, Joy. *Divine Feminine: Theosophy and Feminism in England*. Johns Hopkins University Press, 2001; and BURFIELD, Dana. 'Theosophy and Feminism: Some Exploration in Nineteenth-Century Biography', in HOLDEN, Pat, ed. *Women's Religious Experiences: Cross-cultural Perspectives*. London: Croom Helm, 1983, pp. 27–56.

feminists under Besant's presidency. Historian Olive Banks estimated that approximately ten percent of British feminists were Theosophists at one time or another between the 1890s and the 1930s, a proportion one hundred times higher than among the rest of the population[34]. Joy Dixon studied the list of members of the English section of the Theosophical Society and discovered that, while men were in the significant majority in 1890, half of the members were women by 1895, two-thirds between 1900 and 1910, and nearly three-fourth between 1915 and 1925.

The list of Theosophist feminists under Besant's presidency would be too long to quote in full, but included writer and militant for animal rights Mabel Collins, suffragettes Isabel Cooper-Oakley and Ursula Mellor Bright, socialist educational reformer Margaret McMillan, suffragette and socialist Dora B. Montefiore, avant-garde actress, novelist and occultist Florence Farr, and socialist journalist Constance Lloyd, Oscar Wilde's wife. When the Theosophists launched an Art Circle in 1908, Caroline F. E. Spurgeon joined them and gave a series of lectures on mysticism in English literature. In 1913, she became the first female British university professor at Bedford College, London. During Besant's presidency, the Theosophical Society also included among its members Emmeline Pethick-Lawrence[35], another socialist suffragette, as well as Emily Lutyens[36], granddaughter of Edward Bulwer-Lytton — author of *Zanoni* and *Last Days Of Pompeii* — and daughter of Robert Bulwer-Lytton, Viceroy of India from 1876 to 1880. Emily Lutyens, a socialist and a member of the WSPU, had converted to Theosophy in 1910, after attending one of Besant's lectures. She was a militant suffragette, as was her sister, Constance Lytton, who died, paralyzed, some years after being force-fed in prison while operating under the false identity of a poor seamstress, which she had adopted in order not to receive special treatment as an upper-class woman. Working closely with Besant,

---

[34] BANKS, Olive. *Becoming a Feminist: The Social Origins of 'First Wave' Feminism*. Brighton: Wheatsheaf Books, 1986, pp. 168–70.

[35] Her husband Frederick Pethick-Lawrence was the Labour Minister in charge of India and Burma when India achieved independence in 1947.

[36] RIDLEY, Jane. 'Lutyens, Lady Emily (1874–1964)', in *Oxford Dictionary of National Biography*. Oxford University Press, 2004.

Emily Lutyens took on the education in England of Besant's adopted son Jiddu Krishnamurti and his little brother Nitya from 1911, before becoming involved in India's fight for Home Rule. The Labour Party asked her, as it did Besant, to run for Parliament under their banner in 1918.

Under Besant's presidency, the Theosophical Society developed a more feminine, even feminist, spirituality. Charlotte Despard, co-founder of the Women's Freedom League, also was a Theosophist, and published *Theosophy and the Woman's Movement* in 1913. In the introduction to this essay, she explained the link that she saw between the woman's movement and this spiritual revival: 'How has it all come about and why is the movement so strong? because it is in the direct line of spiritual evolution.' Despard, like Besant and other feminist Theosophists, based her belief in a 'common humanity of man and woman', an ontological definition that included spirituality: 'in nature, in essence and in aims, albeit unconsciously, they are one.' The Theosophical belief in reincarnation allowed to overcome the illusory difference between men and women, for as Despard explained:

> Every kind of Experience has to be gained by the Soul before it can consciously return to its Eternal Source. Every quality has to be evolved. The body which is merely the temporary form of the indwelling spirit, functions here through sex. In spiritual qualities there is no sex. The traveller [...] as he passes from life to life, may come to-day as a man and in the distant to-morrow as a woman.

Despard, who also shared in Besant's socialism, defined materialism as a masculine value, the contribution of which to humanity's evolution had reached its limits. In 1913, she wrote, in a visionary way:

> The nineteenth century boasted of its culture, its science, its far-reaching civilisation. The twentieth century is taking stock of these things. What, after all, has modern civilisation done? It has not brought peace; it has not brought happiness. To some, for a brief time, a pale satisfaction; to the vast multitudes of the human race, toil, monotonous, ill-paid drudgery or sheer misery.

Theosophy strove, therefore, for a necessary spiritual renewal, which had to be feminine, in the broader sense of the term. Such spirituality, more intuitive and emotional, almost mystical, was clearly set apart from established religions, for, as Despard explained: 'The religious, in common with the industrial ideal, was male and woman accepted it from man.' For this reason, a number of Theosophists had been, like Besant, agnostic, or even atheist, before turning to a more feminine form of spirituality, perfectly summarized by Theosophist Minnie Theobald, who wrote, in 1904:

> Put aside your books, stop the ceaseless working of your brains and learn to feel! To feel the rhythm of the universe, to feel life and love flow from every object that surrounds you, and by experience know Universal Brotherhood[37].

Besant never turned away from the path of action and service to favour devotion exclusively, although she considered devotion as central. Under Besant's influence, as well as that of the female Theosophists she inspired, Theosophy contributed to a redefinition of Western spiritual values as eminently feminine. This evolution, among others, led to Jungian psychology[38], but also to what is commonly called the New Age[39] movement.

[37] Quoted in DIXON, Joy. *Divine Feminine: Theosophy and Feminism in England.* Johns Hopkins University Press, 2001, p. 69.

[38] See JUNG, Carl Gustav. *Modern Man in Search of a Soul.* Oxford: Routledge Classics, 2001 (1933); and SOUZENELLE, Annick. *Le Féminin de l'être: pour en finir avec la côte d'Adam.* Paris: Albin Michel, Col. Spiritualités vivantes, 2000.

[39] See BEVIR, Mark. 'Annie Besant's Quest for Truth: Christianity, Secularism and New Age Thought'. *Journal of Ecclesiastical History* 50.1, 1999, pp. 62–93.

Co-Masonry[40]

Besides Theosophy, Annie Besant also fought for Freemasonry to be open to both men and women on an equal basis, i.e. Co-Masonry. She already knew Freemasonry well, for Charles Bradlaugh was a Freemason, at least until the Prince of Wales was initiated as Grand Master of the United Grand Lodge of England in 1874. This initiation went against Bradlaugh's republican ideal, but he remained close to the Grand Orient de France instead, especially since British Freemasons required belief in a Supreme Being.

In 1911, suffragette and Theosophist Ursula Bright violently criticized Freemasons' discrimination against women, a point of view shared by Besant: 'Male Masonry is the expression of power, wealth, social influence and exclusiveness. Co-Masonry is the expression of service, tolerance, freedom of speech on all subjects.' In 1902, Besant had founded the first Co-Masonic Lodge of the Universal Order of Co-Freemasonry, in London. It was modelled after the Grande Loge Symbolique Écossaise de France, Le Droit Humain (The Great Symbolic Scottish Lodge of France, The Human Right), founded in 1893 by French feminist, freethinker, and republican Maria Deraisme. Theosophist Francesca Arundale[41] had been the first British woman to be initiated into it, soon followed by Besant and Charlotte Despard. Besant's Universal Order of Co-Freemasonry admitted women on the same terms as men, for, as the *Co-Mason*, the order's journal explained in 1909: 'a movement which professes to be a Brotherhood of

[40] See BUISINE, Andrée. *La Franc-maçonnerie anglo-saxonne et les femmes.* Paris: Trédaniel, 1995; GEOFFROY Sophie. 'Une *New Woman* théosophe aux origines du Droit Humain britannique: Annie Besant (London 1847–Adyar 1933)', in RÉVAUGER, Cécile, ed. *Les Femmes et la franc-maçonnerie des Lumières à nos jours.* Bruxelles: La Pensée et les Hommes, 2012, pp. 121–46; PILCHER-DAYTON, Ann, *The Open Door: the History of the Order of Women Freemasons 1908–2008.* London: Order of Women Freemasons, 2008; PRESCOT, A. 'Builders of the Temple of the New Civilisation: Annie Besant and Freemasonry', in HEIDLE A. & J. SNOEK, eds. *Women's Agency and Rituals in Mixed and Female Masonic Orders.* Leiden: Brill, 2008, pp. 359–92.

[41] Mother of George Arundale, who succeeded Besant as international president of the Theosophical Society after her death.

Humanity cannot accomplish its object if it refuses entry to one half of the human family.' Although that year, in the first issue of the journal, feminist Theosophist Edith Ward had affirmed that Co-Masonry was part of 'that great stirring of the whole world which is known as the woman movement'[42].

In September 1911, a few weeks after the Women's Coronation Procession, Co-Masons organized a Co-Masonic Order's parade in Tavistock Square, in Bloomsbury, to celebrate the laying of the foundation stone of the London headquarters of the Theosophical Society[43], a building designed by Emily Lutyens' husband, Edward, the architect of New Delhi. Besant was the first Englishwoman to perform this masonic ritual. Incidentally, Besant had marched in full masonic regalia in the Women's Coronation Procession, in June. The *Co-Mason* had described the Women's Coronation Procession as a 'sacramental' public action on the part of women, and claimed that sex should not be an obstacle to the quest for Truth, while hoping that the success of the procession was a sign that women would soon be granted political independence. The open feminism of Co-Masonry was also embodied by Charlotte Despard, who had marched in June at the head of the members of the Women's Freedom League, and who led the Order's parade in September.

Co-Masonry as devised by Besant was highly ritualized: women and men had equal access to a complex hierarchy of multiple ranks, titles, and attributions. Such equality was exceptional in a spiritual movement: only a few Methodist female preachers, women within the occult Order of the Golden Dawn, and spiritualist female mediums could perform the same rituals as men. As a result, Co-Masonry also appealed to women who rejected the patriarchy of Catholicism but were still fascinated by Catholic rituals, along with a number of artists, writers, and aesthetes. Co-Masonry's ritualism and hierarchy were felt by some of its members to be reassuring

[42] Quoted in DIXON, Joy. *Divine Feminine: Theosophy and Feminism in England*. Johns Hopkins University Press, 2001, p. 80.

[43] Since 1925, the building has housed the British Medical Association under the name of BMA House.

during the Great Unrest of the 1910s, to which many contributed with their militant feminism. Gertrude Baillie-Weaver, Theosophist and Co-Mason, expressed as much in the *Co-Mason* in 1913: 'an ordered ritual that images [...] THAT which can never pass'[44].

By the 1920s, under Besant's leadership, Co-Masonry could boast forty lodges in England, ten of which in London, and several others in the Empire at large, especially in India. In 1925, Besant still explained:

> If [Masonry] is really anything, it is a presentment by symbol and by legend of the great fundamental truths of human life and human evolution; and therefore [...] — no distinction of sex is permitted; and because of that act in what we call Co-Masonry, it came into the position of being a possible instrument for helping in the evolution of mankind [...] into the really Universal Brotherhood which it proclaims.[45]

Fights for Women's Rights in India[46]

Annie Besant immediately fascinated Indian women, who turned out in droves to her first lectures there, in 1893. In December of that year, the Indian section of the Theosophical Society allowed women to attend the annual convention for the first time. It took place in Madras, and Besant addressed it. She did not, however, immediately allow herself to criticize the traditional customs that weighed on Indian women[47], such as child

[44] Quoted in DIXON, Joy. *Divine Feminine: Theosophy and Feminism in England*. Johns Hopkins University Press, 2001, p. 83–4.

[45] BESANT, Annie. *The Theosophical Society and the Occult Hierarchy: Three Lectures Delivered in the Kensington Town Hall, London, to Fellows of the Theosophical Society, October 1925*. London: Theosophical Publishing House, 1925.

[46] See ANDERSON, Nancy Fix. 'Bridging Cross-cultural Feminisms: Annie Besant and Women's Rights in England and India, 1874–1933'. *Women's History Review* 3, 1994, pp. 563–80.

[47] See PAXTON, Nancy L. 'Feminism under the Raj: Complicity and Resistance in the Writings of Flora Annie Steel and Annie Besant'. *Women's Studies International Forum*. 13.4, 1990, pp. 333–46.

marriage, or widows being prohibited from remarrying and ostracized. She was then striving for a cultural and spiritual Indian revival, while the so-called civilizing reforms imposed by the British had already incited violent reactions among the Indian population. The 1856 law allowing widows to remarry was even considered to be one of the causes of the Indian Rebellion of 1857[48]. As a result, British authorities did not introduce any social reform in India after the Rebellion until the Age of Consent Act 1891, which raised the age of sexual consent for Indian girls from ten to twelve, but did not address the issue of child marriage. Christian missionaries also used the argument of women's condition in India over and over again to justify their rejection of Hinduism, which they presented as barbaric and primitive. Although Besant suffered attacks from the Missionary Society for encouraging a Hindu revival, she feared that the Indians would associate her with those same missionaries.

In 1894, after returning from her first visit to India, Besant tried to justify her caution as regarded Indian women's position:

> Customs vary enormously in different parts of India, and the question of woman's position is far more complicated than many English reformers are inclined to think. [...] as a matter of fact the Hindus look with great disapproval on many of the ways and customs of European women, and consider that the Western ideal of womanhood is far lower than their own.

The *Woman's Signal*, an English feminist paper, reported Besant's remarks, and expressed their concern, recalling the significance of Besant's feminist fights up to then:

> It were wiser, surely, if Mrs Besant, who in the past has so nobly stood for women, were to face the evils, as she finds them and as they exist, and to throw the weight of her fine intellect into the work of Eastern reform [...].[49]

[48] Also known as the Sepoy or Indian Mutiny, it is often called the First War of Independence.

[49] 'Mrs Besant v. Mrs Bishop'. *Woman's Signal*, 12 April 1894.

Eventually, Indian reformers, such as Kaliprasanna Kavyabisharad, or the liberal newspaper the *Indian Social Reformer* in Madras[50], also ended up criticizing Besant's tolerance of Indian women's condition. So, in 1901, Besant gave a lecture entitled 'Womanhood'. As the advocate of a cultural and spiritual Indian revival, Besant was inspired by an idealized past, that of the Vedic society, when women did not suffer discrimination and oppression, because of traditional practices that she believed to have been imported later. Besant therefore held that the reforms she proposed did not stem from a wish to westernize India, but from a desire to return to original Hinduism, which, according to her, valued strong and educated women. By giving women more freedom, she told Indians, 'you would not be following the West, but following your own ancestral culture'; and of conservative, orthodox Hindus, she said: 'those men are as dangerous to India's religious future as those who would utterly westernise her.'

In 1903, Besant tackled the difficult issue of widows, with the essay 'Widow-Remarriage', still drawing her arguments from what she believed to be the real values of Hinduism:

> Hinduism presents man and woman as complementary halves of a single whole, each supplying what the other lacks. [...] It considers husband and wife as spiritually one, even as they are physically united.

Still cautious, however, she demanded that only widows whose marriage had never been consummated could remarry. She explained that this was also the view of Narayan Ganesh Chandavarkar, a Hindu reformer, president of the 1900 Indian National Congress, as well as a judge of the Bombay High Court. Besant, however, asked that the other widows would be able to become teachers or nurses. She nevertheless concluded, subversively: 'Some who take the highest view of marriage urge that the widower should not remarry any more than [should] the widow.'

Besant leaned on the educational needs of Indian girls to advance her arguments against child marriages. In 1904, in *The Education of Indian*

---

[50] Now called Chennai.

Girls, she violently opposed such marriages, speaking of 'These helpless victims, sold into slavery by their own fathers to purchased husbands', and wondering 'is it possible that India shall become free so long as this child-slavery remains?' In a 1915 article, 'Girls' Education', Besant again asserted: 'For any education beyond the most elementary, it is obvious that pre-puberty marriage must be abolished.' Eleven years earlier, she had founded the Central Hindu Girls' School, with a curriculum that remained respectful of traditions. In the year of its foundation, she explained in *The Education of Indian Girls*:

> Indian greatness will not return until Indian womanhood obtains a larger, a freer, and a fuller life, for largely in the hands of Indian women must lie the redemption of India. [...] man and woman must walk forward hand-in-hand to the raising of India [...]. The battle for the education of girls is just beginning.

While her precise views on the kind of elementary education necessary for Indian girls may sound conservative, Besant explained nonetheless: 'For those who desire higher education, the curriculum will necessarily be much the same as for boys.' In 1906, Narayan Chandavarkar, then vice-chancellor of the University of Bombay, wrote to the *Indian National Reformer* to express his admiration of the way Besant was able to make her reforms accepted through this gradual and tactful approach.

In 1913, Besant expressed her desire for reform even more clearly, with a series of lectures given in Madras, published as *Wake up, India: a Plea for Social Reform*. Now involved in the struggle for Indian Home Rule, she affirmed that only a reformed India would be able to reach political autonomy, and that any form of oppression and inequality such as the caste system and the inferior status and ignorance imposed on women ought to be abolished: 'Indian men do not deserve to be free politically, until they give freedom socially to Indian women.' In response to those who accused her of cultural imperialism, she said that she was fighting just as much against British culture by affirming equality between men and women. Given the violence of the Police repression against English suffragettes that year, her comparison was quite justified.

In 1917, Besant accepted the presidency of the Women's India Association, founded that year by feminist Theosophists Dorothy Jinarajadasa and Margaret Cousins. The latter had already launched the Irish Women's Franchise League in 1908. In 1919, Besant was elected president of the Indian Ladies' Conference, to whom she once again gave a speech on Indian women's rights and need for education.

Besant was by then one of the main leaders of the Indian nationalist movement, alongside Gandhi and Nehru, to the point of being put under house arrest by the British authorities in 1917. Upon her release, in December, she became the first woman to be elected president of the Indian National Congress[51]. She immediately added women's right to vote to its resolutions, underlining their importance in the struggle for Home Rule during her inaugural speech. As a member of the delegation received by Edwin Montagu, the Secretary of State for India, during his visit to Madras in 1918, Besant once again demanded that women's right to vote be included in any plan for Indian Home Rule. When the local Madras parliament decided to grant women the right to vote in 1921, Besant was invited to speak during the celebrations that followed.

Many Indian women honoured Besant's memory when she died in Madras in 1933. Poet and nationalist Sarojini Naid, who had been the first Indian woman to preside over the Indian National Congress in 1925, and the second woman in this post after Besant, said about her sister-in-fight: 'for the women of India she had done more in her time than any other single Indian woman'[52]. Before that, Besant had also done a great deal for British women, and her feminism greatly deserves to be re-evaluated today.

---

[51] See also FORBES, Geraldine. 'The Politics of Respectability: Indian Women and the Indian National Congress', in LOW, D. A., ed. *The Indian National Congress: Centenary Hindsights*. Oxford University Press, 1988, pp. 55–97.

[52] Quoted in ANDERSON, Nancy Fix. 'Bridging Cross-cultural Feminisms: Annie Besant and Women's Rights in England and India, 1874–1933'. *Women's History Review* 3.4, 1994, p. 576.

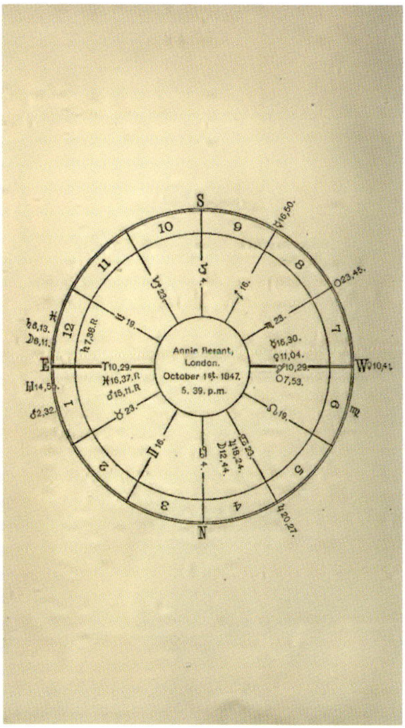

Fig. 1 — Horoscope of Annie Besant

Fig. 2 — Annie Wood at sixteen

Fig. 3 — The Bride, 1867

Fig. 4 — Mrs Besant and her Mother, 1867

Fig. 5 — Annie Besant in 1878

Fig. 6 — Annie Besant in 1885, in the dress she wore when she lectured for the NSS

Fig. 7 — Annie Besant in 1892
(wearing Madame Blavatsky's ring)

Fig. 8 — Strike Committee of the Matchmakers' Union
(with Herbert Burrows on her left, 1888)

Fig. 9 — Annie Besant in 1889

Fig. 10 — Annie Besant photographed by her son Digby in 1890

Fig. 11 — Annie Besant with her son Digby in 1890

Fig. 12 — Mrs Besant, her daughter Mabel (Mrs Besant-Scott), and her grand-daughter Muriel (Scott), Melbourne, 1894.

Fig. 13 — Annie Besant, Colonel H.S. Olcott and William Q. Judge in 1891

Fig. 14 — Mrs. Annie Besant and C. W. Leadbeater in 1900

Fig. 15 — Annie Besant and Rudolf Steiner, Munich, 1907

Fig. 16 — Annie Besant at fifty

Fig. 17 — Annie Besant, Co-Mason,
with her Scottish Rite 33rd degree sash
and double headed eagle adorned hat (n.d.)

Fig. 18 — The All India Home Rule League, 1916–1917

Fig. 19 — Annie Besant with Mohammed Ali Jinnah (on her left), 1917

Fig. 20 — Annie Besant upon her release from house arrest in India, 1917

Fig. 21 — Annie Besant with Gandhi, Madras, 1921

Fig. 22 — Annie Besant on Trafalgar Square, 1924

Fig. 23 — Annie Besant visits Cardiff, June 1924
(Cardiff Theosophical Society archives)

Fig. 24 — Golden Jubilee of the Theosophical Society,
Adyar, 1925

Fig. 25 — Annie Besant with Krishnamurti in Ojai, California, 1926

Fig. 26 — Annie Besant with Krishnamurti at the Star Camp in Ommen, 1929

Fig. 27 — Annie Besant arrives in Finland, 1927

Fig. 28 — Cornerstone ceremony at Helsinki, Finland, 1927

Fig. 29 — Annie Besant in 1927

Fig. 30 — Annie Besant's
funeral pyre, 1933

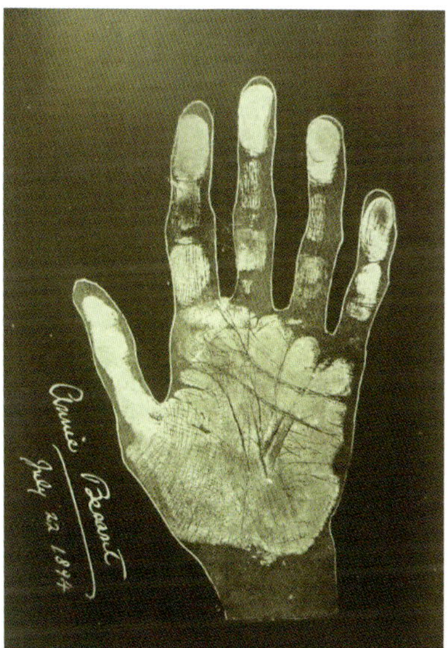

Fig. 31 — Annie Besant's hand,
July 1894

Fig. 32 — Indian commemorative stamp, 1963

Fig. 33 — State Bank of India's publicity campaign, 2011

Fig. 34 — Google Doodle of Annie Besant on her 168th Birthday in 2015

4

Annie Besant's Struggles against Political and Social Inequalities: From Radicalism to Socialism (1874–1890)[1]

by Marie Terrier[2]

Political Struggles within the Radical Movement

When Annie Besant became a member of the National Secular Society (NSS) in July 1874, she not only joined freethinkers, but also Radicals[3]. Secularists led two simultaneous fights: against religious dogmas, and against the exclusion of the working classes from political power. In the *National Reformer*, Charles Bradlaugh attempted to maintain a balance between theological and political questions, and so did Besant in her writings and lectures: she fought for freedom of speech and conscience,

[1] See SAVILLE, John and Joyce M. BELLAMY, then Keith GILDART and David HOWELL, eds. *Dictionary of Labour Biography*. Basingstoke: Palgrave Macmillan, 13 vols., 1972–2010; BESANT, Annie: *Autobiographical Sketches*. London: Freethought Publishing Co., 1885 (republished and annotated by MACKAY, Carole Hanbery, ed. Peterborough, Ont.: Broadview Press Ltd, 2009) and *Annie Besant: An Autobiography*. London: T. Fisher Unwin, 1893; NETHERCOT, Arthur Hobart. *The First Five Lives of Annie Besant*. University of Chicago Press, 1960; and SAVILLE, John, ed. *A Selection of the Social and Political Pamphlets of Annie Besant*. New York: Augustus M. Kelley, 1970.
[2] See TERRIER, Marie. *La Contribution théorique et militante d'Annie Besant (1847–1933) au renouveau socialiste des années 1880 en Grande-Bretagne. Genèse et prolongements*. PhD dissertation (n.p.). Université Sorbonne-Nouvelle, Paris 3, 2015.
[3] See ROYLE, Edward. *Radicals, Secularists and Republicans: Popular Freethought in Britain, 1866–1915*. Manchester University Press, 1980.

demanded political equality between men and women, defended the Irish, denounced imperialism and attacked the monarchy as well as the political and social privileges enjoyed by the aristocracy. All her fights were conducted in the name of the republican values 'liberty, equality, fraternity'.

Besant defined 'liberty' in the same way as John Stuart Mill in his 1859 essay *On Liberty*: the possibility of using all of one's faculties to improve oneself without infringing on other people's freedom. Besant believed liberty to be a condition of individual and collective progress. In 1875, in *Civil and Religious Liberty*, she presented the conquest of liberty as a never-ending struggle that required complete selflessness: 'to her we must sacrifice our time, and, if need be, our comfort and our happiness.'

For Besant, 'equality' meant justice and fairness. Human beings might not be born naturally equal, but Besant equalled civilization with the protection of all individuals' rights, as opposed to the rights of the strongest. This was the only way to allow humanity as a whole to progress, Besant explained in 1875, in *Liberty, Equality, Fraternity*: 'when equality of right is recognised, we shall gradually decrease inequalities of Nature, and we shall raise the race itself to a higher level.'

As a Radical, Besant considered 'fraternity' as essential: when human beings acknowledged each other as brothers and sisters, they fought for the liberty and equality of all. According to her, unity and co-operation were necessary for each man and woman to progress, and thus society as a whole. So, in *Liberty, Equality, Fraternity*, she insisted on 'fraternity', that could only be reached 'by joyful self-sacrifice for the common good, and glad free labour for the benefit of all.'

To attain this ideal, Besant first demanded that a Republic be established in Britain, notably in *English Republicanism*, written in 1877. She rejected the principle of heredity, preferring that of meritocracy. Besant's ideas on how to implement this political system were daring — but she voiced them at a time when republicanism was losing ground because of Queen Victoria's renewed popularity, so Besant came to focus on the democratization of the existing political system instead.

Besant frequently expressed her faith in the parliamentary system, but she added that all political and social groups ought to be represented in Parliament, so that diverging interests could be expressed until an agreement was reached. Besant was therefore in favour of universal suffrage: to her, only the franchise would allow women and the working classes to amend or repeal the laws which restricted their freedom. As Besant strongly believed in self-determination, she was in favour of a federal political system, and criticized any excessive centralization of power, be it within Britain or the Empire.

Even though Besant criticized the flaws of the British political system, she admired it — especially Parliament. As a consequence, she had confidence in the system's ability to evolve towards true democracy. The way Besant imagined Britain becoming a Republic was emblematic of her reformist frame of mind: she predicted gradual reforms, accompanied by laws that would prevent the continuation of the monarchy after the death of Queen Victoria. According to her, thanks to the 'English political genius', Britain was at the forefront of such political progress. Besant asserted that a republican and democratic system 'would be the orderly and peaceful completion of our national growth.' Fearing abrupt change, she believed that her mission consisted of promoting political and social reforms in order to avoid a revolution. Besant's involvement with radicalism allowed her to define the political ideas that became prominent in her forthcoming public commitments. It also led her to ponder the 'Condition of England Question'[4], which came again to the fore with the economic depression from the end of the 1870s.

Fighting for Land Reform

Annie Besant's interest in land reform dated back to her support of the agricultural workers in Lincolnshire who had joined the National

[4] This phrase was first used by Thomas Carlyle in *Chartism* (1839) to describe the dreadful condition of the British working classes, and the dangerous gap between the rich and the poor.

Agricultural Labourer's Union, created by Joseph Arch in 1872. In 1874, in *Landlords, Tenant Farmers and Labourers*, she described those labourers' terrible working and living conditions, and she encouraged farmers to join them in resisting their landlords, whom she held responsible for their plight.

The last twenty-five years of the nineteenth century were marked by a great depression in British agriculture, and consequent agitation. It was in that context that Besant took part in organizing a large conference on the issue of land reform in February 1880: it gathered around 5000 delegates from a number of progressive movements. Charles Bradlaugh opened the debate with a triumphal speech, in which he defended compulsory cultivation — if uncultivated, farmable land would be seized by the State —, thus criticizing absentee landlords who only cared about their own interests. In spite of this proposal, and while some in the audience supported complete land nationalization, Bradlaugh still came strongly in favour of peasant ownership. Besant and Joseph Arch followed him on the platform, as well as Edward Aveling, who had recently joined the NSS, and Christian socialist Rev. Stewart Headlam, who had founded the Guild of St Matthew in Bethnal Green, in 1877. The Land Law Reform League was launched in the wake of the conference, with Besant as one of its vice-presidents. In addition to the principle of compulsory cultivation of farmable land, the League demanded more protection for the farmers. It also proposed a system of progressive taxation, in order to incite landlords to sell small plots of land to their farmers. Unfortunately, the League never was very active, because Bradlaugh got caught up in his parliamentary struggle from May 1880. Then, once he was allowed to sit in 1886, he became less interested in extra-parliamentary agitation. Bradlaugh formulated a detailed agenda for land reform, that he defended in Westminster with little success.

The Land Law Reform League was far from being the only organization agitating for land reform: during the summer of 1880, more militant Radicals founded the Land Nationalisation Society, with Alfred Russell Wallace and Helen Taylor among its leaders. Land reformers were also concerned about the renewed agitation in Ireland. The word 'boycott' was first used to describe farmers and agricultural workers' resistance in County

Mayo in 1880: crushed by exorbitant rents, they responded to Charles Parnell's appeal — the president of the Irish National Land League — and refused to harvest the lands managed by Charles Cunningham Boycott. It was also in 1880 that the Liberals discussed the Irish Land Act 1881. It led to the creation of courts that would not only set fair rents, but also fight the arbitrary evictions that dissuaded farmers from investing in the lands they cultivated.

Besant gave a series of lectures in support of the Land Law Reform League[5]. As a Radical, she saw a return to the land as a solution to the situation of the industrial working classes. Besant castigated the landlords who did not care about the common good; she even called into question their property right, quoting John Stuart Mill: 'No man made the land. It is the original inheritance of the whole species. Its appropriation is wholly a question of general expediency. When private property in land is not expedient, it is unjust'[6]. Besant also demanded tax reforms, as well as changes in the laws that governed inheritance, in order to better allocate the land. Additionally, she favoured a redistribution of wealth, insisting on the fact that wealth was a product of labour. Even though, like Bradlaugh, she supported the idea of peasant ownership, her pamphlets show her increased interest in land nationalization.

Neo-Malthusianism and the Causes of Poverty

To Annie Besant, neo-Malthusianism was a means of fighting poverty: her 1877 essay *The Law of Population* was dedicated 'TO THE POOR.' In order to understand the Victorian ideological controversy around birth control[7],

---

[5] See BESANT, Annie. *Labour and Land: Their Burdens, Duties and Rights*. London: Freethought Publishing Co., 1881.

[6] Besant took this quote from *Principles of Political Economy* (1848).

[7] The term 'birth-control' was widely used only from the 1920s. To speak about fertility limitation, Victorian Malthusians spoke of 'limitation of the family', 'preventive checks', 'scientific checks to population' or 'conjugal prudence'. The term 'birth control' is used here to avoid circumlocutions.

it is necessary to recall the traditional working-class opposition to Malthusian theories, perceived as 'anti-poor'. Later historians tried to redeem Malthus by underlining the progressive aspects of his ideas, making a distinction between Malthus and those Victorian Malthusians, who attempted to limit poor relief under the pretext that it encouraged the poor to breed. Victorian Malthusians presented overpopulation in working-class neighbourhoods as the sole cause of poverty, and believed poverty could disappear thanks to individual efforts to limit family size. Most Radicals and socialists, for their part, argued that poverty originated in an unequal distribution of wealth, and that it was necessary to reform the economic and social system. Some Radicals tried to combine the two, such as Francis Place (1777–1854): while he supported birth control, he was also actively involved in trade-unionism and Chartism, although both movements – trade-unionism (starting in the 1820s)[8] and Chartism (1838–1858)[9] – were generally hostile to Malthusian theories. In the 1880s, this battle was taken up by the socialists, who were very critical of the Malthusian League[10].

Even though Besant was one of the vice-presidents of the Malthusian League, she did not agree with the individualism and social conservatism of some of its leaders, and there were tensions within the League. Besant fully supported the League's desire to limit religious influence on sexual matters, as well as its eagerness to spread medical knowledge as widely as possible. She was also drawn to the League's fight against prostitution and their defence of women's rights. However, while its president, Charles Drysdale, was a typical Victorian Malthusian, others, such as Besant, outlined the multiple causes of poverty, and advocated social reforms too.

---

[8] Trade unions developed after the Combination Acts (forbidding working-class associations) were repealed in 1824.

[9] In his study on Chartism, Malcolm Chase recalls this opposition to Malthusian theories. See CHASE Malcolm, *Chartism: A New History*. Manchester University Press, 2007, p. 15.

[10] See the chapter entitled 'Labour and the Malthusian League', in LEDBETTER, Rosanna. *A History of the Malthusian League, 1877–1927*. Columbus: Ohio State University Press, 1976, pp. 87–119.

In *The Landlord's Attempt to Mislead the Landless* (1881), Besant explained that the causes of poverty were: '(1st) the number of laborers [*sic*]; (2nd) the tenure of the land, and so closely allied with this as to be part of it, the distribution of the wealth produced by the workers.' Besant constantly argued that birth control and social reform were complementary, but, as reforming the social and political system was a long process, she insisted on the necessity of fewer mouths to feed in the meantime, in order to avoid a violent revolution:

> Land reform is sorely needed, but, to meet the immediate needs of the present, land revolution would be necessary; it is surely wiser to lessen the population-pressure, and to work steadily at the same time towards Reform of the Land Laws, instead of allowing the population-pressure to increase until the starving multitudes precipitate us into a revolution.

After she became a socialist, Besant logically removed this paragraph from *The Law of Population*, but she went on stressing that land reform and birth control were complementary. To her, fewer children meant that their parents would have more time and energy to fight for social reform. Besant also strongly opposed social Darwinism: she explained that birth control would help reduce competition for work and the social struggle for survival. Far from being a fight to maintain the existing economic and social order, neo-Malthusianism was, for Besant, an opportunity to look for solutions to the issue of poverty, but also to call into question her militant affiliations when these solutions were found wanting.

Crisis of Confidence in the Liberal Party

As Edward Royle explained: 'politically, Bradlaugh and his followers stood on the extreme left of the Gladstonian Liberal Party'[11]. Radicals allied

[11] ROYLE, Edward. *Radicals, Secularists and Republicans: Popular Freethought in Britain, 1866–1915*. Manchester University Press, 1980, pp. x–xi.

themselves with Liberals during elections: it was thanks to such an alliance that Bradlaugh was first elected MP in Northampton in 1880, after several unsuccessful attempts as an independent candidate. So, as many Radicals, Besant supported the Liberals in 1880.

Nevertheless, this alliance soon began to splinter. While the Radicals expected a land reform in Ireland, Gladstone's Liberal government reinforced coercion and suspended Habeas Corpus there instead. In 1882, Besant wrote *Coercion in Ireland and Its Results*, to denounce this suppression of individual freedom, stressing that repression would never solve social issues in Ireland. Many Radicals were also disappointed to see that Gladstone's foreign policy hardly differed from Disraeli's imperialist agenda. The militants of the NSS finally bitterly observed that Gladstone barely supported Bradlaugh in his battle to be allowed to sit in Parliament in spite of his atheism.

Not only did the Liberal Party thus failed to meet the aspirations of many Radicals like Besant, but she began to feel cramped within the NSS and the Malthusian League: two organizations very keen on individualism, whereas she longed for more altruism. Additionally, their leaders opposed increased State intervention in the economy, and rejected further social reforms. Besant therefore turned to other progressive movements.

New Radicalism, Trade Unionism and the Co-operative Movement

The NSS was only one trend in the broad and varied Radical movement. Radicalism experienced a revival in the 1870s and 1880s, as the 'new Radicals' no longer limited their demands to political and land reforms; rather, they underlined the necessity of State intervention to ensure social progress. Joseph Chamberlain was emblematic of this new radicalism: as mayor of Birmingham from 1874, he had the city forcibly purchase water and gas companies, thereby improving these services while reducing their costs. Chamberlain undertook slums clearance and built working-class lodgings in their place. Public and private funds were raised to build schools, as well as public libraries, swimming pools and baths. Besant was most interested in the reforms of those she called 'advanced Radicals'. She nevertheless felt that they remained too close to the Liberal Party and that their social and ethical thinking ought to go further.

At that time, the working classes were also supported by the expanding trade-union movement[12]. New model, or craft, unions — as they were referred to — had appeared in the 1850s, but they only gathered male skilled workers and artisans, i.e. the working-class aristocracy. Hardly influenced by socialist ideas, those unions did not challenge economic liberalism. In order to protect their members' wages, they controlled the labour supply in their trades. They also dubbed as friendly societies, with relief funds meant to support their members in case of unemployment, illness or disability. Their federation, the Trades Union Congress, was founded in 1868 in Manchester. As the trade-union movement became increasingly institutional, a Parliamentary Committee was created in order to encourage the working-class vote in the wake of the Second Reform Act 1867, and to lobby in favour of pro-working-class legislation. The Trade Union Act 1871 legalized trade unions for the first time in Britain, although the right to strike was not recognized yet, and picketing remained illegal until 1875. In 1874, the first 'Lib-Lab' (Liberal-Labour) MPs entered Parliament: in exchange for their loyalty to the Liberal Party, these Labour candidates had enjoyed the much needed Liberal support during the general election. In 1880, twelve 'Lib-Lab' MPs were thus returned to Parliament.

Besant acknowledged the importance of trade unions, who had demonstrated 'the value of combination, the force of united action [and] the strength of self-reliance.' She nevertheless believed that the movement was too focused on controlling labour supply: she blamed the craft unions

[12] See PELLING, Henry. *A History of British Trade Unionism*. Harmondsworth: Penguin Books, 1963; ALASTAIR, J. Reid. *United We Stand: A History of Britain's Trade Unions*. London: Penguin Allen Lane, 2004; BANTMAN, Constance. 'Du *lib-labism* à la grande fièvre ouvrière: les *trade unions* entre libéralisme, travaillisme et action directe', in MOTARD, Anne-Marie, ed. *Les Syndicats britanniques: déclin ou renouveau ? Revue française de civilisation britannique*, 15.2, 2009, pp. 45–57.

for defending their own members only, thereby neglecting the majority of the working class, composed of women and unskilled workers. Besant, nevertheless, did not support strike action: not only was she wary of such acts of defiance against employers, but she was also concerned about consequent wage loss that might result in the pauperization of striking workers' families.

Instead, Besant favoured the co-operative movement, initiated by industrial philanthropist and social reformer Robert Owen (1771–1858), considered as the father of British socialism[13]. Because of Owen's idealism and focus on ethics, Marx and Engels saw him as one of the founders of utopian socialism. From the outset of his career in Manchester, Owen was deeply concerned about the ghastly consequences of the Industrial Revolution on the working classes. According to him, one's environment determined one's physical, intellectual and moral tendencies, and only favourable conditions would allow self-reform. Improving the workers' situation was therefore seen by Owen as a precondition to build a better society. In 1800, he put his theories into practice in his New Lanark factory, in Scotland: working conditions were improved, the ten-hour day was implemented, young children were sent to school, and adults were provided with leisure activities, as well as dining halls and sick rooms. As a laboratory of social reform, New Lanark soon drew visitors from throughout Europe[14].

Owen fought for social reforms, working with MPs and reformers to improve education and to fight against child labour. He demanded laws to protect exploited workers, left defenceless in the new capitalist system. Owen grew frustrated at how slow the economic and social system was to reform, however. So, from the 1820s, he supported the establishment of utopian communities, such as New Harmony, Indiana (USA), a completely secular community, where private ownership was abolished. Owen's communities were meant as the starting points of a broader social reorganization, based

[13] See SIMÉON, Ophélie. 'Robert Owen, père du socialisme britannique ?'. *La Vie des idées*, 4 September 2012. http://www.laviedesidees.fr/Robert-Owen-pere-du-socialisme.html; and HARRISON, J. F. C. 'A New View of Mr Owen', in POLLARD, Sidney & John SALT, eds. *Robert Owen: Prophet of the Poor*. London: Macmillan, 1971.

[14] New Lanark is now a UNESCO World Heritage site.

on ethics and co-operation instead of competition. Owen also launched the British co-operative movement in the 1820s: co-operative shops, workshops and companies were to ensure the fair remuneration of labour and to abolish individual profit — profits were to be put towards working-class education and agricultural communities instead. Despite the failure of organized Owenism in the mid-1840s, Owen's ideas had a long-term influence on working-class movements, especially on Chartism.

In the 1870s and 1880s, Besant still praised the co-operative movement: it 'has prepared men to think of a possible future in which co-operation should wholly replace competition, and Owen's dream of universal brotherhood become a living reality'[15]. Incidentally, secularism had been launched by former Owenists and co-operators, including George Jacob Holyoake. Besant insisted on the importance of the co-operative movement on working-class education, but she was critical of the inefficiency of some co-operatives, and blamed others for having reintroduced individual profit. She was also opposed to those who cut themselves off from the world by withdrawing to utopian communities, instead of working on reforming the whole of society.

The Socialist Revival of the 1880s

For many social and political reformers, the campaign for land reform proved a gateway to socialism. The Land Law Reform League was not the only organization to take on the issue. In 1882, American Radical Henry George toured Britain and Ireland to promote land nationalization. In his book, *Progress and Poverty*[16], and in his lectures, George denounced economic liberalism. He rejected the idea that poverty was caused by overpopulation and the supposed moral failures of the working classes, arguing instead that

[15] BESANT, Annie. *The Socialist Movement*. London: Freethought Publishing Co., 1886.
[16] GEORGE, Henry. *Progress and Poverty: An Enquiry into the Cause of Industrial Depression and of Increase of Want with Increase of Wealth*. London: Paul Kegan, 1881 (1879).

the economic and social system was at the origin of their poverty. The crux of his argument was that modern civilization produced material progress at the cost of increasing poverty for the working classes. In order to solve this paradox, George called for fraternity and economic co-operation. Historians showed that George's followers could easily adhere to socialist ideas, after he thus insisted on the structural causes of poverty[17].

Besant was wary of Henry George, because he criticized Malthusianism. Nevertheless, she supported some of his followers, especially those who defined themselves as Christian socialists. In 1883, they founded the Land Reform Union, with Stewart Headlam, Helen Taylor and a few of those who were to create or join the Fabian Society.

At the beginning of the 1880s, Henry Mayers Hyndman was one of the most vocal advocates of socialism. In 1881, he had founded the Democratic Federation to promote political reform, and his organization officially embraced socialism in 1883, becoming the Social Democratic Federation (SDF). The SDF soon had 500 members, and launched its own weekly, *Justice*, the following January. Hyndman was openly inspired by Karl Marx, calling for a social revolution resulting in the abolition of private ownership of the means of production[18]. In the long run, Hyndman wanted the State to take control of the economy, but in the short run he hoped to create a socialist party based on the German model, in order to promote social reforms in Parliament, as so many 'stepping stones' — decent homes for workers, free education, free school meals, the eight-hour day and the nationalization of railway companies.

Alongside Hyndman, another essential figure of the socialist revival was William Morris — by then a famous a poet, artist, craftsman and designer. Morris wanted to democratize arts and crafts, and ensure their

[17] See PELLING, Henry. *The Origins of the Labour Party, 1880–1900*. Oxford University Press, 1966 (1954), p. 10; WOLFE, Willard. *From Radicalism to Socialism: Men and Ideas in the Formation of Fabian Socialist Doctrines, 1881–1889*. Yale University Press, 1975, p. 79.

[18] For his part, Karl Marx (1818–1883), who lived in exile in London, did not trust Hyndman, who was a journalist, businessman and politician, too close to imperialist Conservative circles to his taste.

survival in a modern civilization increasingly standardized by industrial mass-production. Pleasure and self-development through creative, meaningful work were crucial to his thinking. Morris was inspired by art critic and social thinker John Ruskin, and rejected the Victorian society for not allowing individuals to create and develop freely. He strongly criticized machines and the factory system which fragmented work and dehumanized workers. In 1883, Morris, disappointed by the Liberals whom he used to support, joined the SDF.

Nonetheless, Morris's relations with authoritarian Hyndman were immediately tense. Morris believed Hyndman delayed a necessary revolution by fighting for parliamentary representation and reforms instead. Morris rejected social reforms, considering that they could never bring about a complete change in the production and distribution of wealth. He feared that such reforms would divert the working classes from the ultimate objective: controlling the means of production. So, at the end of December 1884, Morris led away a splinter group, that included Ernest Belfort Bax, Eleanor Marx[19] and her partner Edward Aveling (who had left the NSS during the summer of 1884). In its manifesto, Morris's Socialist League advocated revolutionary socialism and the abolition of social classes. Unlike Hyndman, Morris and his supporters believed that it was necessary to work with existing labour organizations, because a true social revolution could not come from the State only. Their motto famously was: 'Educate, Agitate, Organise', but they saw their role as primarily educational: they had to prepare the people for socialism.

Even though the Socialist League only gathered 230 members, its monthly, *Commonweal*, sold around 2000 copies, and influential figures joined — such as the poet and early activist for homosexuals' rights Edward Carpenter, or the artist and engraver Walter Crane. Friedrich Engels, a close friend of Marx's, who edited Marx's unpublished writings after his death, supported the League, even though he was wary of its anarchist tendencies. Indeed, the Socialist League was characterized by ideological diversity: gathering revolutionary Marxists, like Eleanor Marx and Ernst Belfort Bax,

[19] Karl Marx's youngest daughter.

as well as anarchists, and ethical socialists interested in the moral, rather than economic side of socialism[20].

In the 1880s, socialist ideals and strategies were still in the process of being defined, and the socialist movement was characterized by dialogue, exchange and cross-fertilization between its different brands. This intellectual fervour resulted in the creation of numerous organizations, among which the Fellowship of the New Life. At the beginning of 1883, a group of about thirty London Liberals, Radicals, socialists and other progressive intellectuals came together to denounce the competitive system and to encourage the moral reconstruction of society. They were unable to agree on which actions to take, however: while some favoured the creation of communities where to carry out their ethical principles, others wanted to encourage both structural and moral reforms within society at large. The Fabian Society emerged from the latter group in January 1884. Frank Podmore, one of its founding members, suggested its name in reference to the third-century BCE Roman general, Quintus Fabius Maximus Verrucosus, nicknamed 'Cunctator' (the 'Delayer'), because he had postponed confrontation with Hannibal in favour of a strategy of harassment which allowed him to choose the right time for his attack.

Twentieth-century Fabians are known for defending a gradualist and constitutional brand of socialism. However, in 1884–1885, the Fabian Society was only a debating group of around fifty, who compared ideas on how best to reorganize society. There was no Fabian ideology as such, and Fabians rarely belonged to the Fabian Society only: George Bernard Shaw remained a member of the SDF when he joined the Society in September 1884. As for Charlotte Wilson, who joined the Fabians at the beginning of 1885, she was a staunch anarchist. Sidney Webb joined the Fabians in May 1885, though, as a Positivist, he still believed in a possible moral reform of capitalism. It is indeed important to recall that the differences between the various organizations of the socialist revival were moving lines rather than fixed boundaries. It is also crucial to underline the constant dialogue

[20] See the section 'Ethical Socialists', in BEVIR, Mark. *The Making of British Socialism.* Princeton University Press, 2011.

between radicalism and socialism in order to understand Besant's part in the socialist revival.

Conversion to Socialism (1883–1884)

When Annie Besant discovered socialism, the movement was not fully organized yet, but socialists soon found themselves at the heart of the social agitation in London. Indignation about persistent poverty helps explain the intellectual and moral appeal of socialism in Radical circles. The great depression in agriculture had intensified migration towards large industrial cities — where the workers' economic situation hardly was any better, and many actually found themselves unemployed. Besant was appalled by working-class families' living conditions in the slums of the East End of London. She came to realize that the moral judgement the ruling classes passed on the poor was completely out of touch with social reality, and that the working classes could not overcome the limitations of their social environment by themselves. She understood that the poor were not morally 'undeserving'; rather, they were the victims of a hypocritical society. As she explained in *Why I Am a Socialist*: 'I am a Socialist because of the failure of our present civilisation.'

From 1883, Besant paid more and more attention to socialist arguments, while Bradlaugh, for his part, was still fiercely opposed to socialism, which he considered as a dangerous, unrealistic and violent ideology. In January 1883, Besant attended a lecture by French anarchist and former *Communarde* Louise Michel. In her report for the *National Reformer*, Besant said she understood Michel's wish to abolish poverty, but she distanced herself from Michel's asceticism, believing that, as dreadful as the situation was, it was necessary 'to cultivate grace and beauty in life.' In the two years that led to Besant's joining socialism, she kept apprised of the activities of the SDF, whose members often used harsh words against Bradlaugh. In her autobiography, Besant explained that the criticism she then voiced against socialists was more personal than ideological: 'I must confess that my deep attachment to him [Bradlaugh] led me into injustice to his Socialist foes in those early days.' Besant was torn between what she called 'a conflict between personal tie and a call of duty.' Even though she was increasingly interested in socialism, she kept denouncing the Marxist socialists who preached violence — arguing instead that Britain was a free country, so that people could use political agitation and elections if they wanted to have their say.

Bradlaugh encouraged debate with socialists, believing it was the best strategy to prove them wrong. Ironically, this was how Besant was drawn to their ideas. In April 1884, a debate between Hyndman and Bradlaugh led Besant to reconsider her stance. Answering to the question 'Will Socialism Benefit the English People?', Hyndman heavily drew on Radical values — especially that of work as opposed to privileges — and expounded an altruistic ethic. He defined socialism as 'an endeavour to substitute for anarchical struggle or fight for existence an organized co-operation for existence.' Hyndman wanted to promote the interest of the community and to abolish individualism, whereas Bradlaugh supported individualism, because he believed that individuals only, rather than the State, could remedy social ills[21].

Besant met George Bernard Shaw during one of those debates in the spring of 1884. She was initially critical of him, believing that he was a middle-class 'loafer' who just wanted to teach lessons to the working class. She soon discovered that the young, impoverished writer was actually living according to his socialist principles. Besant then offered to publish Shaw's novel, *The Irrational Knot,* by instalment in *Our Corner*, the monthly she had launched in 1883. Publication started in April 1885 and, two months later, she entrusted the 'Art Corner' to Shaw, who soon proved himself a talented art critic.

Once Besant agreed with the socialists' moral arguments, she decided

---

[21] HYNDMAN, Henry Mayers, & BRADLAUGH, Charles. *Will Socialism Benefit the English People? Verbatim Report of a Debate between Henry M. Hyndman and Charles Bradlaugh Held at St. James' Hall on April 17th, 1884*. London: Freethought Publishing Company, 1884.

to study their economic theories. In her autobiography, she explained that having read only Liberal economists so far, she knew nothing of socialist economic principles. She started analysing the production and distribution of wealth from a socialist perspective, and soon came to realize that the capitalist system of production, which relied on private ownership of the means of production and the pursuit of personal profit, dispossessed workers, contributed to their physical and moral degradation, and destroyed Nature. As a consequence, from the summer of 1884, Besant demanded increased State intervention to protect the working classes. She supported higher taxes on capital and the eight-hour day — reforms that were part of the SDF agenda. *Justice* therefore noted: 'Mrs Annie Besant is finding it necessary to turn Socialist; but does not like anyone to tell her so.'

It was eventually the issue of free school meals which led Besant to move explicitly closer to socialists. In December 1884, she used her *National Reformer* column 'Daybreak' to support free school meals. She drew the attention of William Platt Ball, a regular contributor to the *National Reformer*, who feared that this measure would encourage the poor to depend on public relief or charity. His individualist and typically Malthusian arguments — which occasionally verged on eugenics — did not keep Besant from going on defending the principle of State intervention. She showed remarkable courage, because she thus defied most of the NSS, especially her friend Bradlaugh. Soon after, Besant officially announced she would join the socialists.

In January 1885, Besant attended a lecture given by Shaw to the Dialectical Society, a bastion of Liberal economists and Malthusian reformers. Shaw explained in his autobiography[22] how much he feared Besant would rise up at the end of his lecture to destroy his arguments one by one. Contrary to what Shaw expected, Besant agreed with him and asked him to submit her name for election to the Fabian Society — to which she was admitted in June 1885. In her own autobiography, Besant explained she had chosen to join the Fabian Society: 'Because it was less hotly antagonistic

[22] SHAW, George Bernard. *An Autobiography, 1856–1898. Selected from His Writings.* WEINTRAUB, Stanley, ed. London: Reinhardt, 1969.

to the Radicals than the two other Socialist organisations.' In fact, Besant was critical of the SDF's ambiguous stance as concerned violence; and she disagreed with the Socialist League's rejection of gradual reforms. So she most probably chose to join the Fabian Society as a means to express her own views.

In 1917, when Shaw commented on Besant's conversion to socialism, with all of his usual condescension towards women, he asserted that she threw herself into it 'with her accustomed suddenness and impetuosity.' He could not be more wrong, as Besant's decision to join the socialist movement was the outcome of a long personal study and reflection.

Her Socialist Views on the Reorganization of Society

In *History of the Fabian Society* (1916), Edward Pease asserted that Annie Besant was, above all, a propagandist, and suggested that her socialist thinking was limited. Yet, Besant's socialist essays prove her ability, not only to conduct in-depth reflection on socialism, but also to adapt its ideology to a British public.

Besant asked for a complete reorganization of society, carried out mainly by the State — but that she redefined as a community, organized to promote the public good, not as an institution designed to control the people: 'In the modern Democracy the People are the State. Parliament is no longer a class, making laws for a Nation; but it is the Nation in its legislative activity'[23]. According to Besant, the extension of the political franchise allowed for social reforms, and she encouraged people to vote, to use whatever constitutional power was available to them, in order to promote policies that truly protected their interests.

During her first lecture at the Fabian Society, in December 1885, Besant made a clear statement in favour of collectivism: for her, the State would have to nationalize land and capital. Pragmatically, however, she insisted

[23] BESANT, Annie. *The Trades Union Movement*. London: Freethought Publishing Co., 1890.

on devolution, and stressed that global solutions would emerge from small-scale experiments. She even hesitated at first between production being managed directly by the workers' trade unions, or administratively, by elected representatives. The main task, however, was to put an end to competition, by doing away with the private ownership of the means of production. In *Why I Am a Socialist*, Besant asserted that 'Socialism claims for the whole community control of its land and its capital.' Still, rather than wiping the slate clean, she wanted to retain large companies, but with completely different functioning and purpose. Besant's socialist industry would thus heavily rely on machines, but so as to reduce the working day and to protect workers' health. In *The Socialist Movement*, Besant recommended increased mechanization of exhausting and dangerous tasks, such as mining. She was also in favour of sharing unwanted tasks among workers, and she proposed compensatory measures for those who worked in the harshest conditions. Besant's desire to make work less hard and alienating for everyone attests to her ability to tackle fundamental social and ethical questions.

In the system Besant advocated, workers would enjoy the benefits of the entirety of the wealth they produced — directly, thanks to wages, and indirectly, thanks to public services. 'All profits made would come back to the nation as a whole', she assured in *Radicalism and Socialism*. The aim of her new economic organization was to offer equal access to health, education, justice and leisure. Contrary to the capitalist system of production which dehumanized workers, Besant's socialism would allow them to progress as individuals. Besant strongly insisted on the right to a favourable environment: in an article entitled 'Hanging', she denounced the death penalty, insofar as criminals were the result of unfavourable circumstances. Besant believed crime could be eradicated, and she asked for a judicial system whose motto would be 'help instead of punish'. She claimed that, thanks to socialism: 'the day will surely dawn when none will be found vile enough to murder a man for hire, and when the last gallows shall be presented as a historical relic of past barbarism to the successors of Madame Tussaud.'

Besant wanted Parliament to pass laws that would 'spread sufficiency and comfort throughout the community.' She supported the movement for an eight-hour working day, launched in 1886 by Tom Mann, a trade unionist and SDF militant. She was anxious to improve working conditions as quickly as possible, so she asked for more factory inspectors in order to ensure that the Factory Acts truly were implemented. Besant insisted on decent wages, comfortable housing and leisure for everyone. She also asserted that 'children and workers incapacitated by age or sickness should receive an equal share [of the wealth produced] with the communal employees'[24]. Though Besant did not refer to social benefits, this bold assertion helped pave the way for the Liberal reforms of the 1910s and the Welfare State.

Education was central to Besant's thinking. She developed a reformist educational programme that was ahead of its time in many regards. She rejected rigid and mechanical instruction, preferring teaching methods meant to develop individual intelligence instead. Besant also believed girls and boys should receive the same education, in order to encourage sex equality and understanding. Besant wanted education to fight against national prejudices too, and to encourage open-mindedness. She refused to see the cost of education as an issue, because she considered it, first and foremost, as the lever to help society forward. All in all, Besant fought for an educational system that would be free, compulsory, mixed and secular.

Besant also sought to integrate her feminist principles into her socialist thinking. She insisted on women's economic independence as a means of emancipation — contrary to those mostly male socialists and trade unionists who supported the concept of 'family wage', which allowed the husband to provide for the needs of his wife and children. Besant fought against sexual prejudices when she explained to male workers that they should not perceive women's labour as a threat. Capitalists used female workers to lower wages, but Besant encouraged male and female workers to struggle together against their exploiters, and to demand equal wages

[24] BESANT, Annie. 'Industry under Socialism', in SHAW, Bernard, ed. *Fabian Essays in Socialism* (1889). Garden City, NY: Doubleday, 1961.

and working conditions.

So, Besant's socialist society would protect individual rights, but there would also be duties, especially that of working. She still maintained that it was necessary 'to subordinate the individual to the general good.' Besant concluded 'Industry under Socialism' on the assertion that the success of socialism depended on the development of 'social instincts', an ethical stance of the utmost importance in her thinking.

Through her search for a balance between individual rights and the general good, Besant contributed a valuable reflection on social organization. Admittedly, she drew on some of the ideas and theories that were being circulated at the time, but she formulated a personal synthesis, that was at times very original and daring.

Use of the Theory of Evolution to Justify Socialism

Although Annie Besant encouraged men and women to take an active part in the building of socialism, she also explained that all societies evolved towards it anyway. This 'inevitability of socialism' was a widespread concept at the time, but it took on different forms. Socialists inspired by Marx believed that capitalism was to collapse under the weight of its inner contradictions. Others thought that traditional political parties had reached their limits and would surely be replaced by a new socialist one. Finally, some socialists, including Besant, explained that the political and economic evolutions of their time already were setting the stage for socialism. Besant was not alone in believing in a smooth, gradual transition towards socialism as opposed to a violent revolution, but she was one of the first to rely explicitly on the theory of evolution to justify her belief[25]. In *Why I Am a Socialist*, Besant explained that the evolutionary forces at work within society were paving the way for socialism, and that this belief was the main reason why she had converted to socialism. By declaring 'I am a

[25] STACK, David. *The First Darwinian Left: Socialism and Darwinism 1859–1914*. Cheltenham: New Clarion Press, 2003, pp. 6 & 48–50.

Socialist because I am a believer in Evolution', Besant presented socialism as natural and inevitable.

Even though it can be argued that socialism rested on ideals, to Besant it was grounded in scientific facts: her views were meant as the scientific continuation of Darwin's and Spencer's work. Besant's vision of the theory of evolution also drew on Jean-Baptiste de Lamarck's own biological theory and Auguste Comte's Positivism, but the conclusion that society naturally evolved towards socialism was entirely her own.

According to Besant, if the struggle for existence in 'Nature' generated progress, this did not apply to human societies. For her, competition and individualism were 'the evil fruits of the perpetuation among men of the struggle for existence: a struggle which however inevitable among brutes, is […] unworthy of human civilisation' — whereas the progress of civilization depended on 'social tendencies' such as co-operation. Besant explained that society needed sympathy, fraternity, respect for others and love in order to progress. Besant was defending a position close to Darwinian anthropology: according to French philosopher Patrick Tort, who commented on *The Descent of Man* (1871), Darwin came to the conclusion that contrary to what occurs in 'Nature', the survival and progress of human societies did not depend on the struggle for existence, but rather on the triumph of sympathy[26].

Besant also relied on historical analysis to show that society had already initiated its march toward socialism. She explained in *The Evolution of Society*, that she wanted to '[judge] the future by the past.' To her, the electoral reforms of 1832, 1867 and 1884, already paved the way of socialism. The increasing State intervention in the economy was another encouraging sign. Besant added that the principle of co-operation was already at work with the division of labour: in the factory system each worker needed his co-workers to make a product. Besant also explained that, as capitalists tended to delegate the management of their companies to employees, they had unwittingly proved that good managers did not need to own the means of production. As a consequence, such managers could easily be replaced

[26] TORT, Patrick. *L'Effet Darwin. Sélection naturelle et naissance de la civilisation*. Paris: Éditions du Seuil, 2008.

by civil servants working for the public good.

Significantly, Besant sometimes resorted to religious vocabulary to present her socialist theories, comparing socialism to the Promised Land or a form of redemption, for instance. Like many Victorian social thinkers, Besant believed that history was animated by a guiding principle, leading society toward a better future often presented as a form of salvation, thus revealing her faith in 'Progress'[27].

Fabian (1885–1890)

Most historians of the Fabian Society have concluded that Annie Besant's part was marginal — taking Shaw's comments for granted, when he claimed, for instance, that during theoretical discussions, she was 'the fifth wheel to the coach.' In 1971, Eric Hobsbawm thus justified excluding Besant from his study on 'The Lesser Fabians'[28]: 'She can hardly be classified as a Fabian and her connexion with the society was short-lived anyway.' Yet, Besant's role among the Fabians deserves to be reappraised.

When Besant became a member in June 1885, the Fabian Society was a small organization in search of an identity. It was a discussion group without a clear ideology, gathering about fifty middle- or lower-middle-class intellectuals. Not just anybody could join: new members had to be proposed by two existing ones, and then elected during a meeting. The Fabians' first collective publication, the *Fabian Tracts*, argued that the economic system created poverty, and that it had to be changed. However, while the Fabians agreed on this core socialist principle, they were torn between reformist and revolutionary strategies. Additionally, they only

[27] Karl Löwith insists on the legacy of Christian theology in the secular idea of progress: LÖWITH, Karl. *Meaning in History: The Theological Implications of the Philosophy of History*. Chicago University Press, 1949. For the debate on the interpretation of socialism as a new form of religion, see YEO, Stephen. 'A New Life: The Religion of Socialism in Britain, 1883–1896'. *History Workshop* 4, 1977, pp. 5–56.

[28] HOBSBAWM, Eric. 'The Lesser Fabians', in MUNBY, Lionel M., ed. *The Luddites and other Essays*. London: Michael Katanka, 1971, pp. 231–44.

had a vague idea of what the role of the State should be. As for the ethical socialists among them, they maintained that moral reform had to precede structural changes in society.

By the Edwardian Era, the Fabians had devised a strategy of permeating Liberal elites as a means to establish socialism gradually — almost without anyone noticing it. The Fabian Society later played a decisive part in defining the collectivist ideology of the Labour Party. However, in the 1880s, the Fabians' strategy was still unclear, and they were a marginal group, especially when compared with the 700 members of the Social Democratic Federation, and the 25,000 members of London Radical clubs. Though, today, George Bernard Shaw and Sidney Webb are considered as two of the most important theoreticians of British socialism, they were hardly known in the 1880s, and their theories not yet fully developed. As for other famous Fabians: Beatrice Webb joined the Society in 1890 only, while H. G. Wells was a member from 1903 to 1908.

So, in 1885, Besant's joining the Fabians was a major asset for them. She was ten years older than most of them, and much better known and influential — including among Radical circles, whom the Fabians wanted to draw away from the Liberal Party towards socialism. Fabian Hubert Bland, acknowledging Besant's experience, then declared that 'Mrs. Besant, [...] probably knows more of the views of the working classes than all the other leading Socialists put together.' In April 1886, Besant was elected to the Fabian Society's Executive Committee, and thereafter took it upon herself to extend the Fabians' influence. First of all, she devised a national network of provincial sections, using the National Secular Society's own local ones, although some Fabians were not pleased with this alliance. The Fabians eventually adopted her strategy during their 1890 'Lancashire Campaign', with a lecture tour and the creation of provincial sections that were to play a major part in the rise of the Labour Party.

Besant organized with fellow Fabians a three-day conference in June 1886. She wanted socialists and Radicals to join them to discuss the issue of the distribution of wealth — but she also saw the conference as a means to consider united political action, and fifty-eight progressive associations from all over the country sent delegates. However, while they all agreed on the cause of poverty and wished to remedy it, no common strategy emerged. The conference drew public attention on the Fabians, but they still felt ill prepared to put their ideas into practice. They needed to express their vision of socialism more clearly, and to define their strategy to build a socialist society.

Besant took an active part in the theoretical debates that led the Fabians to clarify their position. First, their hesitating between anarchism and collectivism had to be settled. The Fabians explained the difference between the two in their 1886 'Tract 4', entitled *What Socialism Is*: Besant wrote the section on collectivism, while Charlotte Wilson wrote the one on anarchism. As in her lectures at the Fabian Society, Besant clearly supported collectivism: in a context of economic and social crisis, she emphasized the necessity for State intervention, if only to solve the issue of unemployment. Though they were not anarchists, the Fabians proved reluctant towards Besant's proposals. Some of them still favoured private enterprise, and feared excessive State intervention in the economy — a view they expressed in *The Government Organisation of Unemployed Labour*, a collective report published in June 1886. Ethical Socialists among the Fabians also warned against the dangers of materialist determinism, and of a bureaucratic system that would deprive individuals of all initiative. In the end, however the Fabians adopted a clear collectivist approach, detailed in the *Fabian Essays in Socialism* (1889), meant to offer a general and coherent definition of their socialism. They proposed an alternative form of socialism, drawing both on Owenism and Marxism. They defined not only the moral basis of their socialism, but also its political and economic foundations, in order to persuade Radicals away from the Liberals. The Fabians' gradualist and constitutional approach proved highly successful, and the collection of their essays soon had to be republished.

Besant contributed 'Industry under Socialism' to the *Fabian Essays*. The *Graphic* — the influential British illustrated weekly — described Besant as 'the chief orator' of the Fabian Society, when it reviewed *The Fabian Essays* in March 1890[29]. Even Besant's rather critical biographer Arthur Nethercot conceded that 'her inclusion in this significant volume showed the respect in which she was held as an authority on labour, industry, and trade unions'[30]. Indeed, far from being marginal, Besant's essay was emblematic of Fabian socialism as it progressively emerged at the end of the 1880s. Just like the other Fabians, she defended the idea that political and economic evolution paved the way for socialism — of the 'the inevitability of socialism' — and she presented the role of the State and of local authorities as central to its gradual implementation.

Not only did Besant work at justifying and defining socialism, but she also encouraged the Fabians to state a clear political strategy. From her first lecture at the Fabian Society, in December 1885, Besant had underlined the benefits of parliamentary action to implement socialism, and defended gradualism: 'Society is to be reformed by a slow process of evolution, not by revolution and bloodshed, it is you revolutionists who stem and block the evolutionary progress.' Even though her position was still marginal within the Fabian Society, it must be noted that other groups already wanted to defend an overtly socialist programme in Parliament: SDF Henry Hyde Champion wanted to launch an independent socialist party, and he encouraged the SDF to present candidates to Parliament in 1885. As for Keir Hardie, he moved away from the Liberals, and founded the Scottish Parliamentary Labour Party in 1888. Besant sought to unite those socialists who favoured parliamentary action. To that purpose, she organized a debate on 17 September 1886 at the Fabian Society. She submitted the following motion to vote: 'It is advisable that Socialists should organise themselves as a political party, for the purpose of transferring into the hands of the whole community full control over the soil and the means of production as well as over the production and distribution of wealth'[31]. There was resistance to this proposal, however. William Morris, for one, rejected

[29] 'The Reader'. *Graphic*, 8 March 1890, p. 14.
[30] NETHERCOT, Arthur Hobart. *The First Five Lives of Annie Besant.* University of Chicago Press, 1960, pp. 292–3.
[31] In the *Practical Socialist*, January 1886.

parliamentary action because it involved compromises that he considered detrimental to the socialist mission of education. Charlotte Wilson, as an anarchist, also opposed Besant's collectivist strategy, as it entailed the creation of a political party. Besant's motion, seconded by Hubert Bland, was eventually adopted with forty-seven votes against twenty-seven, but the debate had been so heated that the manager of Anderton's Hotel, where the conference took place, informed the organizers that they would have to hold their meetings elsewhere from then on.

In spite of Besant's ideological victory, the Fabians, as a whole, were not yet ready to position themselves on the front line of socialist parliamentary action. In order not to cause a rift within the Society, Sidney Webb suggested that the Fabians who sided with Besant found an independent group: the Fabian Parliamentary League, which came into being in November 1886. Though most of the Fabian Society's leaders had seemed reluctant towards Besant's ideas, they proved ready to work with her to define a political strategy. The Fabian Parliamentary League did not seek to become a new political party, but rather to delineate a programme of specific reforms in order to reach out to Radicals. Its manifesto also encouraged socialists to run in elections, especially local ones, and to support the candidates who favoured socialist ideas: in 1892, Sidney Webb was elected to the London County Council, where he served for eighteen years. Besant also hoped to build a militant network to organize the working-class vote. The League dissolved in April 1888, but its agenda was taken up by the Political Committee that replaced it as an integral part of the Fabian Society.

During the summer of 1887, Besant founded the Charing Cross Parliament, in which the Fabians' involvement showed their growing interest in parliamentary politics. A mock parliament, it enabled socialists to form a cabinet, with Henry Hyde Champion as Prime Minister, Besant as Home Secretary, Bland as Foreign Secretary and Webb and Graham Wallas respectively as Chancellor of the Exchequer and President of the Board of Trade. Shaw was appointed President of the Local Government Board; and as for Sydney Olivier, foreseeing his career in the imperial administration, he was appointed Colonial Secretary. During the meetings of the Charing

Cross Parliament, those 'Cabinet Ministers' introduced the Bills meant to implement socialism. The mock parliament thus became a laboratory where the Fabians debated the ideas at the heart of the 1889 *Fabian Essays*.

Even though Besant played a leading part in organizing the debates that led to a clear definition of Fabianism, there was also a militant side to her activities, most of which were not directly undertaken on behalf of the Fabian Society.

Supporting the Unemployed and Defending Freedom of Speech

From 1885, Annie Besant fought energetically to spread socialism among the working classes, and to defend the workers' interests: *Justice* even referred to her as the 'Joan of Arc of the proletariat.'

The social and political context was particularly tense: coercion in Ireland was violently resisted, and the unemployed in London organized numerous meetings and demonstrations. The SDF and the Socialist League in particular stirred up crowds from street corners, in parks or in public squares. Riots sometimes broke out, as in February 1886, and the upper and middle classes grew nervous. The Conservative Home Secretary, Henry Matthew, took steps to interfere with, or even ban, those socialist open air gatherings, and he appointed Sir Charles Warren at the head of the London Metropolitan Police to that purpose.

Besant regularly attended these demonstrations, often with Shaw at her side. She understood that this working-class agitation was not only a protest against poverty, but also a battle for freedom of speech. Besant denounced police violence and the judicial persecutions that befell socialist protesters. From September 1885, she decided to bail out those who had been unjustly arrested, to secure their right to a fair trial, and to help them prepare their defence. Many years later, Shaw still remembered her determination 'when she would march into a police court, make her way to the witness stand, and compel the magistrate to listen to her by sheer force of style and character.' Eventually unable to cope with the number of such cases alone, Besant launched the Socialist Defence Association in October 1887.

Tension further increased when the Government decided to forbid all public meetings on Trafalgar Square — the traditional London forum for free speech. This decision came out only a few days before a huge demonstration, planned for Sunday, 13 November 1887. The Metropolitan Radical Federation (MRF), as well as socialists and Irish nationalists, decided to defy the ban. They hoped that the pressure of a peaceful crowd would force the police to withdraw. That Sunday, Besant, alongside Shaw and Morris, was in one of the four separate marches converging on Trafalgar Square. The police did not wait for the protesters to reach Trafalgar Square, and Besant's march was stopped at Holborn. Musical instruments were broken, banners were torn, and protesters brutalized. Besant managed to reach Trafalgar Square along with some small, disorganized groups of protesters. She tried to build a barricade to resist police assault, but to no avail: the protest was violently dispersed. Many demonstrators were arrested, and hundreds of people injured.

The socialist militants were dismayed. The event, thereafter referred to as 'Bloody Sunday', made them aware of the fact that a working-class revolution would entail the use of physical force. Most, including William Morris, then came to the conclusion that it was necessary to devise another political strategy to avoid a blood bath. Meanwhile, Besant denounced police violence, and demanded, in the name of freedom of speech, for peaceful protests to be allowed back on Trafalgar Square, but in vain. Her Socialist Defence Association had to come to the defence of the many demonstrators who had been arrested, and Morris, Crane, Headlam and Eleanor Marx helped her in this. Besant also played a major part in organizing a public funeral for Alfred Linnell, a clerk who had died after being run down by a police horse during another banned demonstration on Trafalgar Square the following Sunday. With Headlam, Morris, members of the SDF such as Herbert Burrows, and the Radicals, Besant wanted to pay homage to a man she considered as a martyr. Despite the restrictions imposed by the police, the procession gathered 100,000 people on 18 December 1887, and stretched as long as a mile and a half.

This was when Besant met the celebrated journalist W. T. Stead, who had launched the Law and Liberty League (LLL) on 19 November, also to fight against the unfair trials imposed on protesters. In February 1888, Besant was elected to the Executive Committee of the LLL, alongside Stead, Morris, Burrows, James Tims of the MRF and George Foote of the NSS. Under Besant's influence the LLL became a fully-fledged political organization, relying on 'Vigilance Circles' to implement the decisions of its 'Ironside Circles' — an explicit reference to Oliver Cromwell. At the top of LLL there was an Executive Committee, whose aim was to influence public life through this network. Not only police violence, but all of the injustice suffered by workers would be denounced. LLL militants were also asked to take an active part in local political life.

Not every socialist or Radical supported the LLL: some harboured an unfounded fear that it would become a secret society and prepare a coup; others were reluctant towards the LLL's advocacy of boycott as a means of social and political resistance. Nevertheless, the League continued its activities, and extended its influence — especially with its weekly the *Link*, launched by Besant and Stead in February 1888.

The *Link* (February–December 1888)

The *Link* was first launched mainly to explain and support the action of the LLL. Some historians have presented the weekly as merely the product of Besant's personal ambition, explaining that she wanted to create her own organization and needed a newspaper in order to rule over it. Worse still, Nethercot clearly did not pay any attention to the content of the articles in the *Link* and went so far to identify 'fascistic' tendencies in Besant's venture. In fact, the *Link* was above all the result of Besant's enthusiasm for her cause, and her weekly was meant to unite LLL militants[32] — for, as Besant proudly recalled in her autobiography, the LLL had allowed people, from different

[32] The paper was called the *Link* as a reference to one of the etymologies of the word 'religion', from the Latin word *ligare*, meaning to bind, to unite. See Chapter 5.

classes and religious backgrounds, to work together 'to aid and relieve the oppressed.'

The *Link*, subtitled *A Journal for the Servants of Man*, drew on various sources of inspiration. First of all, the subtitle referred to Auguste Comte's Religion of Humanity. Next, when presenting the paper, Besant cultivated the analogy with Cromwell's Republican army — even though she did not in the least consider the creation of an actual army. In one of the *Link*'s first editorials, Besant and Stead explained that they wanted to use religious-like strategies to 'work for the temporal redemption of mankind, in the secular sphere of politics and of industry.' They also made an explicit reference to Victor Hugo in the epigraph, taken from his novel *L'Homme qui rit* (1869) (*The Man Who Laughs*): 'The People are silence. I will be the advocate of this silence. [...] I will speak of the small to the great, and of the feeble to the strong. [...] I will be the bleeding mouth where the gag is snatched out. I will say everything.'[33] — perfectly encapsulating Stead and Besant's vision of their mission.

Since the 1870s, first with the *Northern Echo*, then the *Pall Mall Gazette*, Stead had used the press to defend the oppressed. A staunch Christian, Stead believed that serving man meant serving God. To that purpose, he inaugurated what became known as 'new journalism': Stead brought formal innovation to make his papers appealing to a broader readership, and reformed their contents — leaving aside parliamentary reports, for instance, in order to focus on common people's lives and concerns, and to reveal scandals. Considered as the father of investigative journalism, Stead researched poverty, crime and vice. In 1885, working alongside Josephine Butler, who had asked him to launch a press campaign on the subject, Stead published a series of articles entitled 'The Maiden Tribute of Modern Babylon', in which he denounced the forced prostitution of very young girls in London[34]. The popular outrage provoked by these articles

[33] Besant and Stead would likely have known that Hugo actually drew from the Bible: 'Open thy mouth for the dumb in the cause of all such as are appointed to destruction. / Open thy mouth, judge righteously, and plead the cause of the poor and needy.' (Proverbs 31: 8–9, King James Version).

[34] See ROBINSON, W. Sydney. *Muckraker: The Scandalous Life and Times of W. T. Stead:*

led Parliament to pass the Criminal Law Amendment Act 1885, that raised the age of sexual consent from thirteen to sixteen[35], as hoped by Stead and Butler. During his investigation, however, Stead had decided to prove the existence of child prostitution by buying a thirteen-year-old girl himself: he was consequently tried and sentenced to three months in jail. Upon his release, Stead resumed his moral crusades as before.

The *Link* was typical of Stead's 'new journalism', as Besant and he hoped to move their readers by appealing to their moral conscience. Although the weekly was first meant to pass on information concerning the LLL's struggle for freedom of speech and the right to demonstrate on Trafalgar Square, it also aimed at organizing the working-class vote in London, and at exposing scandals concerning working conditions, so as to shame employers into reforming their ways.

Though the *Link* was launched by both Besant and Stead, it was Besant who was the most involved in the two fights that made the paper famous: the matchgirls' strike, and her election on the London School Board.

The Bryant & May Matchgirls' Strike (July 1888)[36]

In 1888, the appalling working conditions for young women employed by the Bryant & May match factory were brought to the attention of the House of Lords Select Committee on the Sweating System. So, when trade-unionist Clementina Black gave a lecture at the Fabian Society on 'Female Labour', Champion and Burrows denounced the starvation wages of the female

Britain's First Investigative Journalist. London: Robson Press, 2012.

[35] Unfortunately, the Criminal Law Amendment Act 1885 also included the infamous Section 11, commonly known as the Labouchere Amendment, which targeted male homosexuals by making so-called 'gross indecency' a crime. It was only repealed in 1967.

[36] Louise Raw has rightly stressed that many of the strikers were women in their twenties and thirties. She therefore refers to them 'matchwomen' in RAW, Louise. *Striking a Light: The Bryant and May Matchwomen and their Place in Labour History.* London: Continuum, 2009. For the sake of coherence with Besant's writings, the traditional term 'matchgirls' has been retained here.

matchbox makers who worked at home for Bryant & May in the ensuing debate. Annie Besant then decided to investigate a case that involved one of the most important companies in the East End of London: in all, Bryant & May employed almost 5000 people in their four factories and workshops, but also from home — and they presented themselves as model employers.

Besant went to interview the matchgirls as they left the factory at the end of the day. She published the resulting article entitled 'White Slavery in London' in the *Link* of 23 June 1888. Besant meant to shame Bryant & May, and to call for a boycott of their matches. In a very detailed account, she insisted on the matchgirls' starvation wages, revealing that while shareholders earned dividends of over twenty per cent, the vast majority of the matchgirls earned between four and nine shillings a week at most — at a time when a male labourer could ask for thirteen shillings a week, and a male skilled worker for twenty-eight. Besant also discovered that some matchgirls had to pay up to two shillings a week for cramped lodgings. She denounced instances of malnutrition among of some the younger girls, with a moving example clearly aimed at arousing the sympathy of her middle-class readers: 'the child lives on only bread-and-butter and tea, alike for breakfast and dinner, but related with dancing eyes that once a month she went to a meal where "you get coffee, and bread and butter, and jam, and marmalade, and lots of it."' Besant also resorted to sarcasm when she described the way a foreman treated the matchgirls, using their own words: 'The wage covers the duty of submitting to an occasional blow from a foreman; one, who appears to be a gentleman of variable temper, "clouts" them "when he is mad".' She reported the managers' callousness when accidents occurred:

> One girl was fined 1s. for letting the web twist round a machine in the endeavour to save her fingers from being cut, and was sharply told to take care of the machine, 'never mind your fingers'. Another, who carried out the instructions and lost a finger thereby, was left unsupported while she was helpless.

What was most damaging to Bryant and May, however, was Besant's revelation that the matchgirls were still 'subject to deductions in the shape of fines', which had been recently forbidden by the Truck Act Amendment Act 1887.

Besant sent her article to the company directors, who immediately threatened to sue her for libel, though nothing came of it. She also sent it to a factory inspector and invited him to confirm her statements. Finally, she asked Charles Bradlaugh and Robert Cunninghame Graham, both MPs by then, to call on the Government, which they did, twice, on 6 and 12 July. Besant also informed the matchgirls of her actions in their behalf: she went back to their factory with Herbert Burrows on 26 June, to hand out copies of the *Link* to them — to which she added roses as a gift. In the following days, the foremen tried to pressure the matchgirls into revealing who had given information to Besant. They also tried to make the matchgirls sign a document stating that they were satisfied with their working conditions, which they refused to do. As a result, the alleged ringleaders were reduced to part-time work, and eventually fired. So, on 5 July, their colleagues went out on strike in support: no less than 1400 matchgirls took to the streets and began to organize.

The next day, a delegation of matchgirls went to the *Link*'s headquarters to ask for Besant's help. She had not imagined that they would go on strike, and she had certainly not encouraged them to do so. Nevertheless, she decided to support them with all the means available to her. That same evening, she began a strike fund, and embarked on a campaign against Bryant & May, maintaining her statements regarding the fines and deductions. With Burrows, she also accompanied a delegation of matchgirls to Parliament, so that they could testify to sympathetic MPs.

The first strike wage was paid on Saturday, 14 July. Besant relied on a workers' committee, as well as on her socialist friends. Thankfully, many of matchgirls then left London to go and harvest hops, as they usually did in the summer — but 600 of them still had to share the £130 that had been collected. This, however, allowed them to continue their struggle. The box-makers who worked from home on piece-work also received a share of the strike fund because the strike affected them too.

The following Saturday, the strike fund totalled £205. The contributions came from Liberal politicians, Radical clubs and socialist groups from all over the country, but also — crucially — from trade unions. The London Trades Council decided to support the strike, and its member unions collected £80. Their contribution symbolically connected two social groups that so far had found it hard to co-operate: that of male skilled union workers with regular incomes, and that of unskilled and unorganized female workers, who strove for a living.

The noose tightened around Bryant & May, as the issue of the illegal fines was brought before Parliament. Besant directly appealed to their shareholders in an open letter published on the front page of the *Link*. Once again, she denounced the matchgirls' starvation wages, fines and deductions, and the fact that matchbox makers had to pay for paint and brushes. Besant also dwelt on the phosphorus poisoning which caused 'phossy jaw', a necrosis in the jaw that could cause death. True to her secularism, Besant revealed that prominent Anglican clergymen were among the shareholders, underlying their moral hypocrisy:

> You know me as a heretic to your creed, alien from your Church. But if all you say be true, I had rather be heretic and helper of the poor, than orthodox and oppressor of the weak. [....] I hold you up to the public opprobrium you deserve, and brand you with the shame that is your rightful doom.

What tipped the scale in favour of the matchgirls was an independent investigation published in *The Times* that vindicated Besant's findings concerning wages, fines and deductions — even though the paper had been hostile to her at the beginning of the strike. *The Times* concluded on the poor relations between Bryant & May and their workers as central to the conflict. At that stage, the company felt they had no choice but to negotiate, as urged by the London Trades Council.

The strike committee and representatives of the London Trades Council met with Bryant & May on 16 July. The latter agreed to do away with the system of fines and deductions. They promised to provide carts to carry the heaviest loads, and to open a dining hall so that the matchgirls could eat away from the toxic fumes. Most importantly, they allowed a union to be formed. Finally, all of the striking workers, even the ringleaders, were to be reinstated. The ten-day matchgirls' strike thus ended in a resounding victory. No one had yet imagined that young, unqualified female workers, mostly Irish immigrants, would win against so powerful a company as Bryant & May. Their courage and determination, as well as the press coverage of their fight and the financial support that they received had been decisive.

Today, Besant is probably best remembered in Britain for her support of the matchgirls' strike, which still arouses interest and curiosity among historians, as well as the general public. In July 2013, on the 125th anniversary of the strike, Louise Raw organized a festival, during which Bill Owen and Tony Russell's 1965 musical *The Matchgirls* was performed. Many articles were then published in the mainstream press, underlining the long-term significance of the strike[37].

Involvement in New Unionism

'New unionism' — as the unskilled workers' movement was called — intensified when the London gas workers and dockers followed in the matchgirls' footsteps[38], and went on victorious strikes in the spring and summer of 1889. They were led by young, militant trade unionists, such as James Keir Hardie, John Burns and Tom Mann. Inspired by socialism, they wanted Parliament to regulate working conditions, rather than trade unions just negotiating with employers, and they logically pushed for working-class representation in Parliament. At first, older and more conservative trade-union leaders were rather hostile to this new generation's views and strategies, but new unionism gained momentum all the same, and paved

---

[37] See for instance BROWN, Lyn, MP. 'Out of the Shadows: the Women who Sparked the Labour Movement'. *The Guardian*, 4 November 2013.

[38] As underlined by Louise Raw, many of the dockers were related to the matchgirls, and came from the same Irish community in the East End.

the way for the creation of the Labour Party.

Annie Besant helped the Bryant & May matchgirls form a trade union as early as July 1888. She and Herbert Burrows were elected secretary and treasurer, respectively, and sat alongside twelve matchgirls on the union committee. The union soon gathered over 600 members. In addition to managing a relief fund and defending the interests of all female workers in the match industry, Besant wanted the union to undertake social and cultural activities. She launched a subscription and the East London Working Women's Club was opened in August 1890 — largely thanks to a donation of £1000 Madame Blavatsky had received and decided to pass on to Besant. Besant was secretary of the club, and Mrs. Lloyd, a Theosophist, was put in charge: rooms were let and cheap meals served to some 150 club members, mostly young female workers from the match, rubber and confectionary factories of the East End. Concerts, dances and lectures were given in the club, and Besant visited it every week.

In November 1888, Besant was sent as a delegate of the Matchmaker's Union to the International Trades Congress organized in London. She used this opportunity to call for British trade unions to accept women and unskilled workers among their members. Along with John Burns, who represented the Amalgamated Society of Engineers, Besant encouraged trade unions to define a political agenda, and to defend their ideas in elections.

Following the highly publicized success of the matchgirls's strike, many other exploited unskilled female workers appealed to Besant for help. Sporting a shortened skirt to ease movement, thick lace-up boots and a red scarf to signal her political allegiance, Besant was soon nicknamed 'Red Annie' among London workers. In August 1888, she supported the South London tin-box makers whose wages were illegally subjected to fines and deductions; in November, she came to the help of Midlands chain-makers; and during the winter, she helped the East End rabbit fur-pullers organize. By September 1890, the Radical Sunday paper *Reynolds's Newspaper* concluded: 'The success of Mrs Besant and Mr Herbert Burrows in bringing strikes of women in London to a satisfactory issue ought to encourage our friends in the country to do likewise'[39].

Besant did not neglect male workers, for whom she fought with the same energy: she led an investigation into the working conditions of tramway and omnibus companies' employees, and she paid close attention to the gas workers'[40] and the dockers' strikes. The *Morning Post* of 31 August 1889 also read that: 'Mrs Besant addressed a large meeting of [the printers' labourers] on Clerkenwell-green that morning, and supported the proposition for the formation of a union'[41]; and the London *Globe* reported on Besant joining the strike committee of the East End tailors on 28 September[42]. According to the *London Evening Standard*, when Besant delivered a speech in favour of the eight-hour day from the platform of the Social Democratic Federation during the Hyde Park demonstration of Sunday 4 May 1890, 'she was loudly cheered' by the crowd[43].

The Social Democratic Federation and the International Workers' Congress in Paris (1889)

Annie Besant had worked closely with SDF socialists in the aftermath of Bloody Sunday on Trafalgar Square, and during the matchgirls' strike. She eventually joined the SDF, because, contrary to the Fabians, they worked actively at organizing working-class protest, and were willing to present candidates in elections. From September 1888 to June 1890, the SDF paper *Justice* reported on the numerous lectures Besant gave to their local sections, and regularly published articles she wrote, including monthly editorials. These were a lifeline for Besant who, due to increasing financial difficulties, had to stop publishing her own periodicals *Our Corner* and the *Link* at the end of 1888. In *Justice*, Besant commented on current events and continued

[39] 'The Democratic World'. *Reynolds's Newspaper*, 14 September 1890, p. 8.

[40] On 28 July 1889, Besant was invited by the gas workers to celebrate the eight-hour working day they had just been granted.

[41] 'The Great Strike'. *Morning Post,* 31 August 1889, p. 5.

[42] 'The Taylors' Strike'. *Globe*, 28 September 1889, p. 7.

[43] 'The Hyde Park Meeting'. *London Evening Standard*, 5 May 1890, p. 3.

to discuss the same issues as in her Fabian essays and lectures. Though still a gradualist, Besant used a more Marxist rhetoric, as when speaking of a class struggle between capitalists and the proletariat.

The SDF trusted Besant to the point of electing her as one of their representatives to the International Workers' Congress organized in Paris in July 1889 — to coincide with the Universal Exhibition there, and the centenary of the storming of the Bastille. Nearly two decades after the dissolution of the International Workingmen's Association (or First International), this Congress was meant to bring about the Second International[44]. The project was the brain child of the French socialists who supported Paul Brousse — known as 'Possibilists', because they were in favour of implementing reforms gradually. Supporters of French Marxist Jules Guesde, who wanted to lay the groundwork for collectivist socialism by means of the class struggle, feared that the Second International would be launched without them, so they suggested a parallel congress. Personal conflicts, among French socialists and beyond, added to those ideological and strategic divisions and, despite attempts at conciliation, two congresses were finally held.

The British socialists ended up divided. While Besant, Burrows, Burns and Hyndman attended the Possibilist congress, Aveling, Cunninghame Graham, Hardie, Eleanor Marx and Morris took part in the Marxist one, dominated by German Social-Democrats. Besant was on the committee responsible for checking delegates' credentials to the Possibilist congress. She took her role very seriously because she wanted the congress to be truly representative of the workers. Besant took part in debates on labour legislation — particularly on the eight-hour day and on a compulsory minimum wage —, on the role of the State, and on international co-operation between trade unions. On the first day, Besant also defended sex equality among workers when it came to wages and working conditions. She was elected by acclamation a vice-president and chairperson of the second day. She then gave a brief speech in French 'amid great enthusiasm',

[44] See DROZ, Jacques. *L'Internationale ouvrière de 1864 à 1920*. Paris: Centre de documentation universitaire, 1968.

according to the *Pall Mall Gazette*[45]. She was among the delegates who attended a ceremony to commemorate the massacre of the *Communards* in 1871 – and reported that it was particularly moving.

In the end, both congresses passed relatively similar resolutions, but the Marxist one is considered the originator of the Second International. In 1891, all of the main socialist leaders were reunited at the Second International Congress of Brussels, but Besant did not take part in it.

Upon her return to London, Besant went on promoting some of the principles she had defended at the Paris congress, especially on the London School Board, to which she had been elected at the end of 1888.

Election to the London School Board[46]

The Elementary Education Act 1870 — commonly known as the Forster Act after its sponsor, Liberal MP William Forster — created School Boards: locally-elected institutions responsible for implementing elementary education in their district[47]. These School Boards faced a number of challenges: they had to identify needs, purchase buildings or even build schools when necessary, recruit and pay teachers and other staff, and provide furniture and school supplies. School Boards were financed by local taxes and the fees parents still had to pay, but the extreme poverty of the part of the population in need of elementary schools complicated matters. Not only had parents to pay between 1d and 4d per week, but sending their children to school instead of work meant a loss of income for the family, so the Boards found it difficult to enforce compulsory education. The London School Board (LSB) gathered fifty members, who supervised 400 schools with over 350,000 students.

In School Board elections, each local ratepayer had a number of votes

[45] 'The International Congress of Workers. The Closing Sitting'. *Pall Mall Gazette*, 23 July 1889. See also 'The Workmen's Congresses in London'. *St James's Gazette*, 17 July 1889.

[46] See chapter 3.

[47] They were abolished by the Education (or Balfour) Act 1902.

equal to the number of seats in their constituency; and it was possible to give all of one's votes to a single candidate. This voting system, nicknamed 'plumping', was designed to make sure religious minorities would be represented on the Boards — but it made it possible for well-organized militant groups to get representatives elected too: Aveling thus managed to be returned to the London School Board in 1882. The LSB was dominated by Anglican Conservatives, led by Rev. Joseph Diggle. The Liberal, Radical and Non-Conformist opposition sought to limit their influence on education, and to extend the prerogatives of the Board. They worked as an informal alliance, known as the 'Progressive Party', which Besant supported from the start.

As early as May 1888, Besant used the *Link* to incite working-class organizations to prepare for local elections by drafting manifestos, electing committees and getting workers to vote. Sidney Webb supported Besant's call for more local democracy: he asked the London Liberal and Radical clubs, the working men's clubs and the socialist groups to elect two representatives to sit on Democratic Joint Committees in their constituencies. As the matchgirls' strike was hitting the headlines, Besant still found time and energy to work on this plan. At the end of September 1888, the Central Democratic Committee published a joint manifesto drafted by Besant, Burrows, Foote, Tims and Wallas. It asked for free, secular and compulsory elementary education, denouncing an educational system that both reflected and worsened social inequalities. Their manifesto also aimed at democratizing the management of elementary schools, asked for more evening classes and demanded free school meals.

At the end of October 1888, Besant was chosen by the Tower Hamlets Joint Committee to run as a candidate to the London School Board. She was selected by local working-class militants who knew and admired her, because of her tireless fights in their support. Besant's electoral manifesto took up the one drafted by the Central Democratic Committee, but she added a demand similar to what is called 'fair trade' today: 'I shall, if elected, steadily oppose any of the works of the Board being given to the firms who treat their workpeople unfairly, or who pay less than Trade Union rates of wages.' Besant believed the public sector should be exemplary when it came to implementing labour legislation. She also insisted on democracy in her manifesto: 'As a Democrat, I believe in the government of the people by the people, and if you elect me I shall go to the Board as your delegate.' In keeping with Hugo's quote used as an epigraph in the *Link* — 'I will speak of the small to the great, and of the feeble to the strong' —, she wrote: 'In order that the delegation may be a real one, I shall ask you to meet me, when any question of principle or of public interest arises, so that I may act as your mouthpiece on the Board.'

Besant used the London press and public meetings to spread her ideas: her campaign was much publicized and stirred up a number of controversies. 'I am speaking nearly every night', she explained to the *Pall Mall Gazette* which interviewed her in her office on Fleet Street the week before the vote. Besant was helped by Herbert Burrows during her campaign, and she could rely on her friends from the Fabian Society and the SDF, with whom she held meetings. A support committee that included a number of matchgirls also helped Besant with leafleting and canvassing.

Annie Besant and Stewart Headlam were the only two Central Democratic Committee candidates to the London School Board supported by the Liberal and Radical clubs in their constituencies — and both were returned. In 1924, the Labour leader, George Lansbury, still remembered: 'Although [Besant] was to all intents and purposes a Socialist candidate, with Herbert Burrows as her agent, it was the members of the Tower Hamlets Radical Clubs who secured her triumphant return.' He also highlighted her courage and determination in the face of 'a campaign of calumny, lying, and vilification such as [he] never remember[ed] taking place before or since'[48].

During the two years Besant served on the LSB, she attended an endless list of weekly council meetings, committee meetings, school visits, meetings with school headmasters and with parents — especially concerning fees and attendance. As promised in her manifesto, she investigated LSB suppliers, working closely with the Radicals and trade

---

[48] LANSBURY, George. 'Annie Besant as a Politician', in *Dr. Annie Besant: Fifty Years in Public Work*. London: privately printed, 1924.

unionists on the Board to ensure that those suppliers paid their workers a decent wage and produced quality work. Besant encouraged their employees to organize, to report abuse and to call on her to publicize their case. This was how she discovered and denounced the working conditions at Eyre & Spottiswoode[49], the London firm that printed the elementary school Bibles — only to be threatened with libel again. Commenting on this, she explained that 'the path of the member of the School Board who seeks to serve the oppressed is not altogether one of roses.' Nevertheless, Besant proudly announced in November 1889 that the LSB had decided to entrust their printing work to another firm. The London County Council adopted Besant's principle of monitoring working conditions among their suppliers a few years later. In 1924, in the homage Lansbury paid to Besant, he stressed how much of a 'pioneering' part she had played in this area.

Besant also fought for elementary education to be free in Board schools, which proved at first legally impossible. She therefore demanded that the LSB send a petition to Parliament to demand that School Boards be allowed to abolish fees, to which Parliament eventually agreed in 1891. In the meantime, with Headlam's support, Besant managed to get rules concerning fees remittal considerably relaxed, and to get the LSB to prohibit the exclusion of pupils whose fees had not been paid.

The implementation of free school meals by the Board also proved legally impossible. So, in January 1889, Besant launched a subscription that allowed the distribution of 36,000 free school meals to the poorest pupils in Tower Hamlets during that winter. The following November, she took part in the creation of the London School Dinners Association, which served 236,000 free meals and 26,000 cheap ones during the winter of 1889–1890. Meanwhile, Besant supported Headlam when he asked for pianos to be provided in all Board schools.

Significantly, Besant asked for School Board meetings not to start before five p.m., so that workers could attend. She found it regrettable that

[49] In 1920 the firm enjoyed the dubious distinction of being the first to print in English *The Protocols of the Elders of Zion*, a notorious fake designed to fuel anti-Semitic propaganda.

Board schools management was entrusted to middle-class people, whose own children did not even attend those schools, asserting: 'The more we can throw the control of the Schools into the hands of those who use them, the better for Public Education.' Besant believed that the schools had to play an active part in local life, and supported the victorious motion stating that playgrounds should be opened on Sundays. She also asked that school buildings be rented out to local associations in the evening, on weekends, and during holidays. Besant voiced what were then daring positions, in favour of a comprehensive and secularist elementary education system, or for teachers to be better paid.

Besant progressively earned the trust and respect of the other members of the LSB, to the point of forging pragmatic ad-hoc alliances both with Progressive and Conservative members. She knew when to make concessions or to praise her opponents' work — but she could also be very convincing. Besant benefited from the support of her constituents, with whom she met regularly. They even collected enough money to pay her a wage — for School Board members were not paid, and so dedicated was she to her work on the LSB, that she hardly had any time left to lecture or publish essays and articles, her only sources of income.

Her Socialism after her Conversion to Theosophy

After Annie Besant joined the Theosophical Society in May 1889, her socialist work went on almost as usual throughout 1889 and 1890. To her, socialism and Theosophy — whose first object was to promote 'Universal Brotherhood of Humanity' — were perfectly compatible. Significantly, Besant's first published article as a Theosophist, in the 15 June issue of *Lucifer* was 'Practical Work for Theosophists', thus bridging her socialism and her newly-found spirituality[50]. In September 1890, the *South London Press*, when reporting on a lecture on 'The Class War' Besant gave to the Newington Reform Club, explained to their readers that 'Mrs Besant

50 'Practical Work for Theosophists'. *Lucifer* 4:271, June 1889, pp. 271–4.

[was] an eloquent advocate of Theosophism [*sic*] as well as socialism, and the doctrine of universal brotherhood belongs to both "isms"'[51]. Besant delivered socialist lectures to Theosophists too, as on 'Capital and Labour', in August 1890, in the meeting room of the Blavatsky Lodge[52].

Besant's conversion to Theosophy was generally well accepted by her socialist comrades, many of whom had embraced a form of ethical socialism: a number, like Lansbury, were deeply Christian; others, like Carpenter, were fascinated by transcendentalism or Eastern spiritualities; and some also converted to Theosophy, like Fabian John Brailsford Bright, in 1887, or SDF member Herbert Burrows, in 1888[53].

Besant was still an active member of the Fabian society in July 1890, chairing 'a crowded meeting', during which 'she made a very strong appeal on behalf of the locked-out chocolate makers [...] at Bow, which resulted in a total of £10', according to the *Pall Mall Gazette*[54]. She also was still treasurer of the SDF parliamentary fund in September 1890[55]. Besant resigned from the Fabian Society in November that year, but still lectured to the SDF on 'Past Labour Struggles' in November, and on 'Legalised Trade Unions' as late as December 1890[56].

Besant had obviously worked hard on the London School Board that year, for *Reynolds's Newspaper* commented on the LSB's annual report in October 1890, saying: 'Good work has been done, largely through Mrs. Besant'[57]. So, it came as a shock when she announced on 21 June 1891 that she would 'not be able to present herself as candidate at the coming School Board election'. She explained why in an official statement that was widely

---

[51] 'Notes and Comments'. *South London Press*, 27 September 1890, p. 1.

[52] 'Theosophy in Relation to the Problems of Modern Life'. *Women's Penny Paper* 92, 26 July 1890, p. 471.

[53] See Chapter 5; and the section 'Ethical Socialists', in BEVIR, Mark. *The Making of British Socialism*. Princeton University Press, 2011.

[54] *Pall Mall Gazette*, 19 July 1890, p. 4.

[55] SHAW, G. B. 'Radicals and Social-Democrats'. *Pall Mall Gazette*, 17 September 1890, p. 2.

[56] *London Daily News*, 29 November 1890, p. 2; and 20 December 1890, p. 3.

[57] 'Special Notes'. *Reynolds's Newspaper*, 12 October 1890, p. 8.

reprinted in the London press:

> The death of my honoured friend and chief Mdme. Blavatsky, throws on me heavy additional work in connection with the Theosophical movement, and believing, as I do, that in the progress of that movement lies the hope of a better religious, moral, and social order than we have to-day, I elect to leave the more popular work in other hands and devote myself wholly to the less understood and less attractive duty of pressing the claims of a spiritual philosophy on a public largely dominated by materialism.[58]

Though her Theosophical commitments came to the fore, Besant never disavowed socialism. In *The Future Socialism*, published in 1908, she still maintained that socialists were right to call for structural reforms. However, she had come to the conclusion that a socialist society could not rest on an economic system alone, that moral and spiritual reforms were absolutely necessary for socialism to be implemented and to succeed. As she explained: 'it is this point which, more than anything else, led me outside the paths of Socialist propaganda into trying to form the material which the Socialist needs for the building of his State.'

Besant later tried to integrate her ethical socialist principles into her plans for the political and social reorganization of India[59], and she publicly lent her support to B. P. Wadia in 1918, when he founded the Madras Labour Union, one of India's first trade unions.

---

[58] 'Mrs. Besant to Retire from the School Board'. *Pall Mall Gazette*, 25 June 1891, p. 4; and 'Mrs. Besant's New Mission'. *St James's Gazette*, 26 June 1891, p. 9.

[59] See Chapter 6.

5

Annie Besant, Theosophist (1889–1933)[1]

In his biography of Annie Besant, published in 1929[2], Geoffrey Harry Wells asserted: 'with regard to Mrs Besant's conversion to Theosophy nothing needs more to be stressed than that it was, absolutely, a logical conclusion to all that had gone before. It might almost have been prophesied.' Besant herself wrote, in her second autobiography: 'I have been told that I plunged headlong into Theosophy and let my enthusiasm carry me away. I think the charge is true, in so far as the decision was swiftly taken; but it had been long led up to.' Her second autobiography was marked by her desire to make sense of the path that led her to Theosophy in the spring of 1889. In it, Besant developed a perceptive reflection on her personal evolution, that was at the same time retrospective and introspective: 'Looking back to-day over my life, I see that its keynote — through all the blunders, and the blind mistakes, and clumsy follies — has been this longing for sacrifice to something felt as greater than the self.' From then on, Besant added a spiritual dimension to her fights, but her 1893 autobiography did not contradict the 1885 version: the themes of duty, self-sacrifice and quest for Truth informed both of them equally — leading to Besant's socialism in

[1] See BESANT, Annie. *Annie Besant: An Autobiography*. London: T. Fisher Unwin, 1893; BEVIR, Mark. 'Annie Besant's Quest for Truth: Christianity, Secularism and New Age Thought'. *Journal of Ecclesiastical History* 50.1, 1999, pp. 62–93; HARRIS, Philip S., general ed. *The Theosophical Encyclopedia*. Manila: Theosophical Publishing House, 2006; NETHERCOT, Arthur Hobart. *The Last Four Lives of Annie Besant*. University of Chicago Press, 1963.

[2] WEST, Geoffrey [Geoffrey Harry Wells]. *Mrs. Annie Besant*. London: Gerald Howe, 1929.

1885, and to her conversion to Theosophy in 1893. It does not mean that she formulated two different answers to the same issues, since Theosophy, her second one, transcended the first, but did not cancel it. It also does not mean that Besant's ethical, scientific and spiritual questionings were over. As David Nash wrote, speaking of Victorian secularists: 'these figures show an essential capacity as religious / philosophical *seekers*[3]', adding that we should consider their religious positions 'not so much as stages or milestones on a journey as complex journeys in themselves'[4]. This was especially true of Annie Besant.

The Theosophical Society in 1889[5]

The Theosophical Society, which Annie Besant joined in May 1889, had been founded in New York in November 1875, by Helena Petrovna Blavatsky[6], along with Colonel Henry Steel Olcott, a journalist and lawyer, and William Q. Judge, also a lawyer. Madame Blavatsky, or HPB, was born in Ukraine in 1831. She was the daughter of a Russian army colonel, Peter von Hahn, and a novelist, Helena Andreevna Fadeyeva. Blavatsky was raised by her maternal grandfather, the Governor of Saratov, after the early death of her mother in 1842. Her grandfather gave her an aristocratic education,

[3] Original emphasis.

[4] NASH, David. 'Reassessing the 'Crisis of Faith' in the Victorian Age: Eclecticism and the Spirit of Moral Inquiry'. *Journal of Victorian Culture* 16.1, 2011, pp. 70–3.

[5] See BEVIR, Mark. 'The West Turns Eastward: Madame Blavatsky and the Transformation of the Occult Tradition'. *Journal of the American Academy of Religion* 62.3, 1994, pp. 747–67; CAMPBELL, Bruce F. *Ancient Wisdom Revived: A History of the Theosophical Movement*. University of California Press, 1980.

[6] See DAVENPORT-HINES, Richard. 'Blavatsky, Helena Petrovna (1831–1891)', in *Oxford Dictionary of National Biography*. Oxford University Press, 2004; HARRIS, Philip S. 'Blavatsky, Helena Petrovna (1831–1891)', in *The Theosophical Encyclopedia*. Manila: Theosophical Publishing House, 2006; MEADE, Marion. *Madame Blavatsky: The Woman Behind the Myth*. New York, G. P. Putnam's Sons, 1980; and SANTUCCI, James A., 'Blavatsky, Helena Petrovna' in *Dictionary of Gnosis & Western Esotericism*. Leiden and Boston: Brill, 2005.

with English and French governesses. Helena had just turned seventeen when she married Nicephore Blavatsky, the vice-governor of Erevan, who was over twice her age. She left him almost immediately to embark upon a Bohemian and errant lifestyle, self-supported thanks to her talents as a musician and occasionally as a medium[7]. Some parts of her life are well documented: Blavatsky travelled across Europe, the Middle East, and the American continent, returning to visit her family in Ukraine several times; other events still divide her biographers, especially her stay in Tibet. Facts and allegories probably intertwined in Blavatsky's accounts, but this should not cast doubt on the sincerity of her spiritual message. Anyway, on the subject of her Tibetan retreat, she once answered in a letter: 'Really, it is quite useless to go to Tibet or India to recover some knowledge or power that are hidden in any human soul.' What is certain is that Blavatsky went through a series of mystical crises, interspersed with decisive encounters. She thus met the man she thereafter called 'Master Morya' during the Great Exhibition of 1851 in London. The long conversation she had with this young Indian prince, on a bench in Hyde Park, constituted a major turning point in her life. She eventually lost her Russian Orthodox faith in 1870, and first turned toward Spiritualism. Inspired by Allan Kardec, she founded the Société Spirite in Cairo in 1871, with Emma and Alexis Coulomb. The Société was a failure, but Spiritualism led her to meet Colonel Olcott in 1874, on a farm in Vermont, where they both had come to observe spirit phenomena.

In 1875, Olcott became the first president of the Theosophical Society. By 1889, the year of Besant's conversion, the 'three objects' of the Theosophical Society were thus defined by Blavatsky, in *The Key to Theosophy*[8]:

> FIRST. – To form the nucleus of a Universal Brotherhood of Humanity, without distinction of race, creed, sex, caste, or colour.

---

[7] See LAVOIE, Jeffrey D. *The Theosophical Society: The History of a Spiritualist Movement*. Boca Raton, Fla.: Brown Walker Press, 2012.

[8] BLAVATSKY, H. P. *The Key to Theosophy*. London: Theosophical Publishing Co., 1889.

> SECOND. – To promote the study of Aryan[9] and other Eastern literatures, religions, philosophies and sciences and demonstrate the importance of that study.
> THIRD. – To investigate unexplained laws of Nature and the psychic powers latent in man.

HPB added: 'the First – Universal Brotherhood – being the only one which is expected all applicants will subscribe to,' and explained:

> [...] a careful study of the religions and philosophies of the past as well as of the present day will reveal the common basis upon which all rest and therefore the truth underlying them all. The organization is therefore wholly unsectarian, with no creed or dogma to enforce or impose, its motto being: *There is no Religion higher than Truth*[10].

Madame Blavatsky published her first major book, *Isis Unveiled,* in New York in 1877[11]. It was divided into two volumes, respectively entitled 'Science' and 'Theology'. Far from pitting them against each other, Blavatsky aimed to reconcile them, thanks to the 'Ancient Wisdom' at the origin of all religions. Like Jacob Boehme, William Law or Emanuel Swedenborg, Blavatsky studied Hermeticism, Kabbalah, and neo-Platonism, but she also drew from Eastern spiritualities, especially from Buddhism and Hinduism. Blavatsky left for Ceylon[12] and India with Colonel Olcott in 1878. Living in Bombay[13] in 1879, they launched the magazine the *Theosophist* with the help of Alfred Percy Sinnett. In May 1882, they discovered a large colonial house in Adyar, near Madras[14], which they immediately bought to create

---

[9] Meaning relating to the Vedic period in India, (c. 1500 – c. 500 BCE) when the Vedas, the oldest sacred texts of Hinduism, were composed.
[10] Original emphasis.
[11] BLAVATSKY, H. P. *Isis Unveiled: A Master-Key to the Mysteries of Ancient and Modern Science and Theology*. New York: W. J. Bouton, 1877.
[12] Now called Sri Lanka.
[13] Now called Mumbai.
[14] Now called Chennai.

what are still to this day the international headquarters of the Theosophical Society.

Madame Blavatsky left India in 1885 for Europe, never to return, and settled in London in 1887. There, she founded the Blavatsky Lodge of the Theosophical Society and, in October 1888, her monthly *Lucifer* ('the Lightbringer') announced the creation of the Esoteric Section of the Theosophical Society[15]. In 1887, Blavatsky explained in a letter: 'I have to form [...] a nucleus of true Theosophists, a school of my own [...] with as many mystics as I can get to teach them.' In a further letter, she added that they had to be 'exclusively occult students, willing to accept [...] the teachings of which I am the channel and which I cannot impart except to pledged members'[16]. Blavatsky here referred to messages from the 'Mahatmas' or 'Masters', gathered in a brotherhood to which Morya belonged. It proved the most controversial point of modern Theosophy, and was hotly debated within the Society itself. William Q. Judge eventually concluded in 1893 that 'The Society has no dogma as to the existence of such Masters'[17]. To the question 'Who are they, finally, those whom you call your "Masters"?', Blavatsky answered in 1889, in *The Key to Theosophy*:

> In the first place they are *living men*[18], born as we are born, and doomed to die like every other mortal. [...] We call them 'Masters' because they are our teachers; and because from them we have derived all the Theosophical truths, however inadequately some of us may have expressed, and others understood, them. They are men of great learning, and still greater holiness of life, whom we term Initiates. They are not ascetics in the ordinary sense, though they certainly remain apart from the turmoil and strife of your Western world. [...] The powers which they exercise are simply the development of potencies

---

[15] a.k.a the Eastern or Esoteric School of Theosophy.

[16] Both letters quoted by The Blavatsky Archives. Online ed., 1998–2008 (http://www.blavatskyarchives.com/).

[17] JUDGE, William Q. 'Convention Reports of the TS American Section. April 22–23, 1894', in *Issues in the T.S.: Articles by William Q. Judge*. William Q. Judge Series 27. Bangalore: Theosophy Company, nd. p. 14.

[18] Original emphasis.

> lying latent in every man and woman, and the existence of which even official science begins to recognise.

These 'powers' would be telepathy, the ability to project their 'astral body', but also to 'precipitate' communications out of the air, in letter form, such as those received in India by Theosophist Alfred Percy Sinnett, and that formed the basis of his 1883 book *Esoteric Buddhism*.

In 1888, Madame Blavatsky published her most famous production: *The Secret Doctrine*[19], inspired, she said, by the Mahatmas. The work refined and completed *Isis Unveiled*, while reaffirming the existence of a single occult source for all religions, that which Aldous Huxley famously called in 1945 'the Perennial Philosophy'[20]. The book, over 1500 pages long, was again divided into two volumes: 'Cosmogenesis', on the creation and cycles of the universe, and 'Anthropogenesis', on the evolution of earth and humanity. Extremely well-researched, *The Secret Doctrine* appealed to Victorian science and spirituality. In an article on Blavatsky published in 1892, the Fabian socialist and psychical researcher Frank Podmore, an acquaintance of Besant's who was sceptical of the existence of the Mahatmas and of Blavatsky's occult powers, provided a synopsis of Sinnett's *Esoteric Buddhism* that could apply equally well to *The Secret Doctrine*[21]:

> The main thesis is the Buddhist dogma of re-incarnation, in the light of modern ideas of evolution. The individual man, the human soul and body, is composed of seven parts. Of these the four lower constitute the perishable envelope of the higher – the human soul. With the process of death comes a separation; the lower principles, being earthly in their affinities, cling to the earth, and make their presence felt, sometimes as ghosts, as the so-called 'spirits' of mediumistic séances, or as evil influences obsessing the minds of these who open themselves

[19] BLAVATSKY, H. P. *The Secret Doctrine: The Synthesis of Science, Religion and Philosophy*. London: Theosophical Publishing Co., 1888.
[20] See HUXLEY, Aldous. *The Perennial Philosophy*. London: Chatto & Windus, 1946 (1945).
[21] PODMORE, Frank. 'Madame Blavatsky and the Theosophical Society'. *Good Words*, February 1892, pp. 82–6.

> to such intercourse. But the spiritual part of man first undergoes a process of oblivion and purgation, and thereafter a period, shorter or longer according to the merits of the life preceding, of beatific contemplation and enjoyment. With the end of this period of Devachan[22] comes ever another sleep and ever renewed life on earth. This continual systole and diastole which makes up the little life of man — 'a watch or a vision between a sleep and a sleep' — is but a representation in miniature of vaster cosmic pulsations. These are the days and nights of Brahma, when the whole universe slumbers and wakes again to renewed activity. And through the long-drawn chain of suns and circling planets, through all the stupendous cycle of the ages, throughout the waxing and waning of all things from life to nothingness and back again to larger life, the human soul, a spark of the Central Spirit, retains its identity, and bears with it in all re-births the inevitable burden of *Karma* — the fate which each man by his own acts and thoughts has ordained for himself. 'Quisque suos patimur manes'[23]. The man is the thing which he has made; he reaps now the crop of which the seed was sown in another age and another country, and yet sown by himself.

Aware of how dense and sometimes difficult her two vast esoteric essays were, Blavatsky published *The Key to Theosophy* in 1889, in the form of an interview, in order to explain the main principles of her philosophy to a general public in a more concise manner.

Ethical Dilemmas before 1889

It should be recalled that in many respects, Annie Besant remained a Victorian middle-class woman. While she rejected the most absurd Victorian constraints, especially the patriarchal and religious ones, she always did so in the name of Victorian ethical and spiritual values. Besant

[22] *Devachan* is a theosophical term borrowed from Tibetan Buddhism for a heaven-like phase of the afterlife.
[23] From Book VI of Virgil's *Aeneid*: 'Each of us suffers his own spirit.' (i.e., 'Each of us suffers his own Hell.')

denounced hypocritical moral compromises, as well as the rigid formalizing of Victorian morality into a code stripped of all substance. This is why she rebelled against the Christian dogma of eternal punishment, which forbade any possibility of redemption. The idea of a universe devoid of moral meaning revolted her. Besant lost faith in Victorian Christianity because she judged it irrational, but also morally incoherent. Until her conversion to Theosophy, her dilemma consisted in reconciling secularism and moral duty, in discovering a Truth outside Christianity that would justify the self-sacrifice to which she had aspired since childhood, and which she repeatedly called on even as an atheist and a socialist.

When her mother, on her deathbed, asked Besant, to take communion with her in May 1874, Reverend Stanley, the only clergyman who agreed to perform the rite in spite of Besant's atheism, explained to her that: 'The one important matter was the recognition of "duty to God and man"'. Besant retained the humanist side of this as the ethical basis of her struggles before 1889. In her second autobiography, she recalls:

> To a woman of my temperament, filled with passionate desire for the bettering of the world, the elevation of humanity, a lofty system of ethics was of even more importance than a logical, intellectual conception of the universe; and the total loss of all faith in a righteous God only made me more strenuously assertive of the binding nature of duty and the overwhelming importance of conduct. [...] and in all the years of my propaganda on the platform of the National Secular Society no subject was more frequently dealt with in my lectures than that of human ethical growth and the duty of man to man.

However, how could Besant justify this sense of duty and self-sacrifice separately from any transcendence? Like the other secularist thinkers studied by David Nash, her ultimate motivation: 'lay in the search for an all-encompassing moral order that would bind up, heal, revive and transform their lives'; hers was a 'quest for a new universal morality'[24].

[24] NASH, David. 'Reassessing the 'Crisis of Faith' in the Victorian Age: Eclecticism and the Spirit of Moral Inquiry'. *Journal of Victorian Culture* 16.1, 2011, p. 80.

Quest for Universal Brotherhood before 1889[25]

In 1889, Annie Besant was, at forty-two, an influential if controversial figure in British political and social life. However, her frenzy of involvement and activity no longer managed to conceal her discouragement, even her disillusion. In her autobiography, she defined her socialism as 'a new Brotherhood, in which service of Man should take the place erstwhile given to service of God.' Nevertheless, at the end of the 1880s, she began to doubt that socialism, as it was developing in Britain at the time, would ever allow for the advent of that universal brotherhood to which she aspired, so much did she believe it neglected ethics. She recalled:

> The Socialist position sufficed on the economic side, but where to gain the inspiration, the motive, which should lead to the realisation of the Brotherhood of Man? Our efforts to really organise bands of unselfish workers had failed. Much indeed had been done, but there was not a real movement of self-sacrificing devotion, in which men worked for Love's sake only, and asked but to give, not to take. Where was the material for the nobler Social Order, where the hewn stones for the building of the Temple of Man? A great despair would oppress me as I sought for such a movement and found it not.

Besant concluded with this sentence: 'How unconsciously I was marching towards the Theosophy which was to become the glory of my life.'

In 1874, in *The True Basis of Morality*, Besant had defined her ideal of universal brotherhood thus:

> [...] little worth even wider happiness, if that happiness be selfish, if true fraternity, true brotherhood, do not knit man to man, and heart to heart, in loyal service to the common need, and generous self-sacrifice to the common good.

[25] See BESANT, Annie. *Why I Became a Theosophist*. London: Freethought Publishing Co, 1889; and BEVIR, Mark. 'Annie Besant's Quest for Truth: Christianity, Secularism and New Age Thought'. *Journal of Ecclesiastical History* 50.1, 1999, pp. 62–93.

The following year, she wrote her short biography of Auguste Comte[26]. At the time, the 'Religion of Humanity' imagined by Comte seemed to offer a solution to her ethical dilemmas. This final development of Comte's thinking was well-known in London, thanks to philosopher Richard Congreve, who went so far as to found a Comtist Church of Humanity in 1878, attended by both secularists and Christian socialists. In 1875, Besant made a remark presaging the logic behind her conversion to Theosophy fifteen years later:

> Comte's work is by no means sharply divided into two almost antagonistic portions, as some admirers of his philosophy would have us to believe [...] his earliest writings most clearly foreshadow that Positive Polity, the elaboration of which was — according to Comte's own belief — the crowning glory of his life.

In this biography, Besant continuously stressed the similarities between Comte's path and her own: she identified with him, and was fascinated by his thinking. It is therefore difficult to read this essay without discerning in it her hope for a similar outcome of her quest: 'Henceforth he appears no longer as the scientist, the philosopher, the searcher after truth; rather he is a prophet, bringing a new revelation [...] The truth is no longer sought for, it is found [...]; the glory of the struggle is over and the prize is won.' The concept of the Religion of Humanity therefore influenced Besant's thinking as early as 1875.

As seen in Chapter 4, shortly before her conversion to Theosophy, Besant decided to found a 'Socialist Church', and the paper that she launched with the support of the deeply Christian W. T. Stead was called the *Link*, as a reference to one of the etymologies of the word 'religion', from the Latin word *ligare*, meaning to bind. In founding this 'Church', Besant joined a vast school of contemporary thought[27]: in 1885, in the manifesto of

[26] BESANT, Annie. *Auguste Comte; His Philosophy, His Religion and His Sociology*. London: Charles Watts, 1875.

[27] See YEO, Stephen. 'A New Life: The Religion of Socialism in Britain, 1883–1896'. *History Workshop* 4, Oxford University Press: Autumn, 1977, pp. 5–56.

his Socialist League, William Morris spoke of 'the religion of Socialism, the only religion which the Socialist League professes.' Likewise, Ernest Belfort Bax, a member first of the SDF, then of the Socialist League, published a series of essays in 1886 under the title *The Religion of Socialism*[28], where he concluded that humanity was progressing toward a collective conscience that would transcend individual ones. In fact, several new socialists of the 1880s described their 'conversion' to this political movement in religious terms. Such was the case for Henry Snell, the son of a labourer from Nottinghamshire who became a Labour MP and whose testimony also reveals Besant's almost mystical influence even before she was a Theosophist: 'the adhesion to Socialism of Mrs. Besant had helped to sway my mind and in due course I made my confession of faith one Sunday evening from the platform of the SDF at a meeting in the Great Market Place'[29].

Interest in Eastern Spirituality before 1889

In 1872, having just separated from her husband, Annie Besant found refuge in the home of Moncure D. Conway and his wife. Conway appears as an essential early link between Besant, Eastern spirituality and Theosophy. Highly influenced by transcendentalist Ralph Waldo Emerson, Conway studied the Bhagavad Gita. In 1873, he replaced prayer with meditation at his chapel at South Place, London, and the Bible with an anthology of sacred texts, including passages from the Veda. In 1893, Besant wrote: 'I often attended South Place Chapel, where Moncure D. Conway was then preaching, and discussion with him did something towards widening my views on the deeper religious problems.' Conway had developed a mystical vision of the theory of evolution, similar to that of Blavatsky, whom he met in London in 1879. In 1884, he left on a 'pilgrimage' for several months

[28] BAX, Ernest Belford. *The Religion of Socialism, Being Essays in Modern Socialist Criticism*. London: Swan Sonnenschein, 1886.

[29] SNELL, Henry. *Men, Movements and Myself*. London: J. M. Dent and Sons, 1936, p. 55.

in India, during which he visited Blavatsky at Adyar[30]. While Conway remained sceptical about the Mahatmas, he nevertheless concluded the tale of his visit with these words: 'That Mme. Blavatsky without beauty or wealth should be able to bind men to her proves that she possessed some of those "occult" qualities.' Incidentally, he thought the conversion of his friend Annie Besant to be proof of these qualities.

Besant also encountered a form of spirituality derived from Eastern philosophies among those of her socialist friends who believed in what Mark Bevir defined as 'immanentism'[31], also inspired by American transcendentalism[32]. Besant became a member of the Fabian Society in 1885, but the Society came from The Fellowship of the New Life, founded in London in 1883, following the visit of philosopher Thomas Davidson. The Fellowship had defined itself in December 1883, in the following manner:

> Object. – The cultivation of a perfect character in each and all.
> Principle. – The subordination of material things to spiritual.
> Fellowship. – The sole and essential condition of fellowship shall be a single-minded, sincere, and strenuous devotion to the object and principle.

In 1887, in an essay entitled *The Positive Virtues*, Thomas Davidson, who had inspired the Fellowship, gave a definition of human evolution similar to that of the Theosophists:

> The view of man's nature revealed to us by the doctrine of evolution shows us that man is not a fallen creature but a perpetually rising one — that his moral aim is not to attain a zero-point virtue, the state of paradisiac innocence, but to increase forever in positive, active virtue and power.[33]

---

[30] See CONWAY, Moncure Daniel. *My Pilgrimage to the Wise Men of the East*. Boston & New York: Houghton, Mifflin & Co., 1906.

[31] 'Any of several theories according to which God or an abstract mind or spirit pervades the world.' (https://www.merriam-webster.com/dictionary/immanentism).

[32] See the section 'Ethical Socialists', in BEVIR, Mark. *The Making of British Socialism*. Princeton University Press, 2011.

[33] DAVIDSON, Thomas. *The Positive Virtues*. Chicago: Open Court, 1887.

William Jupp, one of the cofounders of the Fellowship, detailed his own spirituality in 1906[34] — and its similarities with Eastern philosophies and Theosophy are evident:

> [...] an impassioned sense of the Unity and Order of the world and of our own personal relation thereto; an emotional apprehension of the Universal Life in which all individual lives are included and by which they are sustained; the communion of the human spirit with the Unseen and Eternal; faith in God as the Principle of Unity.

The Fellowship also included Edward Pease, secretary and then historian of the Fabian Society; as well as the future Labour Prime Minister James Ramsay MacDonald, who joined in 1888, and became its secretary in 1891. Edward Carpenter[35], who fought within the SDF at the same time as Besant, also was close to the Fellowship: a former Anglican priest who had converted to freethinking, Carpenter had adopted the 'Simple Life', advocated in 1854 by Thoreau in *Walden*, to the point of becoming a vegetarian and living as a farmer and artisan near Sheffield. Carpenter also read the Bhagavad Gita before departing on a spiritual pilgrimage to Ceylon and India in 1890.

Besant had already contributed to Victorian orientalism as a member of the National Secular Society. For the *National Reformer*, she wrote a favourable review of Edwin Arnold's narrative poem, *The Light of Asia* (1879) — a free adaptation of the Lalitavistara, a sacred text that tells the story of Buddha's life and presents his philosophy. The great success of the poem allowed a broad Victorian readership to discover Buddhist thought, then little-known. In 1882, the *National Reformer* also published 'The Indebtedness of Popular Christianity to Buddhism', which inaugurated a series of articles on sacred texts of the East. In 1886, Besant herself gave a lecture on Hinduism and Buddhism. The following extract proves not only

---

[34] See JUPP, William. *The Religion of Nature and Human Experience*. London: P. Green, 1906.

[35] See ROWBOTHAM, Sheila. *Edward Carpenter: A life of Liberty and Love*. New York: Verso (New Left Books), 2009.

her erudition, but also her fascination with the subject:

> These mystic Oriental religions are profoundly Pantheistic; one life pulsing through all living things; one existence bodying itself forth in all individual existences; such is the common ground of those mighty religions which number amongst their adherents the vast majority of human kind. And in this magnificent conception they are in accord with modern science; the philosopher and the poet, with the far-reaching glance of genius, caught sight of that unity of all things, the 'one in the many' of Plato, a belief which it is the glory of modern science to have placed on the sure foundation of ascertained fact.

In May 1889, a few days before her conversion to Theosophy, Besant gave another lecture in the Hall of Science entitled: 'Buddha: His Life and Teachings'. Of course, the goal of the National Secular Society was to question the specificity of Christianity by putting it into perspective, but such comparative study of religions was also one of the great principles of Theosophy, and it offered Besant the possibility of truly understanding Eastern spirituality even before she converted to Theosophy. This also explains why the works of Theosophist Alfred Percy Sinnett (*The Occult World*, 1881, and *Esoteric Buddhism*, 1883) had sparked her curiosity upon their publication, as she related in 1891:

> They fascinated me on my scientific side, because for the first time they threw an intelligible light upon, and brought within the realm of law and of natural order, a large number of facts that had always remained to me unexplained in the history of man.[36]

[36] In her address '1875 to 1891: a Fragment of Autobiography', at the Hall of Science on 30 August, 1891.

Scientific Questionings before 1889

Annie Besant began questioning the limits of Victorian scientific knowledge very early on, rejecting all dogma, including scientific ones, as she famously expressed in 1889 in *Why I Became a Theosophist*: 'Refusal to believe until proof is given is a rational position; denial of all outside of our own limited experience is absurd.' She recalled this phase of her quest for Truth in her 1893 autobiography, as well as her frustration:

> Fact after fact came hurtling in upon me, demanding explanation I was incompetent to give. I studied the obscurer sides of consciousness, dreams, hallucinations, illusions, insanity. [...] I added Spiritualism to my studies, experimenting privately [...]. I read a variety of books, but could find little in them that satisfied me. I experimented in various ways suggested in them, and got some (to me) curious results. I finally convinced myself that there was some hidden thing, some hidden power, and resolved to seek until I found.

Besant was far from being alone in exploring the limits of known science[37]. David Nash discovered through his study of Hypathia Bradlaugh's letters that even Charles Bradlaugh 'had experimented with mesmerism as a method of pain relief'[38]. Frank Podmore[39] and Edward Pease, Besant's socialist comrades within the Fabian Society, also belonged to the Society for Psychical Research[40]. The SPR had been founded in London in 1882, to study in a scientific manner such phenomena as telepathy, hypnosis, apparitions and haunted houses, as well as spiritualism and mediumship: 'without prejudice or prepossession of any kind, and in the same spirit

[37] See OWEN, Alex. *The Place of Enchantment: British Occultism and the Culture of the Modern*. University of Chicago Press, 2004.
[38] NASH, David. 'Reassessing the "Crisis of Faith" in the Victorian Age: Eclecticism and the Spirit of Moral Inquiry'. *Journal of Victorian Culture* 16.1, 2011, p. 79.
[39] In 1886, Podmore co-wrote *Phantasms of the Living*, which catalogued and analyzed some 700 cases of paranormal phenomena.
[40] See GRATTAN-GUINNESS, Ivor. *Psychical Research: A Guide to Its History, Principles and Practices*. London: Aquarian Press, 1982.

of exact and unimpassioned enquiry which has enabled Science to solve so many problems, once not less obscure nor less hotly debated', a stated purpose very similar to the third 'object' of the Theosophical Society. In fact, some SPR members, like cofounder F. W. H. Myers, Edward Maitland or Alfred Russel Wallace[41], a forerunner of the modern scientific theory of evolution, were Theosophists at one time or another.

Besant had been interested in these phenomena since the beginning of the 1880s: in the July 1883 issue of her monthly *Our Corner* she wrote the introduction to 'A Curious Ghost Story', subtitled 'A Fact'. She also attended spiritualist séances, going so far as to host some at her home; and, in 1888, she studied telepathy with Anglican clergyman J. Williams Ashman. When in 1889, W. T. Stead asked her to explain to him her reasons for converting to Theosophy, she sent him this detailed answer:

> Could find no answer to problems of life and mind in Materialism, especially as touching —
>
> 1. Hypnotic and mesmeric experiments, clairvoyance, etc.
> 2. Double consciousness, dreams.
> 3. Effect on body of mental conceptions.
> 4. Line between object and subject worlds.
> 5. Memory, especially as studied in disease.
> 6. Diseased keenness of sense-perception.
> 7. Thought transference
> 8. Genius, different types of character in family, etc

In *Isis Unveiled*, Blavatsky had described 'Science and Theology' as 'two conflicting Titans', between which Victorians were crushed to the point of losing faith in man's spiritual dimension. To Blavatsky, however, the Ancient Wisdom, as studied and promoted by Theosophists, could meet the challenge of modern science, thus *Isis Unveiled* was subtitled 'A Master-Key to the Mysteries of Ancient and Modern Science and Theology'. Besant soon came to consider Blavatsky's 'Ancient Wisdom' as an effective key to

---

[41] PRICE, Leslie. 'Did Mr Wallace join the Theosophical Society?'. *Psypioneer Journal* 8.6, June 2012, pp. 193–4.

her scientific questionings.

Discovering *The Secret Doctrine*

In April 1889, W. T. Stead asked Annie Besant to write a review of *The Secret Doctrine* for the *Pall Mall Gazette*, his London evening paper[42]. In 1893, Besant detailed her reaction to discovering this book:

> Home I carried my burden, and sat me down to read. As I turned over page after page the interest became absorbing; but how familiar it seemed; how my mind leapt forward to presage the conclusions, how natural it was, how coherent, how subtle, and yet how intelligible. I was dazzled, blinded by the light in which disjointed facts were seen as parts of a mighty whole, and all my puzzles, riddles, problems, seemed to disappear.

This is a slightly idealized memory of her first reading Blavatsky's opus, for she actually wrote to Stead: 'I am immersed in Mme Blavatsky! If I perish in the attempt to review her, you must write on my tomb, "She has gone to investigate the Secret Doctrine at first hand"'[43]. The review that she eventually published — anonymously — in the *Pall Mall Gazette* of 25 April 1889, acknowledged the hard time she had with the book: 'It would be difficult to find a book presenting more difficulties to the "reviewer with a conscience"', but her review was generally favourable, though still cautious: '[Mme Blavatsky's] book [is] at once remarkable and interesting — remarkable for its wide range of curious and ancient lore, interesting for the light it throws on the religions of the world.' Besant added:

> Mdme. Blavatsky's views may not meet with acceptance, but they are supported by sufficient leaning, acuteness and ability to enforce a respectful

[42] See STEAD, W. T. 'Mrs. Annie Besant'. *Review of Reviews* vol. 4, October, 1891, pp. 349–67.

[43] Quoted in NETHERCOT, Arthur. *The First Five Lives of Annie Besant*. University of Chicago Press, 1960, p. 302.

> hearing. [...] The book deserves to be read; it deserves to be thought over; and none who believes in the progress of humanity has the right to turn away over-hastily from any contribution to knowledge, however new in its form, from any theory, however strange in its aspect.

Yet, she still concluded: 'Of the truth in it our superficial examination is insufficient to decide'[44].

So Besant put her first impression to the test of her scientific intellect: 'The effect was partially illusory in one sense, in that they all had to be slowly unravelled later, the brain gradually assimilating that which the swift intuition had grasped as truth.' Besant, by then, could not have accepted a theory on the nature of the universe if it had not been founded on scientific principles, especially the laws of physics, the principle of causality, and the theory of evolution.

Blavatsky's position on evolution was very clear: 'Modern science insists upon the doctrine of evolution; so do human reason and the "secret doctrine"', she wrote in *Isis Unveiled*. She accepted Darwin's theory, but rejected Thomas Huxley's purely materialistic conclusions on the origin of life. For Blavatsky, evolution was not material only but also immanentist: the 'Divine Principle' unfurled itself over time, according to a process of evolution that Victorian science had only partially discovered, and which suggested that Man could further develop powers still unknown to it. This vision of evolution was the reason why Besant could accept Blavatsky's teachings on the Mahatmas and their occult powers. For her, the Mahatmas were not supernatural beings, but rather highly evolved individuals. As for Karma, Besant interpreted it as the extension of the law of cause and effect; which also offered her a solution to her ethical dilemmas, once she had accepted the principle of reincarnation.

Thus, not only did Theosophy acknowledge Victorian scientific discoveries, but it went beyond them, proposing a metaphysical explanation of the phenomena that had so puzzled Besant.

---

[44] BESANT, Annie, 'Among the Adepts: Madame Blavatsky on The "Secret Doctrine"'. *Pall Mall Gazette*, 25 April, 1889, p. 3.

Conversion to Theosophy

Besant hoped to have a discussion with Blavatsky. Stead, who had met the latter in London the year before through Russian journalist Olga Novikoff, agreed to introduce them. Twenty years later, he looked back on the consequences:

> From that introduction dates the latest evolution in Mrs. Besant's career. Madame Blavatsky became everything to Mrs. Besant. She was proud and glad to kneel at her feet and drink in her teachings as if they were the oracles of Divine Wisdom [...] if Madame Novikoff had not been so insistent in making me call upon Madame Blavatsky, the Theosophical Society might never have secured the adhesion of Annie Besant[45].

Blavatsky was then living with Archibald Keightley, a medical doctor and General Secretary of the Theosophical Society in England. With the help of his nephew Bertram, Keightley had helped her to organize *The Secret Doctrine*, which had been published at their own expense. After only two interviews with Blavatsky, Besant converted to Theosophy on 10 May 1889 — 'to me the never-to-be-forgotten year in which I found my way "Home"', she said in her 1893 autobiography.

On the last page, Besant, wrote as if her quest had then come to a peaceful conclusion:

> And thus I came through storm to peace, not to the peace of an untroubled sea of outer life, which no strong soul can crave, but to an inner peace that outer troubles may not avail to ruffle – a peace which belongs to the eternal not to the transitory, to the depths not to the shallows of life.

Yet, Warren Sylvester Smith stressed Besant's courage when she converted to Theosophy:

---

[45] STEAD, W. T. *The M. P. for Russia: Reminiscences & Correspondence of Madame Olga Novikoff*. London: A. Melrose, 1909, vol. 1, pp. 130–3.

> The move was a real sacrifice to her. After the scandals of *The Fruits of Philosophy* case and the highly publicized removal of her daughter from her custody, she was only now re-establishing her acceptability in the broader London world by her work on the London School Board. She had won her seat on that body scarcely a year before over the vigorous opposition of clergymen and Tories, in a campaign in which ministers circulated handbills recalling the notoriety of the past. [...] She did not look forward to ostracism and derision again [46].

In fact, Besant herself was under no illusion about the reactions that her conversion would provoke. Four years later, she looked back on her anguish: 'Was I to plunge into a new vortex of strife, and make myself a mark for ridicule — worse than hatred — and fight again the weary fight for an unpopular truth?'

She went so far as to speak of 'ridicule', for she could not pretend to be unaware of the climate of suspicion and mockery surrounding Madame Blavatsky, which obscured her spiritual teachings. The British press had seized on the conclusions from the report of the Society for Psychical Research[47], largely written by Australian-born Cambridge graduate Richard Hodgson, after a three-month stay at Adyar in 1884. Frank Podmore, who had been a member of the SPR committee who initiated the investigation, recalled in 1892 what Hodgson was asked to look into:

> These were, first, such feats as the duplication and transportation of material objects; next, there were the transmission of intelligence between persons far apart and the apparitions of the Masters themselves at a distance from their physical bodies; and, finally, there were the letters mysteriously received from them.

---

[46] SMITH, Warren S. *The London Heretics 1870–1914*. London: Constable, 1967, p. 157.

[47] HODGSON, Richard et al. 'Report of the Committee Appointed to Investigate Phenomena Connected with the Theosophical Society', in *Proceedings of the Society for Psychical Research* 3. London: Kegan Paul, Trübner & Co, 1885, pp. 201–400. See also PRICE, Leslie. 'The Hodgson Report (Theosophy)', in *Psi Encyclopedia*, 2016 https://psi-encyclopedia.spr.ac.uk/articles/hodgson-report-theosophy.

The SPR report, published in early 1885, praised Blavatsky in a sarcastic way in its conclusion: 'we regard her neither as the mouthpiece of hidden seers, nor as a mere vulgar adventuress; we think that she has achieved a title to permanent remembrance as one of the most accomplished, ingenious, and interesting impostors in history.' The report did not explore Blavatsky's supposed motivations, however. Yet it is obvious that the social and financial position that her spiritual powers — here cast into doubt — and her writings afforded to her was a far cry from what a woman born into the Russian aristocracy could expcct. By default, the report therefore did not go against the hypothesis that Blavatsky had only attempted to convince people in the most efficient possible ways of a spiritual message in which she sincerely believed. In 1892, Podmore wrote, not without some genuine admiration:

> Madame Blavatsky is dead, and the riddle of her life — a marvel surely greater than all those crude Oriental counterfeits — must remain for ever unsolved. [...] But her greatly daring genius and the marvellous fascination which she exercised over her followers, an influence which even her death has not destroyed, will almost justify the more generous view that she was herself the half creature of her own imaginings. She came too late into too old a world [...][48].

During their first conversation, Blavatsky had asked Besant to read the report, so that she would have full knowledge of the facts before she joined the Theosophical Society. Besant discovered that Hodgson's conclusions were largely founded on Emma and Alexis Coulomb's accounts. The couple, who had been evicted from Adyar, had taken their revenge by denouncing Blavatsky to Christian missionaries, who were strongly opposed to the Theosophists' influence in India. Besant recalled, in 1893:

> I borrowed a copy of the Report, read and re-read it. Quickly I saw how

[48] PODMORE, Frank. 'Madame Blavatsky and the Theosophical Society'. *Good Words*, February 1892, pp. 82–6.

> slender was the foundation on which the imposing structure was built. The continual assumptions on which conclusions were based; the incredible character of the allegations; and – most damning fact of all — the foul source from which the evidence was derived. Everything turned on the veracity of the Coulombs, and they were self-stamped as partners in the alleged frauds […].

Besant also feared 'ridicule' because her conversion could only appear as a reversal, given what she had previously said of the Theosophical Society. As late as November 1887, she had thus written in *Our Corner* that the contents of the theosophical monthly *Lucifer* were 'mere ravings'. In her 1893 autobiography she recalled what she had thought of the Theosophical Society when she had first heard about it, in 1882:

> Into this whirl of political and social strife came the first whisper to me of the Theosophical Society, in the shape of a statement of its principles, which conveyed, I remarked 'no very definite idea of the requirements for membership, beyond a dreamy, emotional, scholarly interest in the religio-philosophic fancies of the past.'

Besant then quoted Blavatsky's answer from the August 1882 issue of the *Theosophist*: 'it must have been written "while labouring under entirely misconceived notions about the real nature of our society"'. Besant wholly agreed by 1893, and explained that at the time:

> I was still too much dazzled by the triumphs of Western Science, too self-assertive, too fond of combat, too much at the mercy of my own emotions, too sensitive to praise and blame. I needed to sound yet more deeply the depths of human misery […] ere I could put aside my prejudices and study the Science of the Soul.

Exclusion from the National Secular Society

'I would not have left your platform had I not been compelled'. These words were part of the concluding lines of Annie Besant's farewell lecture to the National Secular Society, delivered in the Hall of Science on Sunday 30 August, 1891[49]. However, Besant had joined the Theosophical Society over two years before, in May 1889, and the reasons why she was eventually excluded from the NSS in August 1891 are more complex than a simple reaction to her conversion.

As mentioned by Besant herself in the *National Reformer* in 1882[50], Charles Bradlaugh had actually befriended Colonel Olcott, during a lecture tour in the United States in the 1870s, and Olcott had given a speech in Bombay in 1879, favourable to Bradlaugh's secularism. In the early 1880s, the *Theosophist* published advertisement for freethinking literature, and Bradlaugh also advertised the *Theosophist* in the *National Reformer*. Some of the members of the Bombay and Madras sections of the NSS joined the Theosophical Society, including Murugesa Mudaliar, the editor of the Madras *Freethought Journal*. Bradlaugh then grew nervous, and articles criticizing Theosophy began to appear in the columns of the *National Reformer*. Most of them came from Bradlaugh, but he could still be slightly qualified, as when he wrote that he hoped Blavatsky was right when she asserted that Theosophists contributed to break down caste in India[51].

The 1889 annual convention of the NSS was held on 9 June. Bradlaugh was re-elected as president and Besant as one of the vice-presidents. Her work on the London School Board was praised, and her speech on freethought and humanism was greeted with 'loud and long applause', according to the *National Reformer*, but nothing was said about her joining the Theosophical Society just a month before. On 15 June, Besant published

[49] BESANT, Annie, *1875 to 1891: A Fragment of Autobiography*. London: Theosophical Publishing Society, 1891.

[50] BESANT, Annie. 'Daybreak'. *National Reformer*. 18 June 1882.

[51] Quoted by NETHERCOT Arthur Hobart. *The First Five Lives of Annie Besant*. University of Chicago Press, 1960, p. 302.

her first article as a Theosophist, in *Lucifer*. Entitled 'Practical Work for Theosophists,' it bridged her socialism and her newly-found spirituality, and she dared sign it 'Annie Besant, F. T. S.', — but it apparently fell under the radar of the NSS.

Then on 23 June Besant published under her name in the *National Reformer* a long, and this time very favourable review of *The Secret Doctrine*, entitled 'The Evolution of the Universe.' Besant used scientific arguments her secularist readers might respond to, stressing the continuity between occult and Victorian sciences, but her review launched an immediate controversy within the NSS. She never meant it as a provocation: on the contrary, she had introduced her review saying: 'The *National Reformer* reaches so many different types of readers [...] that it seems likely that among them all some will be found to take interest in the unfamiliar views of the universe set forth in this very remarkable work.'

The review was how Bradlaugh learned of Besant's joining the Theosophical Society. He reacted to it — but also to the numerous letters he received about it — in the next issue of the *National Reformer*, under the title 'Some Words of Explanation'[52]. After admitting to not having read *The Secret Doctrine*, Bradlaugh wrote: 'I very deeply regret that my colleague and co-worker has [...] adopted as facts matters which seem to me as unreal as it is possible for any fiction to be.' He added, quite clearly: 'The editorial policy of this paper is unchanged, and is directly antagonistic to all forms of Theosophy', and concluded that: 'An Atheist certainly cannot be a Theosophist.' Besant's answer was printed right below Bradlaugh's violent reaction. She presented Theosophists as freethinkers themselves: 'On matters of religious opinion, the members are absolutely free. The founders of the society deny a personal God, and a somewhat subtle form of Pantheism is taught as the Theosophic view of the universe, though even this is not forced on members of the society.'

The most virulent of Besant's secularist opponents proved to be George W. Foote. He was an old adversary of hers, having already opposed her public support of birth control in 1877, to the point of joining the NSS-

[52] Reprinted in *Lucifer* 4.23, July 1889, p. 355.

breakaway British Secular Union for a while. Like Bradlaugh, Foote also strongly disapproved of Besant's socialism. Foote immediately published a pamphlet entitled *Mrs. Besant's Theosophy: A Candid Criticism*. The text, however, reveals a number of prejudices that had very little to do with Besant's Theosophy, but very much with her sex: 'from the lips of a woman, especially if young or engaging, even commonplaces are apt to pass with men as revelations, and faulty logic is wonderfully convincing.' Foote's misogyny was even more obvious when he asserted: '[Besant] has not the gist of originality. She seems to me very much at the mercy of her emotions, and especially at the mercy of her latest friends.' As for Blavatsky, Foote twice called her a 'sorceress', to whose spell Besant had supposedly succumbed 'body and soul'. Yet, just like Bradlaugh, Foote readily confessed: 'For my own part, I cannot say that I have *read* these volumes; but I have *looked* through them.' He still firmly concluded: 'Mde. Blavatsky's *Secret Doctrine* is the work of an accomplished charlatan.'

Thus it was mostly to Foote that Besant answered with her two lectures jointly entitled *Why I became a Theosophist*, given in August 1889 in the Hall of Science, 'to a crowded audience', according to the *Pall Mall Gazette*. Its report reveals that she still enjoyed considerable support from her fellow secularists: 'In concluding Mrs Besant said [....] she would never give her enemies the right to say that she left the ranks of organized freethought of her own free will. (Applause.) If they wanted her to go, let them say so. ("No, no.")'[53]. In September, *Lucifer* published a report of the debate that had followed Besant's second lecture. Many of the questions were actually candid inquiries into the tenets of Theosophy: 'the gentleman [asked] whether Theosophy is a system which can be grasped by the majority of people'; 'Another gentleman wished to know where the Ego was between the periods of reincarnation'; but other secularists openly called for Besant's exclusion: 'Mrs. Besant must go', a 'Mr. King' exclaimed.

Foote responded with two lectures, both called *Secularism and Theosophy: A Rejoinder to Mrs. Besant's Pamphlet*. Interestingly, in them

[53] 'Why I Became a Theosophist: Mrs Besant offers an explanation to Her Secularist friends'. *Pall Mall Gazette*, 12 August 1889, p. 6.

Foote admitted to having already 'complain[ed] of Mrs. Besant's having used the Freethought platform "in an unjustifiable manner" to propagate Socialism', thus unwittingly showing that Besant's Theosophy only added to his resentment towards her. Foote also revealed his fear of Besant's powers of persuasion, writing: 'she might lead Freethinkers astray. [...] The best of us are human, and many excellent persons have followed a trusted leader into new paths, out of sheer love and admiration.' Foote also was downright threatening: 'Foreign matter will sometimes enter an organism, but the organism tries to expel it, and, if strong enough it succeeds.' As for Theosophy, he just concluded: 'At any rate it is hardly worth discussing.'

Bradlaugh, for his part, only officially expressed his disapproval once more a few weeks later in the *National Reformer* — scornfully asserting that he did not want to waste any more time on a belief that held 'only a very minor place among the world's delusions,' and he went on comparing 'Mme. Blavatsky' to 'M. Jules Verne'. Bradlaugh's further silence on the matter of Besant's Theosophy may have had to do with the fact that he was invited to attend the Indian National Congress (INC) in Bombay in December 1889. There, he met the man who had founded the INC in 1885: Allan Octavian Hume, an Anglo-Indian former civil servant, who had been a member of the Theosophical Society between 1881 and 1883. By 1889, a significant number of Indian and Anglo-Indian members of the INC also were Theosophists, which did not seem to bother Bradlaugh when he was acclaimed by the INC as their 'Member for India'[54].

Still, when Bradlaugh resigned from the Presidency of the NSS in February 1890, shortly after he came back from India, he appointed Foote as his successor until the next annual conference, held in Manchester in May — during which Foote was elected by acclamation. Besant then announced her resignation as vice-president, because she could not 'work harmoniously' with Foote, although the Executive Committee tried to dissuade her. Foote's own paper the *Freethinker* then said it presumably

---

[54] See NASH, David. 'Charles Bradlaugh, India and the Many Chameleon Destinations of Republicanism', in NASH David and Antony TAYLOR, eds. *Republicanism in Victorian Society*. Stroud: Sutton, 2000, pp. 106–24.

meant she had also resigned from the NSS — adding that it did not really matter anyway, since she had resigned *de facto* when she had converted to Theosophy.

This was merely wishful thinking on Foote's part, for not only was Besant still a member, but she still lectured for the NSS, as in August 1890 for its North-West section, on 'Women in Hindostan [*sic*], Compared with Women in Palestine and Christendom'[55]. She also went to Ireland for the first time in her life in October 1890, where she lectured to the NSS sections of Dublin and Belfast. Besant was still fighting for secularism as late as March 1891, on the London School Board, arguing: 'that every freethinker ought to be glad to obtain relief from the duty of giving religious instruction which he did not believe in'[56].

However, Bradlaugh's death on 30 January 1891 deprived Besant at least of symbolic support within the NSS. In April, she left England to attend the annual convention of the American Section of the Theosophical Society, held in Boston, as Blavatsky's personal delegate. Before her departure, she said she would soon be back on the platform of the Hall of Science — but Mme. Blavatsky died on 8 May, while Besant was sailing back from America.

The papers that carried Blavatsky's obituary often dwelled on the Hogdson Report and systematically mentioned Besant. The *London Daily News* of 9 May thus read: 'Madame Blavatsky was openly charged with imposture. For all that, there were many believers in her, and among the most conspicuous and most ardent of these was Mrs Besant'[57]. The *Pall Mall Gazette*, no longer edited by W. T. Stead by then, published on its front page an article on HPB entitled 'The Prophetess of the Buried Tea Cup', referencing one of the events investigated by Hogdson, and said: 'Mrs Annie Besant, revolting from miracles, threw herself upon Mahatmas and atheism ends in theosophy'[58].

After Besant announced on 21 June that she would 'not be able to present

[55] 'Sunday Lectures', *Reynolds's Newspaper*, 31 August 1890, p. 6.

[56] 'London School Board', *South London Press*, 7 March 1891, p. 8.

[57] 'Madame Blavatsky Died Yesterday...'. *London Daily News*, 9 May 1891, p. 5.

[58] 'The Prophetess of the Buried Tea Cup'. *Pall Mall Gazette*, 9 May 1891, p. 1.

herself as candidate at the coming School Board election', explaining that 'The death of my honoured friend and chief Mdme. Blavatsky, throws on me heavy additional work in connection with the Theosophical movement'[59], the *Pall Mall Gazette* published an interview of Besant under the headline: 'I Believe in Madame Blavatsky'. The journalist described Besant as 'a lady of great force of character, quickness of mind, and command of words', and concluded about her unwavering faith in Blavatsky: 'We talk of Mme. Blavatsky's "miracles" — surely, the "miracle of miracles" is here!'[60]

The first annual convention of the Theosophical Society in Europe was held in London, partly at Besant's place, on 9 and 10 July. The context proved perfect for George Foote to launch a renewed attack on Besant. On 17 July, he had a letter sent to her stating that the NSS committee in charge of the Sunday lectures in the Hall of Science 'desire[d] that all lectures from this platform on Sunday evenings shall be upon subjects upon which the lecturer is in agreement with the principles and objects of the National Secular Society.' Besant replied that she could not 'submit to a censorship', and 'must accept [her] exclusion from the platform'[61]. She announced she would give the NSS a farewell address on Sunday 30 August.

It may sound as if Besant used the letter as a convenient opportunity to leave the NSS, but this view runs counter to what she expressed in her address. It was entitled '1875–1891: A Fragment of Autobiography', because Besant summed up her work within the NSS since 1875, as well as her own personal evolution.

'The hall was crowded to its utmost capacity', according to *Reynolds's Newspaper*[62], and there must have been many journalists, judging by the number of other reports in the London papers. Still according to *Reynolds's Newspaper*: 'When Mrs. Besant rose a voice cried "Shame", then there were

[59] 'Mrs. Besant to Retire from the School Board'. *Pall Mall Gazette*, 25 June 1891, p. 4; 'Mrs. Besant's New Mission'. *St James's Gazette*, 26 June 1891, p. 9; *Reynolds's Newspaper*, 28 June 1891, p. 3.

[60] 'I Believe in Madame Blavatsky'. *Pall Mall Gazette*, 13 July 1891, pp. 1–2.

[61] 'Mrs. Besant and the Secularist Society'. *Pall Mall Gazette*, 1 September 1891, p. 6.

[62] 'Mrs. Besant's Farewell Address to Secularism'. *Reynolds's Newspaper*, 6 September 1891, p. 5.

many cries of "No, no," then cheering, which lasted for several minutes.' Her tribute to Bradlaugh also was cheered, and there were 'laughters and cheers', when she said that she was given *The Secret Doctrine* to review because she 'was thought to be more or less mad on such subjects.' But Besant also voiced a powerful denunciation of the paradox of supposed *free*thinkers refusing to listen to different views, and acting as a sect themselves:

> I did not break with the great Church of England, and ruin my social position, and break with all that women hold dear, in order to come to this platform and be dictated to as to what I should say. [...] What is it you are saying? That you will have no word from your platform save that which you already know, echoing back from your brains to the brain of the speaker the truth you have already discovered. [...] If you are right, you ought to be strong enough to hear a lecturer put views you don't agree with.

Reynolds's Newspaper concluded: 'During the closing sentences of her address Mrs. Besant spoke under great emotion — an emotion which was reflected not by a few of her hearers. Having ended, she left the platform with the friends that accompanied her. Meanwhile the place simply rang with cheers' — which once again tends to show that even by then, Besant enjoyed significant support within the NSS. In fact, just as with the socialists, it seems that at least a portion of late Victorian secularists did not consider Theosophy as totally incompatible with their views.

An Immediate Leading Role within the Theosophical Society

Meanwhile, Annie Besant's ascension within the Theosophical Society had been as swift as that which had followed her joining the National Secular Society. She became a co-editor with Blavatsky of the monthly *Lucifer* in September 1889, then president of the Blavatsky Lodge in January 1890. In July of that year, she transferred the lease of her large London house in St. John's Wood to the European Section of the Theosophical Society, at a time when her reduced income no longer allowed her to rent it. Her home thus became the headquarters of the Blavatsky Lodge, and Blavatsky herself, as well as a dozen of the most influential Lodge members came to live there — including G. R. S. Mead, Blavatsky's personal secretary, who had studied mathematics at Cambridge, then Eastern philosophy at Oxford. There was also Isabel Cooper-Oakley, Archibald and Bertram Keightley, and Countess Wachtmeister, a French aristocrat married to a Norwegian diplomat. Lectures took place every Thursday evening, and they were so successful that admission tickets had to be printed. These lectures resulted in several new converts, such as suffragette Ursula Mellor Bright, the wife of Radical MP Jacob Bright, as well as their daughter, Esther.

Besant, accompanied by Archibald Keightley, undertook her first transatlantic voyage in April 1891 to represent Madame Blavatsky at the annual convention of American Theosophists, in Boston, and she took advantage of the journey to make a lecture tour along the East Coast — she even gave a lecture on the liner returning to Europe, at the request of passengers who had recognized her. It was only upon her arrival that Besant learned of Madame Blavatsky's death, just a few months after Bradlaugh's. By a strange coincidence, they had both died of renal failure, and both secular funeral services took place at Brookwood Cemetery, in Woking. Besant and William Q. Judge, now general secretary of the American Section, had been appointed by Blavatsky as 'Joint Outer Heads' of the Esoteric School (the 'Inner Heads' being the Masters themselves).

The World Parliament of Religions of Chicago (1893)

In 1893, Besant travelled to Chicago to take part in the World Parliament of Religions, which was associated with that year's World Columbian Exposition[63]. She was accompanied by two of her socialist and Theosophist friends, Herbert Burrows and Henrietta Müller, and also by a young

[63] It was meant to celebrate the 400th anniversary of Christopher Columbus' so-called discovery of America in 1492, but it was inaugurated one year late.

Brahman from Benares[64], Gyanendra N. Chakravarti. This professor of mathematics at the University of Allahabad became her tutor in Brahmanism. From then on, Hinduism supplanted Buddhism in Besant's spirituality, but mostly in its ancient, traditional form. She also crossed paths with Swami Vivekananda, whose immense success during the Parliament largely contributed to spreading awareness of Hinduism among Westerners.

The Theosophist lectures were very successful too: the Lutherans, less popular, had to exchange their fifteen-hundred-seat hall with the five-hundred-seat one originally meant for the Theosophists. No fewer than 3000 people attempted to squeeze into this hall for the Theosophists' final lecture, on Saturday evening, to the point that an additional one had to be organized on Sunday in Washington Hall, the largest of the Parliament of Religions, where a balcony was hastily erected so that everyone could fit in. Fortified by this triumph, Besant and Müller then left for a lecture tour that took them to Cincinnati, Toronto and New York.

Benares (1895–1907)

Back from America in the autumn of 1893, Annie Besant immediately set off to Marseilles to embark on her first journey to India. After a short stay in Ceylon, she reached India for the first time in November 1893, and went on tour of over 120 lectures in Calcutta[65], Benares, Delhi, Lahore, Bombay and Allahabad among other places. Besant was a triumph, as much among Anglo-Indians as the English-speaking local population, receiving processions, offerings and showers of rose petals along the entire tour. Many joined the Theosophical Society after attending one of her lectures, especially since Besant clearly said that one did not need renounce one's religion to become a Theosophist, as she explained, for example, to Pierre

[64] Now called Varanasi.
[65] Now called Kolkata.

Loti[66] when she met him in Benares in 1900:

> 'Our principles,' she said to me a little later, 'our dogmas! We have none. Amongst the Theosophists (such is the name by which they call us) you will find Buddhists, Brahmins, Mussulmans, Protestants, Catholics and Orthodox people, and even folks like you.'
>
> 'But what must I do to join you?'
>
> 'Swear to regard all men as your brothers and your equals, and meet them with the same love whether they be beggars or princes. Swear to seek spiritual truth by all means in your power. That is all.'

The international headquarters of the Theosophical Society was at Adyar, but the headquarters of the Indian Section was in Benares, which Besant decided to call her home after 1895. The reasons for this decision may have been partly spiritual, as her conversation with Loti in 1900 seemed to indicate. Besant explained to him:

> Those whom you have lately left at Madras are tinged with Buddhism, from whose cold tenets your mystic temperament has recoiled. It is in esoteric Brahmanism in its oldest form that we find our light and peace. To us it seems to offer the purest form of truth which men may know.

Loti stayed in Benares, in order to study Theosophy from Besant[67]. He related his experience in *L'Inde (sans les Anglais)* — India (without the English) —, published in 1903 . The chapter entitled 'The House Where the Masters Dwell' is a description of the Theosophical Society's headquarters, where Besant lived and taught:

> The House of the Masters is always open to those who care to come [...].

---

[66] Pierre Loti (pen-name of Louis Marie-Julien Viaud, 1850–1923) was a well-known French naval officer, travel writer and novelist. English quotes from LOTI, Pierre. *India* (translated from the French by George A.F. Inman). New York: Duffield, 1913.

[67] Kurt Leland found Loti's date of joining the Theosophical Society in the membership records: 24 February 1900, under the name Pierre Loty, with a note: 'Now in Benares.'

> In an inner room there is a platform covered by a white cloth for the numerous guests, who sit upon it in Indian fashion while searching for the hidden things. Brahmins are crouching there, whose brows bear the seals of Vishnu or of Siva, thinkers who wander barefoot and with no garment but a coarse cloth wrapped round their loins but who have looked on everything, and for whom the world has no more snares, learned men who, in their contempt of earthly things look like beggars or labourers in the fields, but who have mastered the latest and most transcendental philosophies of Europe, and who say with tranquil assurance: 'Our philosophy begins where yours ends.'
>
> [...] The plain tables before them are loaded with those Sanskrit books containing the secrets of that Brahmanism which preceded all our religions and philosophies by so many thousand years.
>
> [...] But they simply say: 'We know nothing and simply seek to learn.'

Election to the Presidency of the Theosophical Society (1907)

After the death of Madame Blavatsky in 1891, Besant was caught in a power struggle between William Q. Judge in the United States, and Colonel Olcott in India, respectively vice-president and president of the Theosophical Society. Their conflict led to the schism of a great portion of American Theosophists in 1895. Judge died the following year, and Katherine Tingley succeeded him as the head of the Theosophical Society in America, establishing its headquarters at Point Loma, California, in 1897. Point Loma became a utopian community, with a farming operation, as well as a theatre, schools and a university, which prospered until the Great Depression. Katherine Tingley was a great orator and traveller, and her path crossed Besant's several times. Nevertheless, in 1897, Besant's new American lecture tour encouraged hundreds of Americans to choose the section still loyal to Olcott, now referred to as the Theosophical Society (Adyar).

When Colonel Olcott died in February 1907, Besant should not have had any trouble in succeeding him as president of the Theosophical Society, were it not for the sex scandal that involved her friend Charles

W. Leadbeater. This former Anglican priest had become a Theosophist in 1883, and left for Ceylon in 1884, where he worked with Olcott to revive Buddhist education. Besant met him ten years later in London, when he was the secretary of the London Lodge, then directed by A. P. Sinnett. Sinnett had entrusted Leadbeater with the education of his son, as well as that of young George Arundale. Besant soon began working with Leadbeater on an alternative scientific research method based on meditation, allowing for visions and 'astral travels' at the heart of matter and the human psyche. In 1906, the parents of a fourteen-year-old American boy, whom Leadbeater had tutored, accused him of having taught their son how to masturbate, and they produced a letter that he had written as evidence. Leadbeater did not deny facts, explaining that his advice had been 'prophylactic', intended to relieve the boy of his sexual tensions, and to protect him from 'more serious' temptations. Nonetheless Leadbeater was excluded from the Theosophical Society until 1908, despite Besant's support. Her adversaries used this against her — as well as her somewhat controversial role as Outer Head of the Esoteric School[68]— during the June 1907 election, which she nevertheless won. Constantly re-elected, she remained at the head of the Theosophical Society until her death, in 1933.

The votes cast in 1907 give a reliable estimate of the number of active Theosophists at the time: approximately 11,000 worldwide, including a little over 3600 in India, almost 2000 in the United States, a little less than 1500 in Britain, approximately 800 in the Netherlands, 650 in France, 600 in Germany, 580 in Scandinavia, almost 550 in Australia, 270 in New Zealand, 200 in Cuba and a little over 150 in Italy. In 1928, after twenty-one years of Besant's presidency, the Society could boast 45,000 members throughout the world.

[68] See MEAD, G. R. S '*The Quest* — Old and New: Retrospect and Prospect'. *Quest Reprint Series* 1 April 1926. *Psypioneer Journal* 11.3, March 2015, pp 97–107.

Theosophical Missionary

After her 1907 election, Annie Besant settled at Adyar, where she supervised the extension and embellishment of the headquarters: temples for most of the major religions were erected[69], as well as bungalows and dormitories for members and visitors, a library and printing press, a large conference hall and beautiful gardens stretching for almost a mile along the river, up to the Bay of Bengal. The estate also included a farm, the produce of which was sent to communal kitchens, where vegetarian and Hindu meals were prepared for the whole theosophical community.

Besant continued the rhythm of life that she had adopted in 1895: she resided and travelled in India for most of the year, but, except during the First World War, she left for Europe or the United States during the hottest months. When abroad, she gave lectures on India and Theosophy and recruited members for local sections. She also took advantage of her travels back to Britain to maintain friendships as well as feminist and socialist acquaintances, and often was still actively involved in their struggles. Beginning in 1894, Besant travelled several times to Australia and New Zealand, where Theosophy was well established: Alfred Deakin, Prime Minister of Australia from 1903 to 1910, was a former Theosophist.

Besant used her long journeys on liners and trains to perfect her understanding of Sanskrit and of the sacred texts of Hinduism, and to prepare her lectures. In 1924, she discovered aircraft, which she adopted enthusiastically, despite the discomfort of those very first passenger flights. She also learned how to drive in 1909, at the age of sixty-two, claiming that

[69] An Association of Hebrew Theosophists was founded in Adyar in 1925, and a committee for building a synagogue on the compound was established. Although Annie Besant laid the first stone for the synagogue in 1927, it was never completed. See HUSS, Boaz. '"A Jew Living in an Ashram": The Spiritual Itinerary of S. S. Cohen'. *Journal of Indo-Judaic Studies* 15, 2015; and the picture captioned 'Dr Annie Besant, President of the Theosophical Society, Laying the Foundation Stone for the Adyar Synagogue'. *The Jewish Theosophist* 1.4, July 1927, p. 3.

at the wheel of her automobile[70], she felt like a character in an H. G. Wells novel. In 1927, at nearly eighty, she still gave fifty-six lectures in just over three weeks, in all of the European capitals, travelling from one to the next in a small four-seat plane. Always at the forefront of modern technology, which fascinated her, Besant was filmed during the Theosophical World Conference, in Paris in 1921, and some of her lectures were broadcast over the radio from 1925.

Leadbeater's description of the crowd of Theosophists who flooded Benares for the annual convention of 1911 speaks of Besant's popularity as a spiritual leader, as well as the extraordinary climate of tolerance that reigned within the Theosophical Society:

> There were members from almost every country in Europe, from America and from all parts of India, and it was most striking and beautiful to see white and black alike, Brahmins and Buddhists, Parsis and Christians, haughty Rajput princes and gorgeously apparelled merchants, grey-haired men and young children [...][71].

Scientific Research as a Theosophist

A selection of Annie Besant's Theosophical lectures and articles were gathered between 1911 and 1913 by the Theosophical Publishing Society into three volumes of her *Essays and Addresses*, entitled *Psychology*, *The Spiritual Life,* and *Evolution and Occultism.* The first included Besant's reflections on conscience, memory, hypnosis, emotions, telepathy and the nature of the soul; while in the third, she addressed the answers Theosophy could give to the great scientific questions of the time on the nature of the universe and its evolution. As a Theosophist, Besant continued to keep

[70] The motorcar was a gift from the astrologer and Theosophist Alan Leo, born William Frederick Allan (1860–1917), who visited Besant at Adyar in 1909. See FARNELL, Kim. 'A Brief Biography of Alan Leo', skyscript.co.uk, August 2006.

[71] Letter to Fabrizio Ruspoli, 31 December 1911, quoted in LUTYENS, Mary. *Krishnamurti: The Years of Awakening.* London: John Murray, 1975.

herself informed of the latest scientific discoveries, as is obvious from her 1898 lecture series *Evolution of Life and Forms*: 'some of the greatest problems of modern science are now turning on the nature of the atom, and that scientists are asking, what is it? Is it matter or force? It is a particle or a vortex?' She even seemed to anticipate quantum physics[72], when she affirmed: 'The universe is made up of vibrations.'

In 1907, the year Besant was first elected president of the Theosophical Society, she gave a series of lectures in London that could be considered as her manifesto. This only makes the following extract more meaningful:

> H.P.B. [...] did not give a body of teachings to be swallowed, to be taken on authority, to be accepted by what is called faith; but a body of verifiable teachings, facts to be examined over again, facts to be experimented on, to be carefully studied, as the scientific man studies the part of the world he knows.

In these 1907 lectures, Besant lamented that the Theosophical Society's third object — to investigate unexplained laws of Nature and the psychic powers latent in Man — was, according to her, neglected:

> Therefore I would claim for the Society its place as a seeker after new knowledge, [...] it seems to me that it is a duty of the Theosophical Society, not only to deal with the facts that others have verified, but to carry on researches by properly qualified persons among its own members.

However, she remained very clear: 'There is nothing miraculous or supernatural, but everything is the orderly product of Nature working along definite lines'; and she insisted on the importance of adopting a scientific point of view and scientific method:

> You must try, in all psychical research, in all weighing of observation of phenomena, to cultivate the purely scientific spirit, indifferent save to the truth and the accuracy of the results, [...]; not seeking for facts to verify a

[72] Albert Einstein published his theory of relativity in 1915, and quantum physics began to develop in the 1920s.

doctrine already believed in, but seeking for facts in order to draw conclusions from them as to the laws and truths of the unseen world.

In 1898, in *Evolution of Life and Forms*, Besant explained:

> The fundamental difference between ancient and modern science is that [...] The first studies life, and sees in forms the expressions of life. The second studies forms, and tries, by the process of induction, to find out if there be an underlying principle by which the multiplicity of forms may be explained. The first works from above downwards, the second from below upwards, and in that very fact is the promise of a meeting place where the two will join hand in hand.

In this lecture, Besant called for 'the ultimate union' of Ancient and Modern, Eastern and Western sciences, so as to revive on a solid, scientific basis 'the olden times [when] Religion and Science were wedded together, and there was no discord between the intelligence and the spirit.' To her, the bridge between science and spirituality had been broken, with 'religion on the one side suspicious of science in its progress; science on the other hand apt to be proudly contemptuous of religious claims.' As a scientist and leading Theosophist, Besant believed that reconstructing that bridge was one of her essential missions. She described the scientist of ancient times as an ideal:

> [...] he has to study life, not form; and for such study he must evolve himself, the life that is within him, for only life can measure life, only life can respond to the vibrations of the living; his work is to unfold himself, to bring out of the depths of his own nature the divine powers that lie hidden therein, not in the senses but in the Self. His investigations can only be carried on by means of these powers.

Besant put this ideal into practice with Charles W. Leadbeater. Together they penned two significant studies: *Thought-Forms*, published in bookform[73] in 1905[74], and *Occult Chemistry*, subtitled 'A Series of Clairvoyant Observations on the Chemical Elements', in 1908.

With *Thought-Forms*[75], Besant joined a long Theosophical tradition; Swedenborg already had asserted: 'I could see solid concepts of thought as though they were surrounded by a kind of wave', in his *Arcana Coelestia*, published between 1749 and 1756. In the preface to *Thought-Forms*, Besant nevertheless placed herself at the heart of the preoccupations of the science of her time:

> As knowledge increases, the attitude of science towards the things of the invisible world is undergoing considerable modification. [...] it finds itself compelled to glance further afield, and to construct hypotheses as to the nature of the matter and force which lie in the regions beyond the ken of its instruments. [...] and as the physicist nears the confines of his kingdom he finds himself bewildered by touches and gleams from another realm which interpenetrates his own.

She called this 'realm' the 'astral plane', and justified her work by affirming: 'One of the most interesting of the highroads from the physical to the astral is that of the study of thought.' Besant believed that on the astral plane:

> [...] every thought gives rise to a set of correlated vibrations in the matter of this body, accompanied with a marvellous play of colour, like that in the spray of a waterfall as the sunlight strikes it, [...] Each definite thought produces a double effect – a radiating vibration and a floating form.

---

[73] It was first published as an article: BESANT, Annie. 'Thought-Forms'. *Lucifer* 19, September 1896, pp. 65–75.

[74] 'The first edition of *Thought Forms* was published in both green and red hard covers in 1905. [...] The next edition of *Thought Forms* was published by the Theosophical Publishing House in 1925. It was in this edition that the erroneous date of 1901 was introduced.' CROW, John L., '*Thought Forms:* A Bibliographic Error'. *Theosophical History* 16.3-4, July–October 2012, p. 126.

[75] See PECASTAING-BOISSIERE, Muriel, 'Annie Besant and Charles W. Leadbeater's "Key to the Meanings of Colours", in *Thought-Forms*', in RIBEYROL, Charlotte, ed. *The Colours of the Past in Victorian England*. Oxford: Peter Lang, 2016. pp. 205–33.

In the preface, Besant paid homage to the artists who had drawn the thought-forms that she and Leadbeater had clairvoyantly observed and described to them: 'Mr John Varley, Mr Prince, and Miss Macfarlane'[76]. Indeed, the superbly illustrated book had a considerable influence on modern art[77]. Wassily Kandinsky, who owned a copy, spoke about it in his 1910 manifesto, *Über das Geistige in der Kunst* (*Concerning the Spiritual in Art*)[78], in which he developed his own theory of colours. Several artists were inspired by their study of Theosophy at the dawn of the twentieth century, such as Frantisek Kupka, Piet Mondrian and Kazimer Malevich and composer Arnold Schönberg[79].

Occult Chemistry, for its part, was considered as visionary by scientists in the years following its publication[80]. In his 1919 preface to the second edition, A. P. Sinnett explained that some of Besant and Leadbeater's discoveries had since been confirmed by the work of Russian chemist Dimitri Mendeleïev, inventor of the periodic table of elements, as well as by that of Marie Curie, but also of William Crookes. A member of the Royal Society, Crookes was one of the most respected British chemists and physicists after he discovered thallium in 1861, helium in 1895, and researched uranium and radioactivity. Like Besant, Crookes believed that it was science's duty to study unexplained phenomena. This was the reason why he presided over the Society for Psychical Research between 1896 and 1899, and also joined the Theosophical Society. Crookes actively supported

[76] 'Mr Prince' and 'Miss Macfarlane' keep eluding art historians, but 'Mr John Varley' was the landscape and orientalist painter John Varley, Jr (1850–1933).

[77] See LACHMAN, Gary. 'Kandinsky's Thought Forms and the Occult Roots of Modern Art'. *Quest* 96.2, March–April 2008.

[78] KANDINSKY, Wassily. *Concerning the Spiritual in Art* (translated by Michael T. H. Saddler in 1914). New York: Dover, 1977 (1910).

[79] See HALL, Kathleen. 'Theosophy and the Emergence of Modern Abstract Art'. *Quest* 90.3, May–June 2002; and the catalogue of the 'Traces du Sacré' (Traces of the Sacred) exhibition, which took place at the Centre Pompidou, Paris, in 2008.

[80] See LAMBS, Luc. 'Préface', in BESANT Annie and Charles LEADBEATER. *La Chimie occulte: Série d'observations faites sur les éléments chimiques au moyen de la clairvoyance* (translated by René Allendy). Paris: Adyar, 2004 (1908).

Besant and Leadbeaters's scientific research, to the point of lending them some of his instruments.

Besant's scientific questionings, and some of her conclusions, were still applicable when quantum physicist Fritjof Capra published his famous essay *The Tao of Physics* in 1975, subtitled 'An exploration of the Parallels between Modern Physics and Eastern Mysticism'. Such research method, based on meditation, also interested B. Alan Wallace, who published his doctoral thesis in 1989 with the title *Choosing Reality: A Contemplative View of Physics and the Mind*. He too called for a means 'to transcend the split between science and religion by seeking parallels between insights in modern physics and in mysticism.' Wallace's references, like Besant's, were 'classical India, East Asia and Tibet', civilizations, Wallace explained, that had developed 'a qualitative, contemplative science [...whose] aim is to transform personal experience so as to gain direct insight into reality.'

With Leadbeater, Besant also conducted research on reincarnation and remembrance of past lives, again via meditation. Their conclusions were published in 1913 under the title *Man: Whence, How and Whither*. Besant explained in her introduction that 'Metaphysicians, ancient and modern, declare that Past, Present and Future are ever simultaneously existent in the divine Consciousness, and are only successive as they come into manifestation, i.e., under Time, which is verily the succession of states of consciousness.'

Besant did not neglect Western esotericism in her studies: in keeping with the research of Anna Kingsford, the influential Christian Theosophist who had died in 1888[81], she published a series of exegeses of the Gospels in 1901, under the title *Esoteric Christianity; or The Lesser Mysteries*. In 1907, Besant founded the International Committee for Research into Mystic Tradition with Isabel Cooper-Oakley. The seriousness of Besant's research in this field led her to be invited to lecture on Giordano Bruno at Oxford in 1909, then in the Sorbonne in 1911, two universities where he himself

[81] See PERT, Alan. *Red Cactus: The Life of Anna Kingsford*. Watson Bay, NSW: Books and Writers, 2006; and KINGSFORD, Anna (with MAITLAND, Edward). *The Perfect Way; or, The Finding of Christ*. London: Field & Tuer, 1882.

had taught at the end of the sixteenth century. The latter lecture[82], delivered in French, drew 4000 people to the Sorbonne's Grand Amphithéâtre, while anarchist and Catholic students, united in their opposition to Besant's views, demonstrated noisily outside.

Her Theosophical Ethics

The second volume of Annie Besant's Theosophical texts, *The Spiritual Life*, addressed ethics, especially the questions of duty, devotion, suffering and evil, considered through the lenses of Karma and Dharma[83].

In *A Study in Karma*, published in 1911, Besant presented duty as the result of a karmic debt, which must be repaid before one could hope to progress spiritually. She did not consider this debt as a form of punishment, however, but rather as a necessary experience:

> The knower of Karma will see in these duties the reactions from his own past activities, and will patiently accept and discharge them; he knows that when they are fully paid, they will drop away from him and leave him free, and that meanwhile they have some lessons to teach him which it is incumbent upon him to learn.

This concept of 'lessons' allowed Besant to avoid being accused of fatalism or resignation in the face of Karma. On the contrary, she saw one's environment as a constant challenge, which demanded a free and individual reflection on oneself and on one's possibilities of action. For her, Karma was the condition of an evolving incarnated soul that retained its free will and responsibility.

In *Dharma; or The Meaning of Right and Wrong*, published in 1899, Besant considered that 'morality' was 'a subject closely bound up with

[82] *Giordano Bruno: Theosophy's Apostle in the Sixteenth Century, a Lecture Delivered in the Sorbonne at Paris, on June 15, 1911*. Adyar: Theosophist Office, 1913.

[83] See also LELAND, Kurt, ed. *Invisible Worlds: Annie Besant on Psychic and Spiritual Development*. Wheaton, Ill.: Quest Books, Theosophical Publishing House, 2013.

Dharma, and which cannot be understood without a knowledge of what is meant by Dharma.' She defined Dharma as individual duty, and the foundation of a personal ethic:

> Morality is an individual thing, and it depends upon the Dharma of the man who is acting, and not upon what is sometimes called 'absolute right and wrong.' There is nothing absolute in a conditioned Universe. And right and wrong are relative, and must be judged in relation to the individual and his duties.

In 1895, in *The Path of Discipleship*, Besant already maintained: 'Better to do your own [Dharma], although imperfect, than to try to do the higher Dharma of another. For that into which you are born is that which you need; that into which you are born is your wisest training.' This apparent rejection of absolute moral principles is reminiscent of Friedrich Nietzsche, who affirmed in 1886, in *Beyond Good and Evil*[84]:

> Good is no longer good when one's neighbour takes it into his mouth [...]. In the end things must be as they are and have always been – the great things remain for the great, the abysses for the profound, the delicacies and thrills for the refined, and, to sum up shortly, everything rare for the rare.

And he concluded: 'I now love every fate.' Besant's vision of Dharma also recalls William Blake's famous line from his 1790 poem 'The Marriage of Heaven and Hell': 'One law for the lion and ox is oppression'[85], though this is less surprising, for Blake was much influenced by Swedenborg's Theosophy. In fact, unlike Nietzsche's, Besant's relativism was accompanied by faith in a supreme spiritual Truth, 'beyond good and evil,' but which lent logic to the requirements of Dharma. So, a moral imperative remained: the Socratic 'Know Thyself', but without omitting the end of the precept: 'then

[84] Translated by Helen Zimmern.

[85] On Blake's esotericism, see RAINE, Kathleen. *Blake and Tradition*. London: Routledge & Kegan Paul, 1969.

thou shalt know the Universe and the Gods'[86]. Besant explained:

> My Dharma is the stage of evolution which my nature has reached [...] I must know the stage of my growth, and I must know the law which will enable me to grow further; then I know my Dharma, and by following that Dharma I am going towards perfection. [...] This explains why morality is relative, why duty must differ for every soul, according to the stage of its evolution.

How can one know one's Dharma? In her series of lectures on this topic, Besant refuted the three Western founding principles of ethics: divine revelation, intuition (the voice of conscience) and utilitarianism. Besant's rejection of this last tenet, pronounced in 1893, constituted a turning point in her thinking, for, after losing her Christian faith, she had found an alternative ethical source in John Stuart Mill's philosophical utilitarianism. She now denounced its limits:

> What is the maxim of this school? 'That is right which conduces to the greatest happiness of the greatest number.' [...] This theory does not recognise the irrefragable unity of the human race, and consequently its maxim fails as a basis of morality. It fails because, in consequence of this unity, one man cannot be perfectly happy unless al men are perfectly happy.

Of course, men are not all at the same stage of spiritual evolution, she conceded, but all are on the path to perfection:

> However low, or however high the stage of evolution occupied by the individual, the idea of Dharma gives us the thought of an inner nature unfolding itself in further growth, and we have found that the world is, as a whole, evolving – evolving from the imperfect to the perfect. [...] The world is on the upward trend, although thousands of souls may lag behind.

Besant still expressed an ideal of universal brotherhood, but she now added

---

[86] From Plato's *Charmides*, one of the three precepts engraved above the entrance of the temple at Delphi.

a spiritual dimension to her humanism:

> The ideal now is peace, co-operation, protection, brotherhood and helpfulness. The essence of sin now lies in separateness. [...] We are now on the path towards unity; we are approaching nearer and nearer to each other. We must now unite, in order to grow further. [...] Separation is the mark of descent into matter, and unification is the mark of the ascent to Spirit.

As in the case of siblings, Besant called the most advanced souls, the eldest, to come to the help of the younger ones. As she said in 1900 in *Some Problems of Life*:

> Nor are matters mended if 'equal' be translated to mean 'should have equal opportunities,' for to give equal opportunities to the unequally equipped is to condemn the weaker to perish in the struggle for existence. We have, in our selfishness, left the weaker as a prey to the stronger, instead of training the stronger to regard his strength as imposing on him heavier responsibilities — among which are the helping and protecting of the weaker.

She therefore made the quest for spiritual unity the ethical standard of all life choices:

> But that thought leads us on to another test of conduct. Is the action we are doing one which seeks our own gain, or which helps on the general good? Is our life a self-seeking, useless life, or does it help humanity? If it is selfish, then it is wrong, it is evil, it is against the growth of the world. If you be among those who have seen the beauty of the idea of unity, and have recognised the perfection of the divine manhood that we seek, then you should kill out this heresy of separateness in yourself.

The ultimate goal was to free oneself from Karma and Dharma to achieve a mystical union with the Divine, through altruistic sacrifice and universal love, which was only possible for the most evolved souls. So Besant concluded her 1893 series of lectures with these lines:

> [When] the man desires no longer anything save the Lord. When the soul has reached that stage of evolution, where it asks nothing of the world, but gives itself wholly to God, when it has outgrown all the promptings of desire, when the heart has gained freedom by love [...] – then abandon you all Dharmas; they are no longer for you; no longer for you the law of growth, no longer for you that balancing of duty, no longer for you that scrutiny of conduct. [...] . There is nothing left in you that is not divine.

Her Theosophical Mysticism

In her Theosophical essays and lectures, Annie Besant occasionally touched on the mystical accents of her youth. Thus, like an echo of her teenage fascination for Catholicism, she sounds almost like Saint Teresa of Ávila in this passage taken from *The Three Paths to Union with God*, published in 1897:

> For he who is love is God; he whose whole being is love is the image of the Supreme; in himself he reproduces the divinity, for Love is God and God is Love. What can keep him then apart from that which is himself? What barrier can arise between the soul and its Lord? That soul is filled with the love of the Lord; itself is love unbounded; and as a river joining with other rivers rushes into the ocean, so does that soul that is love fly into the ocean of love, the Supreme.

Incidentally, Besant directly referred to Saint Teresa of Ávila in her 1925 essay *Mysticism*, in which she presented Mystics as solitary 'Dionysian' rebels, who opposed 'Apollonian' religious authorities, often at the cost of their own lives[87]:

> What can the Priest do with this rebel, who places his visions above all

[87] For a definition of the difference between the Dionysian and the Apollonian in this context, see MASLOW, Abraham. *Religions, Values, and Peak-Experiences*. London: Penguin, 1994 (1964).

> scriptures, and asserts an inalienable liberty in the face of the demand for obedience?
>
> So in the ever-recurring conflict, the Priest conquers in the world material, and is defeated in the world spiritual; and the Mystic, rebuked, persecuted, crushed, while dwelling in the body, becomes the Saint. [...] Teresa, rebuked and humbled by her confessor, arises as S. Teresa for unborn generations.

To Besant therefore, Theosophy also was a form of mysticism:

> Theosophy is the reassertion of Mysticism within the bosom of every living religion, the affirmation of the reality of the mystic state of consciousness and of the value of its products. In the midst of a scholarly and critical generation, it reproclaims the superiority of the knowledge which is drawn from the direct experience of the spiritual world.

Yet, in spite of it all, as a Theosophist, Besant still favoured the path of action.

The Path of Action

In *The Three Paths to Union with God*, Annie Besant recalled that:

> THREE Paths have been traced by the Sages along any one of which a man may tread, and, by following, may attain liberation. [...] These three Paths the three Margas as they are called in the Indian Philosophy that of Karma or action, that of Jnana or Wisdom, that of Bhakti or Devotion.

Besant was fascinated by the Bhagavad Gita, to the point of learning Sanskrit to read the original text, before publishing her own translation in 1905. Her fascination for this sacred text can be explained by the fact that she was looking for coherence between action and devotion. Besant did not adhere to a contemplative ideal, the danger and vanity of which she outlined in 1897:

> He may find delight in his meditation, joy from contemplation, and thus may become forgetful of others and may worship for the pleasure of worshipping. But the true Bhakta does not seek to gain; he seeks to give, to give constantly, perpetually, in order that he may overcome the selfishness of human nature and eradicate the grasping tendency of the mind. [...] Not in contemplation is he to find his only employment; his love must flow out towards his fellowman, and his life must be one of constant service, continual assistance, to all who are in need.

She then quoted the Bhagavad Gita: 'Man winneth not freedom from action by abstaining from activity, nor by mere renunciation (of activity) doth he rise to perfection.' Besant also was inspired by the Victorian 'Gospel of Work', which firmly condemned idleness:

> Tamas has first to be overcome; the quality in Nature of darkness, sluggishness, inertia, sloth, has to be mastered, controlled, and brought into entire subjection. [...] Better activity of any kind than no activity at all; better misdirected energy than absolute inertia.

And in 1912, in *Initiation: The Perfecting of Man*, she demanded:

> Give yourself wholly to Service, keeping nothing back; help, wherever help is possible; work, wherever opportunity of work is seen; give yourself to some great ideal; follow it through cloud and sunshine; walk by it in storm and in peace [...], then, man of the world as you may be, knowing nothing of the things of [...] the glories of the occult world, you are beginning to tread those first steps which will bring you up to the beginning of the pathway.

Besant chose the Path of Action, to the point of reviving the tone of some of her last socialist lectures and articles. This is in keeping with Mark Bevir's findings that the Theosophical ideal of Universal Brotherhood attracted ethical socialists who, like Besant, were looking for a spiritual justification for their ideals and struggles[88]. In 1912, Besant prefaced L. Haden Guest's

---

[88] See BEVIR, Mark. *The Making of British Socialism*. Princeton University Press, 2011.

book *Theosophy and Social Reconstruction*, in which Theosophy appeared as the logical outcome of his Fabian socialism — elitist and humanist at once. Charlotte Despard, for her part, believed that Theosophy had inspired her later socialist struggles. Some Victorian and Edwardian socialists joined the League of Theosophical Workers and even more the Theosophical Order of Service, both founded by Besant, in 1891 and in 1908 respectively.

In fact, contrary to what some of her biographers suggested, Besant's conversion to Theosophy did not lead her to renounce the social, moral, and political missions that she had pursued. Such is her summary, in her second autobiography, of the year following her conversion:

> Meanwhile, with this new controversy on my hands, the School Board work went on, [...]. So also went on the vigorous Socialist work, and the continual championship of struggling labour movements, prominent here being the organisation of the South London fur pullers into a union, and the aiding of the movement for shortening the hours of tram and 'bus men, the meetings for which had to be held after midnight. The feeding and clothing of children also occupied much time and attention, for the little ones in my district were, thousands of them, desperately poor. My studies I pursued as best I could, reading in railway carriages, tramcars, omnibuses, and stealing hours for listening to H.P.B. by shortening the nights.

Significantly, Besant's very first article for *Lucifer*, published in June 1889, was entitled 'Practical Work for Theosophists'. In it, she suggested a series of actions intended to promote her ideal of Universal Brotherhood in a very concrete way. She explained why in 1895 in *The Path of Discipleship*:

> [...] and in feeding those who are hungry, and in showing hospitality to those who are in need of it, while you feed one man as a concrete fact you feed all humanity ideally and in intention; when you give hospitality to one man who comes past your door, you open the door of your heart to humanity as one great entity, and in helping and sheltering one you give help and shelter to humanity as a whole.

Besant launched the Theosophical Order of Service (TOS)[89] in February 1908, only six months after being elected president of the Theosophical Society. The TOS motto was 'A Union of Those who Love in the Service of All that Suffers', and its four objects were these:

1) To minimise the sum of misery in the world;
2) To forget self in working for others;
3) To eliminate selfishness and substitute love as the rule of the world; and
4) To live to the highest that is within us.

The TOS — which still exists today[90] — was structured into leagues, each focusing on a particular social mission. By 1910, the TOS had sixty-one leagues worldwide, and an International Council had to be founded to coordinate them. Thus, the TOS fought against child marriage in India, for improved working conditions and universal suffrage in Britain, for prison and hospital reforms in the United States, and more generally against alcoholism and vivisection. Besant justified these actions in 1911 in *The Meaning and Method of Spiritual Life*:

> Activity we must have at all hazards: it is the way of evolution. Without activity the man does not evolve; without effort and struggle he floats in one of the backwaters of life, and makes no progress along the river. Activity is the law of progress; as a man exercises himself, new life flows into him, and for that reason it is written that the slothful man may never find the Self.

Besant's decision to favour the Path of Action became all the more obvious in 1913, when she became fully involved in the political struggle for India's Home Rule[91]. That involvement partially explains some of the Theosophical Society's internal tensions from that point forward, for Besant began to preside over it from a distance, especially as concerned

[89] See DUNNINGHAM-CHAPOTIN, Diana. 'The Theosophical Order of Service', in *The Theosophical Encyclopedia*. Manila: Theosophical Publishing House, 2006.
[90] See http://international.theoservice.org/
[91] See next chapter.

Krishnamurti. Unwillingly, the young man acted as a catalyst for those tensions, and at the time tried but failed to appease them.

Krishnamurti[92]

In 1897, Annie Besant stated that 'humanity specially craves to worship a Being, and seeks in devotional emotion that satisfaction which no abstract conception of infinity can afford.' Two years later, she gave four lectures — published in 1900 under the title *Avataras* — at the annual convention of the Theosophical Society in Adyar. The Sanskrit word *avatâra* means 'descent': in Hinduism, Buddhism, and for Theosophists, an Avatar is the human incarnation of the divine principle, 'descended' in order to spread the teachings intended to guide humanity in its evolution. Krishna, Buddha, Zoroaster, Jesus and Mohammed were thus considered to be Avatars. Following Madame Blavatsky, Leadbeater and Besant believed that so-called Lord Maitreya — also a divinity in the traditional Buddhist pantheon — was the 'World Teacher'. Regularly, they explained, he selected for himself a 'vehicle' — a sufficiently pure human being to incarnate him and act as his mouthpiece. As the Outer Head of the Esoteric School of the Theosophical Society, Besant had explored the occult relationships between humanity and the Mahatmas with Leadbeater, and she believed herself to be in contact with them. Convinced of Leadbeater's gifts as a medium, however, she eventually entrusted him with the privilege of maintaining astral encounters with the Masters, when her more down-to-earth struggle for the liberation of India left her no time for further occult research.

In the Spring of 1909, Leadbeater met a young fourteen-year-old Brahman, Jiddu Krishnamurti, as well as his brother Nityananda, three years his junior, on the beach at Adyar. Their mother had died four years earlier, after giving birth to eleven children, only six of whom had survived. Their father, Jiddu Narianiah, who used to work for the colonial administration,

[92] See LUTYENS, Mary. *Krishnamurti: The Years of Awakening*. London: John Murray, 1975.

lived in poverty in a little house on the edge of the Theosophical Society's headquarters. He had joined the Society in 1882, and had been working there for several months in a secretarial capacity. Krishnamurti was a frail and painfully shy child. His education had been sporadic because of his poor health and his father's constant relocations. Leadbeater, however, claimed to read extraordinary potential in his aura, to the point of seeing Krishnamurti as the future 'vehicle' for the World Teacher.

Besant did not meet Krishnamurti until November 1909, upon her return from a seven-month lecture tour. By then, he and Nitya were living in the Theosophical Society's headquarters, where several members took turns educating them. Besant immediately shared Leadbeater's convictions, and wrote to him a few weeks later: 'So it is definitely fixed that the Lord Maitreya takes this dear child's body. It seems a very heavy responsibility to have to guard and help it, so as to fit it for Him, as He said, and I feel rather overwhelmed.' To better accomplish this mission, Besant decided to adopt Krishnamurti and Nitya in March 1910 — though not without protest, including litigation, from their father. The first text attributed to Krishnamurti, *At the Feet of the Masters*, was published shortly thereafter, signed 'Alcyone'[93]. Besant and Leadbeater felt their intuition was confirmed when they meditated on Krishnamurti's previous lives. The *Theosophist* serialized their findings in 1910–1911, under the general title 'Rents in the Veil of Time'[94].

Early in 1911, Besant launched the Order of the Star in the East, along with its periodical, *Herald of the Star*, to prepare the world for the arrival of its Teacher. The first reactions were mixed amongst the then 16,000 Theosophists worldwide. The creation of the Order even led to the secession of the German and Austrian lodges, whose president, Rudolf Steiner,

[93] Kurt Leland explained to the author: 'This is the name of a star in the Pleiades that at one time in the nineteenth century was thought to be the center of the universe, around which our solar system rotated. That theory is now obsolete, but the choice of this name for Krishnamurti suggests that he was to be the center of the Theosophical universe.'

[94] Later published in two volumes: *The Lives of Alcyone: A Clairvoyant Investigation into the Lives throughout the Ages of a Large Band of Servers*. Adyar: Theosophical Publishing House, 1924.

founded his own spiritual movement, Anthroposophy, in 1913[95]. However, a majority of Theosophists expressed enthusiasm for Krishnamurti and the Order gathered 12,000 members by 1913. The number of people joining the Theosophical Society increased at the same time, to over 36,000 worldwide by 1920, and to 45,000 by 1928.

In the spring of 1911, Krishnamurti and Nitya accompanied Besant to Europe for the first time. Theosophist George Arundale, by then the headmaster of the Central Hindu College, was their tutor. Besant entrusted them to some of her closest Theosophist female friends, who became mother figures for Krishnamurti, especially Esther Bright, Mary Dodge, Countess Muriel de la Warr, and above all Emily Lutyens. The latter's unconditional devotion for Krishnamurti even took precedence over her marriage, and her husband, architect Edwin Lutyens, left alone for India the following year to work on the construction of New Delhi — but only after he had designed the London headquarters of the Theosophical Society in Tavistock Square. Krishnamurti was there when Besant laid the first stone[96]. He and Nitya then followed Besant on her European lecture tour, in order to be introduced to the European Theosophists who could not wait to meet 'Alcyone'. Upon returning to India, the speech Krishnamurti gave at the 1911 annual convention in Benares so impressed the thousands of Theosophists who attended that its date, 28 December, was thereafter celebrated each year by the Order of the Star in the East.

A few weeks later, Narianiah, Krishnamurti's father, filed a suit against Besant to regain custody of his sons, who had just left for Europe again. Manipulated by orthodox Brahmans, who were opposed to the Theosophists' influence in India, Narianiah revived the accusations of sexual abuse brought against Leadbeater in 1906, while Besant had to go through a painful repetition of the trial that had cost her the custody of her daughter twenty-five years earlier. Once again, she conducted her own defence. Krishnamurti wrote to her, in January 1913: 'you know my

---

[95] See WILSON, Colin. *Rudolf Steiner: The Man and His Visions*. London: Aeon Books, 2005 (1985).

[96] See the section on Besant's Co-Masonry in Chapter 3.

devotion and loyalty for you and I love you so much as my dearest Mother [...]. Even if all the world turns against you there is one who will never never abandon his beloved Mother.' She eventually won custody in May 1914, after appealing all the way to the Privy Council in London. When she left England to return to India in June, she did not know that a World War would part her from her adopted sons — who had stayed to study in England — for almost five years. This may be one of the reasons why she became so actively involved in the political struggle for Indian Home Rule during the war. Her fighting alongside Indian nationalists also distanced her from Leadbeater, who had remained staunchly imperialist: he left India without her in 1914 to settle in Sydney, Australia.

Krishnamurti did not forget Besant during the war, to whom he wrote many an affectionate letter. Shortly before seeing her again, he said: 'You will find a great change in me except in one thing, namely that my devotion and love for your dear self has never changed.' When Besant was finally reunited with him in June 1919, she still saw in him the vehicle for the World Teacher. She therefore organized a lecture tour for him throughout Europe. When the first convention of the Order of the Star in the East took place in Paris in 1921, 2000 of the 30,000 members attended it, eager to listen to Krishnamurti's address at the Théâtre des Champs Elysées. Yet, when among close friends, Krishnamurti became increasingly critical of the Theosophical Society's ritualistic drift, of the interpersonal struggles within the Society, and of the cult that was being encouraged around him. He thus wrote to Emily Lutyens: 'Because we can't face the Bigness of life [...] we create Little Bigness which we can see.' The 1921 convention was followed in 1922 by the first Star Camp, a spiritual retreat organized each year for the members of the Order, in the park of Eerde Castle in Ommen, in the Netherlands.

Krishnamurti and Nitya returned to India for the first time in ten years in December 1921. The success of Krishnamurti's Indian lectures did not appease his doubts. Meanwhile, Besant took advantage of Gandhi's presence in jail — her main political competitor in the Indian nationalist movement — to step up her struggle for Home Rule. It was therefore without her that

Krishnamurti and Nitya went to Sydney for the Australian Theosophical convention, where Krishnamurti discovered to his dismay the importance the Liberal Catholic Church had taken within the Theosophical Society. Following Theosophist James Ingall Wedgwood[97], Leadbeater himself had been ordained a bishop of that Church in 1916, and so was George Arundale in 1925. Krishnamurti wrote to Emily Lutyens from Sydney: 'I am not a ceremonialist & I do not appreciate all the paraphernalia with all those prayers and bobbing up & down, the robes etc.' He later publicly expressed his rejection of ritualism during the 1928 Star Camp: 'I still maintain that all ceremonies are unnecessary for spiritual growth.'

Before that, in 1922, Krishnamurti and Nitya discovered the Ojai Valley in California, where they settled in a little cottage given to them by an American Theosophist. There Krishnamurti experienced a long mystical crisis, accompanied by violent physical symptoms. This he later called 'the Process', and it profoundly changed him. 'Like the lake', he explained, 'I felt that my physical body, with its mind and emotions, could be ruffled on the surface but nothing, nay nothing, could disturb the calmness of my soul,' adding: 'I have drunk at the fountain of Joy and eternal Beauty. I am God-intoxicated.'

Even though this 'Process' brought him closer to Besant, to whom he expressed his affection more than ever in his almost daily letters, Krishnamurti began to express an increasingly personal spiritual point of view. During the 1924 Star Camp at Ommen, he thus told the members of the Order: 'You are like people in a dark room waiting for someone to turn on the light for you instead of groping in the dark and turning it on for yourselves.' The death of his brother Nitya in 1925, after years of battling against tuberculosis, devastated him. It doubtless constituted a turning point in Krishnamurti's life, for he expressed his reservations about his role more and more openly afterwards.

Besant spent all of the winter of 1926–1927 in the serenity of Ojai with Krishnamurti and some close friends, including Emily Lutyens, who wrote about Besant as follows, using an Indian term of endearment meaning

[97] From the influential Darwin-Wedgwood family.

mother: 'Amma is so sweet here and so happy. She has not had quiet time like this for years. [...] In the evenings we play bridge and she writes or reads.' Besant left Ojai more certain than ever that the World Teacher was incarnated in Krishnamurti.

However, Krishnamurti declared to the participants of the 1927 Star Camp at Ommen: 'I can be the door but you must pass through the door and find the liberation that is beyond it.' Rejecting the notions of adepts and initiates, he added: 'It lies in the power of each one to enter the flame, to become the flame.' During the 1928 Star Camp, he declared: 'Truth is within yourself', and 'my work is to help you to awaken your desire of attainment, of illumination, of liberation.' He also denounced those people, such as Wedgwood and Arundale, who derived undue influence from their position as intermediaries between Theosophists and the Masters: 'I hope you will not listen to anyone, but will listen only to your own intuition, your own understanding, and give a public refusal to those who would be your interpreters.' Krishnamurti included himself among those interpreters who ought to be rejected, with words that were painful to the members of Order: 'Do not quote me afterwards as an authority. I refuse to be your crutch. I am not going to be brought into a cage for your worship.' Finally, he put the existence of the Masters themselves into question: 'Life itself [is] the guide, the Master and the God.'

Such public expression of his doubts left his followers, including Besant, profoundly distraught. In September 1928, Emily Lutyens wrote in the *International Star Bulletin*, one of the Order's periodicals:

> He is making us do our own work, mentally and emotionally, and that is the last thing we expected of Him. Some people are returning home naked and alone, their foundations shattered, realizing the necessity of reorientating themselves in a world in which every value has changed [...] the tragic side of this Camp has been the way in which the dead past has arisen at every moment to confront the new ideas.

However, Besant's confidence in Krishnamurti remained intact. She dissolved the Esoteric School of the Theosophical Society at the end of 1928, a move which Krishnamurti praised in a letter to Emily Lutyens: 'Amma has done the biggest thing that anyone can do. To build up something & then to put it aside for something bigger is the greatest thing.'

Yet, despite Besant's attempts at conciliation, Krishnamurti announced the dissolution of the Order of the Star to the 3000 participants of the 1929 Star Camp, as well as to the listeners of Dutch radio, which broadcast his address live. He then delivered his famous formula: 'Truth is a pathless land', adding, 'A belief is purely an individual matter, and you cannot and must not organize it. If you do, it becomes dead, crystallized; it becomes a creed, a sect, a religion, to be imposed on others.' He also abdicated his role as World Teacher: 'I do not want followers [...]. The moment you follow someone you cease to follow Truth.' Krishnamurti left the Theosophical Society itself in 1930, when Besant re-launched its Esoteric School.

Thereafter Krishnamurti settled in Ojai, which he nevertheless frequently left for long lecture tours around the world, during which he repeated his message of spiritual freedom[98]. At the end of 1932, he returned to Adyar to see Annie Besant, for he never ceased to love her. He made the trip once again in May 1933, a few weeks before the death of his adopted mother: 'Dear Amma', he wrote, 'It is tragic to see her like this.' He was no longer there when Besant passed away, on 20 September, 1933. Leadbeater, by then nearly eighty years old[99], came all the way from Sydney to be at her side during her last moments. He survived her by only a few months.

George Arundale succeeded Besant as president of the Theosophical Society. His election demonstrated how the majority of the Theosophists

---

[98] See KRISHNAMURTI, Jiddu. *The Collected Works of J. Krishnamurti, 1933–1967* (17 vol). Ojai: Krishnamurti Foundation of America, 1992 (online at www.jkrishnamurti.org).

[99] 'Charles Webster Leadbeater was born on February 16, 1854, at Stockport, Cheshire, England and this is the date given in his birth certificate [and in the 1861 and 1881 Censuses of England and Wales]. For some unknown reason his birth date was later frequently given as February 17, 1847, and that date appeared on his passport.' SHEARMAN, Hugh. *Charles Webster Leadbeater: A Biography*. London: St. Alban Press, 1980, p. 2. See also TILLETT, Gregory. *The Elder Brother: A Biography of Charles Webster Leadbeater*. London: Routledge & Kegan Paul, 1982, p. 16.

of the time had failed to understand Krishnamurti's sober but demanding form of spirituality. Although Krishnamurti had not managed to reform the Theosophical Society from the inside during the 1920s, his teachings became a source of inspiration for the next generation of Theosophists and many other spiritual seekers in the 1970s. Krishnamurti returned to Adyar in 1980, for the first time since 1933, when his friend Radha Burnier was elected president of the Society, a sign of the later evolution of this spiritual movement.

6

Annie Besant's Struggle for Indian Home Rule (1895–1933)[1]

The British Empire[2]

The British Empire achieved global dominance during the century from 1815 to 1914. The end of the Napoleonic Wars, followed by the long *Pax Britannica*, freed the energy necessary for exploration and colonization, while the Industrial Revolution provided — to borrow Eric Hobsbawm's famous phrase — the 'tools of Empire': weapons of course, but also efficient means of transportation, communication and trade, such as trains, steamers and the telegraph, as well as financial institutions that supported British capitalists in their search for raw materials and markets for their industrial products. By 1914, this Empire 'on which the Sun never set' stretched over one fifth of the globe, proudly coloured pink on Victorian and Edwardian world maps, and it probably gathered in almost 400 million people, about one fourth of the world population.

Yet, the Empire is considered by most historians as 'informal', due to the lack of a strong centralized administration, but also because pragmatism and economic opportunism ruled until the 1870s, with no clearly-defined political or ideological ambition. Expansion was not even wanted by the

[1] See BESANT, Annie. *The Birth of New India: A Collection of Writings and Speeches on Indian Affairs*. Adyar, Madras: Theosophical Publishing Society, 1917; KUMAR, Raj, RAMESHWARI Devi and Romila PRUTHI. *Annie Besant: Founder of Home Rule Movement*. Jaipur: Pointer Publishers, 2003.

[2] See PORTER, Andrew, ed. *The Oxford History of the British Empire: the Nineteenth Century*. Oxford University Press, 1999.

majority of British people, who were more concerned about the human and financial cost of the Empire. They feared conflict, as with Russia in Crimea and in Afghanistan, when Britain got caught in the 'Great Game', that followed the declines of the Persian, Chinese and Ottoman Empires. It led to cumbersome takeovers, such as the Suez Canal in 1875, followed by Egypt in 1882, mostly in order to maintain the stability of an Empire that was first and foremost economic.

Imperialism, in the political and moral sense of the term, only developed in the last quarter of the nineteenth century, partly because of the new racial theories derived from Charles Darwin's *On the Origin of Species* (1859) and *The Descent of Man* (1871). The early Victorians who campaigned with William Wilberforce to abolish slavery in the Empire — a goal achieved in 1833 — had been inspired by their Evangelical faith, and their belief that human souls were all equal before God. Some of the late Victorians for their part allowed their materialist philosophy to degenerate from belief in Reason and Science, to scientism and racism.

The symbolic turning point of the imperialist ideology was the 'Crystal Palace Speech', delivered in 1872 by Benjamin Disraeli, then Conservative Leader of the Opposition. Its original title was 'The Maintenance of Empire'[3], and Disraeli attacked those Liberals ready, according to him, to sacrifice parts of the Empire on the altar of pragmatism. Disraeli believed Britain had a moral mission towards the Empire and its peoples, no matter the cost:

> [...] those who advised that policy — and I believe their convictions were sincere — looked upon the colonies of England, looked upon our connection with India, as a burden upon this country, viewing everything in a financial aspect, and totally passing by those moral and political considerations which make nations great, and by the influence of which alone men are distinguished from animals.

[3] KEBBEL, Thomas Edward, ed., *Selected Speeches of the Late Right Honourable the Earl of Beaconsfield* vol. 2. London: Longmans, 1882, pp. 529–34.

Disraeli was convinced of the symbolic and, he hoped, unifying power of the Empire, both at the national and international levels. He wanted to offer a common mission to the British, in order to transcend a class system that he loathed[4]. Though Besant shared this desire for social and international unity, she did not support the arrogance and patriotism with which Disraeli continued his speech:

> It is whether you will be content to be a comfortable England, modelled and moulded upon continental principles and meeting in due course an inevitable fate, or whether you will be a great country, — an imperial country — a country where your sons, when they rise, rise to paramount positions, and obtain not merely the esteem of their countrymen, but command the respect of the world [...].

British imperialism was therefore an ambivalent ideology, a fact that must be fully appreciated in order to understand Besant's position. Alongside an intense, and sometimes racist patriotism — which Besant did not share — a sincere belief in a civilizing mission developed, and that it could supposedly be achieved thanks to the framework and structures of the Empire. This ambiguity is at work in Rudyard Kipling's famous poem 'The White Man's Burden', published in 1899, that presented this civilizing mission as a humanist, even humanitarian duty, of the kind Western NGOs could still identify with today:

> Take up the White Man's burden,
> The savage wars of peace –
> Fill full the mouth of Famine
> And bid the sickness cease;

Kipling went even further, presenting such a mission as a willing sacrifice:

> Take up the White Man's burden,

[4] See Disraeli's 1845 social novel, *Sybil, or the Two Nations*.

No tawdry rule of kings,
But toil of serf and sweeper,
The tale of common things.
The ports ye shall not enter,
The roads ye shall not tread,
Go make them with your living,
And mark them with your dead.

However, in the first stanza of the poem, the peoples to whose aid the 'White Man' must come, to the point of sacrifice, were presented as inferior, with no respect for their civilization: 'Your new-caught, sullen peoples, / Half-devil and half-child.' This is where the profound difference between Kipling's and Besant's visions of India can be perceived most clearly.

The Raj[5]

The conquest of India began in 1600, when Elizabeth I granted a Royal Charter to the East India Company, which founded its first trading post in Surat in 1608. The Company faced competition from Portuguese and Dutch merchants, but managed to establish itself in Madras, Bombay and Calcutta before the end of the eighteenth century. India was a theatre of operations during the War of the Austrian Succession and the Seven Years' War. These 'Carnatic Wars' of 1746–1763 there resulted in the end of French expansion in India, leaving free rein to the East India Company.

The Company's domination extended progressively over the whole sub-continent, thanks to a neo-feudal organization that relied in great part on the landed aristocracy of the *Zamindars*, who were made responsible for tax collection. From 1848, the Company was given direct administrative power over princely states where there was no heir, or where the Rajah

[5] See WOLPERT, Stanley. *A New History of India*. Oxford University Press, 2004 (7th ed.); and MOORE, Robin J. 'Imperial India', in PORTER, Andrew, ed. *The Oxford History of the British Empire: the Nineteenth Century*. Oxford University Press, 1999, pp. 422–45.

was deemed incompetent. It was, however, by military action that Punjab and Burma were conquered shortly thereafter. At the same time, the Company built the railway network, by which cotton and jute were sent to the textile mills of Manchester and Dundee, and British manufactured goods distributed in return. This railway network, along with the telegraph and an efficient postal system, contributed to the geographical unification of India, but also allowed for the rapid transportation of troops. Indeed, the Company also knew how to 'divide and conquer', and made use of local ethnic, social and religious tensions, sometimes even encouraging them, as during the Anglo-Sikh wars. Furthermore, the Company's structural investments in India were financed by arbitrary punitive taxes and tariffs.

By the middle of the nineteenth century, the situation was tense and volatile: only 45,000 British officers were supposed to control over 200 million inhabitants, with the assistance of 230,000 Indian soldiers under their command, the Sepoys. Their violent uprising in 1857–1858 and the terrible suppression that followed forever changed the relationship between India and Britain. Stanley Wolpert wrote that 'Virtually all the bridges so painstakingly erected between the British and Indian Cultures were destroyed by fear and hatred.' While the British spoke of the 'Sepoy Mutiny', many Indians considered it to be their first war of independence. As such, it proved counter-productive: in 1858, the British Parliament passed the Government of India Act, which transferred the political power held by the Company to the Crown. This was accompanied by a proclamation by Queen Victoria to the 'Princes, Chiefs and Peoples', of India, which revealed the same ambiguity as Kipling's — and partly as Besant's. On the one hand, Victoria promised 'prosperity, and that social advancement, which can only be secured by internal peace and good government', as well as 'works of utility and improvement […] for the benefit of all our subjects resident therein'. On the other hand, she also promised to protect traditions, customs, and ancestral land rights, which amounted to maintaining India in the feudal system that had been reinforced by the Company's disastrous administration.

The Government of India Act 1858 founded 'the Raj': from then on

Britain governed the sub-continent through the India Office, with a Secretary of State for India who presided over a council of ten appointed members. Locally, India was managed by a governor-general, thereafter taking the pompous title of Viceroy, appointed for a five-year term by the sovereign, on the advice of the Prime Minister. India was divided into provinces, with a governor for each, as well as local executive and legislative councils. Yet the Raj was still run by a mere 150,000 civil servants and army officers. These were recruited through a competitive exam, and most of them were very young men from the lower middle class, for they were badly paid. Inexperienced and poorly educated, they sought refuge in conservatism and prejudices. The examinations were open to Indians, but held in England, and as a result only about thirty Indians became high-ranking public officials in their own country before 1900. The jurisdiction of British authorities did not extend to the internal administration of the princely states, but these were controlled indirectly by means of treaties made during the time of the Company. In any case, Britain had little to fear from the Rajahs, as Viceroy Lord Lytton explained to Queen Victoria in 1876, the year she was crowned Empress of India, speaking of 'the native aristocracy of the country', whose 'sympathy and cordial allegiance is no inconsiderable guarantee for the stability [...] of the Indian Empire'[6]. The army was reorganized on the basis of one British soldier for every two Indians, often Sikhs or Gurkhas, who had not taken part in the Sepoy Mutiny — meaning that the principle of *divide et impera* was not abandoned despite the universalist tone of the 1858 Proclamation.

Annie Besant first went to India in 1893, but she had been interested in the country's fate since the mid-1870s, when she had first criticized Disraeli's imperialist ideology.

[6] BUCKLE, George Earle, ed. *The Letters of Queen Victoria. Volume 5: 1870–1878.* Cambridge University Press, 1926, pp. 461–3.

The 'Monster Petition' of 1876

Annie Besant's first anti-imperialist action was the 'monster petition' she and Charles Bradlaugh launched in September 1875, against the Prince of Wales' tour of India, organized by Disraeli as a means to promote the Empire. Besant then only saw in the Empire an institution that was as cumbersome, useless and costly as the monarchy, when Prime Minister Disraeli aimed to buttress the symbolic power of both by joining them together. In her autobiography, Besant said that what spurred the petition was the enormous public grant of £142,000 voted by Parliament for the Prince's tour, and she joined in the demonstrations supporting the eighteen MPs who had voted against it. The petition was signed by 100,000 people, and its one-mile-long scroll was carried in a procession to Westminster and presented to the Commons, but to no avail.

While Bengal was on the brink of famine, the Prince of Wales was received in style by Viceroy Lord Northbrook in Bombay, then by several Rajahs in their palaces. His tour went on for several months, and was reported daily in the British press. Disraeli hoped to show that India was now well governed. However, the Prince of Wales himself was shocked to discover the way British authorities treated the local population, and expressed his indignation in private letters. He wrote to Foreign Secretary Lord Granville from India: 'Because a man has a black face and a different religion from our own, there is no reason why he should be treated as a brute'[7]. He nonetheless returned with his arms full of trophies from his tiger hunts on elephants' backs, and sumptuous gifts from Indian aristocrats subservient to British authorities.

Victoria's coronation as Empress of India, also orchestrated by Disraeli, soon followed her son's return. His tour in India had prepared public opinion, to Besant's great displeasure, and three years later she still lamented this 'new title of Empress so foolishly allowed to the Queen by

[7] Quoted by HIBBERT, Christopher. *Edward VII: The Last Victorian King*. Basingstoke: Palgrave Macmillan, 2007, p. 138.

Parliament'[8]. It is important to note that Victoria was Empress 'of India' only; this emphasized the symbolic importance of the Raj, which Disraeli was the first to describe as the 'jewel in the Crown'. Victoria, however, never went to India, and did not even attend the extravagant Delhi Durbar organized in 1877 in her honour by Viceroy Lord Lytton.

'Plea For the Weak against the Strong' (1879)

Annie Besant expressed her rejection of Disraeli's imperialism and foreign policy even more clearly in 1879, during the second Anglo-Afghan war. She reacted to the passing of the Vernacular Press Act, with *The Story of Afghanistan: Or, Why the Tory Government Gags the Indian Press. A Plea for the Weak against the Strong*. Besant's anti-imperialist arguments echoed those of the Liberals, attacked by Disraeli in 1872. William Gladstone himself, then Liberal Leader of the Opposition, wrote to Besant to congratulate her on the quality of her analysis in the article. She had combined pragmatic and humanist criticisms against Disraeli's Conservative Government: 'None voted that [the Tory Government] should embroil us in Europe, in Asia, in Africa. [...] None raised it that it should pour out our money as dross, nor shed human blood as water on three of the four continents of the globe.' Besant demonstrated a scathing sense of irony when she wrote: 'By the light of flaming villages may be traced the blessings of the Empress of India's advancing rule. [...] In this way do we discharge, to use Lord Lytton's words, "our high duties to God and man as the greatest civilising power".' She therefore called for resistance against colonizers: 'These horrors have been committed under the pretence that the Afghans were "rebels." Rebels to whom? Where there is no rightful claim to authority there can be no rebellion in resistance.' Speaking about India, she wrote: 'At least for the sake of common honesty, let us

---

[8] BESANT, Annie. *The Story of Afghanistan: Or, Why the Tory Government Gags the Indian Press. A Plea for the Weak against the Strong*. London: Freethought Publishing Co., 1879.

drop our hypocritical mask and acknowledge that we seized India from lust of conquest, from greed of gain.' She did not reject the concept of civilizing mission, however, providing that it really meant the propagation of those British democratic ideals in which she believed: 'What is our duty to this great land and how may we best remedy our crimes of the past? The answer comes in one word "Liberty". Train India for freedom; educate India for self-government.' *A Plea for the Weak against the Strong* sold tens of thousands of copies in pamphlet form.

In the years that followed, Besant published *The Transvaal* (1881), *Egypt* (1882) and *The Story of Sudan* (1884), all in the same anti-imperialist vein. It is appropriate to add to this list, the children's tale 'Ganga, the River Maid', which Besant wrote in 1885. It thus concludes — strangely foretelling Besant's own funeral half a century later in India:

> And to this day the Hindu, dying afar off from the sacred river, prays that his ashes may be thrown into Ganga's red-brown depths; and dying lips cry with their last breath: 'Ganga, Ganga': and dying eyes fix their last look on Ganga's broad pure stream.

Theosophists in India before 1893[9]

When Annie Besant travelled to India for the first time in 1893, the relationship between the country and the Theosophical Society was complicated. Madame Blavatsky believed Vedic India to be the original source of all spirituality, ancient wisdom and religions. She was, however, critical of some of the Hindu practices she had discovered in 1879. She believed that Hinduism had been led somewhat astray, and called for reforms so that it could get back to the original purity of the Vedas. In his article 'Theosophy as a Political Movement', Mark Bevir showed that

---

[9] See BEVIR, Mark. 'Theosophy as a Political Movement', in COPLEY, Antony, ed. *Gurus and their Followers: New Religious Reform Movements in Colonial India*. Oxford University Press, 2000, pp. 159–76; and 'Theosophy and the Origins of the Indian National Congress'. *International Journal of Hindu Studies* 7.1/3, 2003, pp. 99–115.

the Theosophical Society could not but be critical of the Raj at the time:

> [The Theosophists] needed to explain how Indian society had fallen away from the Aryan ideal. Typically they did so by pointing to the disruptive effects of foreign, and especially British, rule. [...] the British had brought to India a corrupt individualism and decadent materialism [...]. The key political question was [...] how best to return India to its true self.

The Theosophical Society had soon attracted a number of Indian intellectuals, including epigraphist K. V. Subrahmanya Aiyar, historian B. M. Malabari, poet Debendranath Sen, and Sanskrit specialist Kashinath Telang. From her first stay in India, Blavatsky had also fascinated some members of the Anglo-Indian community, especially Alfred Percy Sinnett and Allan Octavian Hume. Sinnett, who became a Theosophist in 1879, was the editor of the *Pioneer*, the most widely read Indian daily in English. His books *The Occult World* (1881) and *Esoteric Buddhism* (1883) — inspired by the Mahatmas' letters he had received during Blavatsky's 1880 visit at his summer house in Simla — played an important part in spreading Theosophical ideas. As for Hume[10], he was a high-ranking reformist public official, who also met Blavatsky in Simla. He too joined the Theosophical Society, and became president of the Simla Eclectic Theosophical Society, when the branch was founded in 1881. Hume also paid for the Indian launch of the periodical the *Theosophist*.

A. O. Hume's spiritual and political involvement was emblematic of the Theosophists' difficult position within the British Raj. In 1912, Hume's friend and biographer, William Wedderburn, recalled India's situation when Hume first met Blavatsky and discovered Theosophy:

> And about the years 1878 and 1879, economic, in combination with political, troubles were actively at work throughout India; the physical suffering of

---

[10] See WEDDERBURN, William. *Allan Octavian Hume: Father of the Indian National Congress. 1829 to 1912.* London: T. Fisher Unwin, 1913; and MOULTON, Edward C. 'Allan O. Hume and the Indian National Congress: a Reassessment'. *South Asia* 8.1–2, June–December 1985, pp. 5–23.

the many, acted on by the intellectual discontent of the few, was rapidly bringing popular unrest to the danger point. For the masses of the peasantry, scourged by poverty, famine, and pestilence, were beginning to give way to despair; they could not make their voices heard, and they saw no hope of relief; while, in the schools and colleges, the leaven of Western education was working among the intellectuals, teaching lessons of political history, and showing them how it was only through storm and stress that the British people had won for themselves the blessings of freedom. Hence the mind of the younger generation was stirred by vague dreams of revolutionary, and even violent, change. This critical condition of affairs was clearly understood by Mr. Hume.

Hume, who had been working in India since 1849, had fought against the Sepoys during their Mutiny, but he believed that the uprising had been the result of the British authorities' incompetence. He had launched a vernacular newspaper: *Lokmitra* (The People's Friend), and founded free elementary schools in the districts in his charge — where he also supported girls' education and opposed child marriage. Responsible for collecting taxes in the north of India from 1867, he openly criticized the most arbitrary among them. Hume also called for a vast land reform, which he detailed in his 1879 essay *Agricultural Reform in India*. He took Indian traditions and social structures into account, and sharply criticized the methods imposed by the British, which caused recurring famines. Hume took early retirement in 1882. The following year, he wrote an open letter to the young graduates of the University of Calcutta, encouraging them to organize themselves in a political movement:

> Every nation secures precisely as good a government as it merits. If you, the picked men, the most highly educated of the nation, cannot, scorning personal ease and selfish objects, make a resolute struggle to secure greater freedom for yourselves and your country, a more impartial administration, a larger share in the management of your own affairs, then we your friends are wrong, and our adversaries right [...] then rightly and inevitably have they become your rulers. And rulers and taskmasters they must continue, let the yoke gall your shoulders never so sorely, until you realise and stand prepared to act upon the eternal truth that, whether in the case of individuals

or nations, self-sacrifice and unselfishness are the only unfailing guides to freedom and happiness.

Indian Theosophists heard this call and asked that a political debate be organized during the annual Theosophical Society convention in Adyar in 1884. Madame Blavatsky and Colonel Olcott refused, for they had been forced to promise the authorities of the Raj that they would limit themselves to spiritual and intellectual activities, and they knew they were being watched. The debate took place nonetheless, but across the street from the Theosophical Society premises. This combination of proximity and separation of the political and the spiritual was emblematic of the dilemma in which Theosophists found themselves. Hume distanced himself from Blavatsky, and resigned from the presidency of the Simla Lodge in 1883, so that he could pursue his political struggles freely, but his later writings show that spiritually he remained a Theosophist.

In 1885, Hume founded the Indian National Congress (INC). The first Congress met in Bombay in December, with seventy-two Indian and Anglo-Indian delegates, many of whom were Theosophists, under the presidency of lawyer Womesh Chunder Bonnerjee. The 1885 INC claimed to be a space for debates only, but its objectives were those formulated by Hume in his 1883 open letter, especially to obtain a fairer portion of Indian administration for educated Indians.

Meanwhile, Charles Bradlaugh fully embraced the Radical honorary title 'MP for India' he had inherited from Henry Fawcett. His unstinting support for India's cause is where the first direct link between Besant and India can be found.

First Meeting between Besant and Gandhi[11]

When Charles Bradlaugh died in 1891, a frail twenty-one-year-old law student joined in the crowd that followed his funeral procession: Mohandas K. Gandhi. Gandhi explained in his autobiography, published at the end of the 1920s: 'Every Indian knew Bradlaugh's name [...]. He was buried in Woking Cemetery[12]. I attended the funeral, as I believe every Indian residing in London did.'

Gandhi was born in Gujarat, on the west coast of India, into a Hindu family of the merchants' and artisans' caste. His father, however, was the *diwan*, the Prime Minister of the small princely State of Porbandar. Gandhi was married at the age of thirteen to a girl barely a year older than him, and he was only fifteen when their first child was born. Gandhi's father died that year, and as his family wanted him to succeed his father as *diwan*, they sent him to study law in London in 1888. Gandhi was not religious, but he had promised his mother to follow the precepts of Hinduism: he therefore joined the Vegetarian Society in London, some members of which were Theosophists.

In his autobiography, Gandhi conceded that it was his discovery of Theosophy that made him want to know more about his own Hindu culture and spirituality:

> Towards the end of my second year in England I came across two Theosophists, brothers, and both unmarried[13]. They talked to me about the Gita. They were reading Sir Edwin Arnold's translation *The Song Celestial* and they invited me to read the original with them. I felt ashamed, as I had read the divine poem neither in Sanskrit nor in Gujarati. I was constrained to tell them that I had not read the Gita, but that I would gladly read it with them, and that

[11] See GANDHI, Mohandras K. *An Autobiography; or, The Story of My Experiments with Truth* (translated from the Gujarati by Mahadey Desai). Ahmedabad: Navajivan Publishing House, 1993 (1927–1928).

[12] Gandhi meant Brookwood Cemetery in Woking.

[13] Archibald and Bertram Keightley who, though of the same age, were actually uncle and nephew.

> though my knowledge of Sanskrit was meagre [...]. I recall having read, at the brothers' insistence, Madame Blavatsky's *Key to Theosophy*. This book stimulated in me the desire to read books on Hinduism, and disabused me of the notion fostered by the missionaries that Hinduism was rife with superstition.

Gandhi's Theosophist friends introduced him to Annie Besant in 1890, shortly after he read her essay *Why I Became a Theosophist*:

> They also took me on one occasion to the Blavatsky Lodge and introduced me to Madame Blavatsky and Mrs. Besant. The latter had just then joined the Theosophical Society, and I was following with great interest the controversy about her conversion.

Gandhi wrote that did not join the Theosophical Society: 'The friends advised me to join the Society, but I politely declined saying, "With my meagre knowledge of my own religion I do not want to belong to any religious body"'. However, although Gandhi did not proceed to full membership, he joined the Blavatsky Lodge as an associate member in 1890[14].

Gandhi became a lawyer in 1891. He briefly returned to India, but, unable to start a practice there, he agreed to go to work in Natal, South Africa, on behalf of an Indian firm. Gandhi left India in 1893, the year of Besant's first visit to the country, and did not settle back there until 1915.

Struggle for a Spiritual and Cultural Hindu Renaissance

Annie Besant, like Madame Blavatsky, saw in India:

> [...] the Holy Land, the land whose great philosophy had been the source of all the philosophies of the Western world, the land whose great religion has

[14] See the Blavatsky Lodge minutes for 1890 in the archives of the Theosophical Society in England.

> been the origin of all religions, the mother of spirituality, the cradle of civilisation.[15]

On her first tour of India, during the winter of 1893–1894, she also asserted: 'If religion perish here, it will perish everywhere, and in India's hand is laid the sacred charge of keeping alight the torch of spirit amid the fogs and storms of increasing materialism'[16]. Besant therefore reversed Victorian spiritual values: according to her, it was up to India to instruct the world. The civilizing mission, the spiritual 'burden' fell to Indians, not to the British 'white man', as she stated in an 1895 lecture entitled 'The Means of India's Regeneration': 'Shall [India] ever again rise from her present degradation, and fulfil the sublime charge laid in her hands? [...] it lies wholly with her children to give back to Humanity the India which may be the Saviour of Spirituality to the world.'

When Besant settled in India for good in 1895, she decided to wear a white sari, explaining in her 1895 lecture that 'here, the wearing of English dress is simply absurd', and that she had chosen white, the colour of mourning in India, as a tribute to the Indian people's sufferings. Such subversive symbolism immediately placed Besant on the margins of the Anglo-Indian community. Pierre Loti, who travelled to India in 1900 to study Theosophy under Besant in Benares, recalled in his 1903 text *L'Inde (sans les Anglais)* (India without the English):

> At the far end of an old garden stands a low and modest Indian house [...]. The Masters work or meditate the whole day [...]. One high amongst them is a European woman, who has come here to seek shelter from the turmoil of the world.
>
> Her face is still beautiful, though crowned with silver hair, and she lives here, barefooted and detached from earthly strife, the thrifty and austere life of an ascetic. [...] she was once of my race [...].

---

15 'India, Her Past and Her Future'. A lecture delivered onboard the Kaisar-i-Hind, in the Indian Ocean, 6 November 1893.

16 'India's Mission Among Nations', in *Essays and Addresses*, vol. 4: *India*. London: Theosophical Publishing Society, 1913 (ca. 1894).

To understand how unusual such a lifestyle was for a European woman in India, one has to recall the consequences that the Sepoy Mutiny had on Anglo-Indian lives and attitudes, as described by Stanley Wolpert:

> New towns and suburbs, called civil lines and camps, were now built for British officials and their wives, with grand 'bungalows' on wide, tree-lined streets. [...] long after Edwardian attitudes and fresh ideas liberated London from the narrow formalism and rigidity of such inhibiting mores [, d]istrust, frustration and fear fed upon one another.

During the closing of the annual Theosophical Society convention of 1909, Besant recalled that, on the contrary, in the 1880s: '[The founders of the Theosophical Society] were suspected by the Government, because they accepted Indians with the social courtesies shown to equals'[17].

Besant was not content with simply adopting the traditional Indian lifestyle. In 1895, she asked, well before Gandhi, 'every patriotic Indian to encourage Indian art, Indian manufactures and Indian labour; and not to go across the seas to bring here endless manufactured articles.' The influence from her friend, the artist and utopian socialist William Morris, can be felt when Besant wondered: 'why should men who have such art on their own soil, why should they go and buy the shoddy productions of Birmingham and Manchester?' In 1884, in *How We Live and How We Might Live*, Morris had already denounced the tragic human consequences of this global capitalism of which the British Empire was the precursor:

> [...] so far-reaching is this curse of commercial war that no country is safe from its ravages; the traditions of a thousand years fall before it in a month; it overruns a weak or semi-barbarous country, and whatever romance or pleasure or art existed there, is trodden down into a mire of sordidness and ugliness; the Indian or Javanese craftsman may no longer ply his craft leisurely, working a few hours a day, in producing a maze of strange beauty on a piece

[17] 'The Work of the T. S. in India', in *The Birth of New India: a Collection of Writings and Speeches on Indian Affairs*. Adyar, Madras: Theosophical Publishing House, 1917 (1909).

> of cloth: a steam-engine is set a-going at Manchester, [...] and the Asiatic worker, if he is not starved to death outright, as plentifully happens, is driven himself into a factory to lower the wages of his Manchester brother worker, and nothing of character is left him except, most like, an accumulation of fear and hatred of that to him most unaccountable evil, his English master.

Morris, and the other utopian socialists alongside whom Besant had fought, had adopted, also well before Gandhi, the ideal of the 'Simple Life', formulated in 1854 by American transcendentalist Henry David Thoreau, in *Walden, or, Life in the Woods*[18]. Thoreau had read the Bhagavad Gita and the Vedas at Walden Pond, and his rejection of materialism was based on the same Eastern spirituality as Besant's, who believed, in 1895, that: '[the Indians] should lead a national, a simple, life with all the noble characteristics of the ancient times; that their houses should have the old simplicity and not be crowded over with a multiplicity of things of foreign manufacture.'

Under Besant's influence, and later her presidency, the Theosophical Society chose to work actively towards India's cultural and spiritual renaissance. Mark Bevir granted an important role to the Theosophists in this, thanks to their religious tolerance:

> Whereas the Arya Samaj had little impact except on Punjabi Hindus, and the Brahmo Sabha except on Bengali Hindus, the Theosophical Society was more of an all-India organisation. Its members came from all over the sub-continent. Besides Hindus, it attracted Parsees, Christians, Sikhs, and even a few Muslims. At least as importantly, it brought members of the western-educated elite of Indian society, such as Aiyar, Rao, and Sen into close contact with liberal members of the British community, such as Sinnett and Hume[19].

---

[18] See the chapter 'The Ethical Socialists', in BEVIR, Mark. *The Making of British Socialism*. Princeton University Press, 2011.

[19] BEVIR, Mark. 'Theosophy as a Political Movement', in COPLEY, A. ed. *Gurus and their Followers: New Religious Reform Movements in Colonial India*. Oxford University Press, 2000, p. 170.

Indeed, despite the emphasis that Besant placed on Hinduism, Indian and Anglo-Indian Theosophists, true to their motto 'There is no religion higher than Truth', came from all of India's religious communities, and the annual Theosophical Society conventions allowed them to meet on common ground, starting in 1881. Besant hoped for a spiritual unification of India, but such an ideal could only conflict with British interests that benefited from the religious divisions of the country — as shown by the partition of Bengal. The partition, decreed in 1905 by Viceroy Lord Curzon, created a Hindu Western Bengal and a Muslim Eastern Bengal (now Bangladesh). Curzon's clearly stated objective was to weaken the powerful nationalist movements of this populous state.

Educational Reforms in India[20]

Annie Besant believed that India's spiritual and cultural renaissance could only be achieved through the awareness, education and example of India's upper classes and castes. She clearly said so in 1909, in 'The Work of the T. S. In India': 'Better to work among those who can influence the masses, than in the masses themselves, as regards reformation and change. Changes should always begin above and work downwards, then they influence powerfully and healthily.' Beyond what can be described as elitism here, actually lay pragmatism, for British authorities relied on the collaboration of the Indian elite. In his previously-cited 1876 letter, Viceroy Lord Lytton explained to Queen Victoria the importance of organizing a *durbar* in these terms: 'If we have with us the princes, we shall have with us the people.' This was the reason why Besant adopted this strategy, which she extended to the new Indian middle classes.

In *The Key to Theosophy*, Blavatsky explained that Western education only resulted in 'an overflooding of the market with money-making

[20] See also the section in Chapter 3 entitled 'Struggles for Women's Rights in India'; and the article 'Theosophy and Education', in HARRIS, Philip S., general ed. *The Theosophical Encyclopedia*. Manila: Theosophical Publishing House, 2006.

machines, with heartless selfish men animals who have been most carefully trained to prey on their fellows and take advantage of the ignorance of their weaker brethren.' According to her:

> Children should above all be taught self-reliance, love for all men, altruism, mutual charity, and more than anything else, to think and reason for themselves. [...] We would endeavour to deal with each child as a unit, and to educate it so as to produce the most harmonious and equal enfoldment of its powers, in order that its special aptitudes should find their full natural development. We should aim at creating free men and women, free intellectually, free morally, unprejudiced in all respects, and above all things, unselfish.

Besant shared Blavatsky's views on education, which also inspired the celebrated educationalist Maria Montessori, who met Besant in London in 1907[21]. Besant wrote in 1912 in *Education in the Light of Theosophy*:

> To the Theosophist each child is a study, and instead of imposing his own will on him and supposing that age and size of body give a right to order and to dominate, he tries to discover through the young body the features of the indwelling owner [...]. He endeavours to aid the indwelling Ruler, not to usurp his throne, to be an adviser, a councillor, not a master.

Applied to Indian children, such educational principles could only sound dangerous to the British authorities of the Raj, anxious to control the Indian elite through education, and to form a compliant educated middle class who could be useful to them.

Besant decided to open a Hindu school, so that Hindu culture and traditions would be transmitted, in accordance with Theosophical values. She toured all of India to extol the merits of her plan, and to collect donations from influential Indians. It must be noted that, until 1904, Besant only accepted donations from Indians. The Maharaja of Benares offered

[21] See WYLIE, Winifred. 'Montessori and the Theosophical Society'. *Quest* 96.2, March–April, 2008, pp. 53–5.

up a portion of the premises and land of his grandfather's summer palace for the school: the Central Hindu College (CHC) was inaugurated there in 1898. Tuition fees were nominal, and in a quasi-monastic atmosphere, students were taught mathematics, English and science, but also Sanskrit, comparative religious studies, history, and logic. Their teachers were Indian and British, and often Theosophists, like Arthur Richardson, the first headmaster, or his successor George Arundale. In 1901, the CHC was officially recognized by the University of Allahabad, and allowed to grant BAs, then MAs in Sanskrit and English from 1905.

Besant rediscovered the joys of teaching that she had experienced at the Hall of Science of the NSS, and often lectured at the CHC. In 'The Indian Nation. An Address Delivered to the Hindu College Boarders' Debating Society' (ca. 1902), Besant stressed the importance of education for the renaissance of the Indian nation: 'How shall the Indian Nation be born? By Sentiment [...]. We must make the history of India a common history, looking on all her great men as a common glory, on all her heroes as a common heritage [...] the story of a common Motherland.' She hoped to educate, in her words, 'the natural leaders of young Hinduism.' Among the young people on whom she had a strong influence was the first Indian Prime Minister Jawaharlal Nehru, whose father had contributed to the foundation of the CHC. The following is what Nehru wrote in his autobiography *Toward Freedom*, published in 1941 — a passage that reveals a generation gap that Besant perfectly understood when she addressed the youth of the Indian elite, but also the elite's anglicization:

> When I was about eleven, a new resident tutor, Ferdinand T. Brooks, came and took charge of me. [...] He was a keen theosophist who had been recommended to my father by Mrs. Annie Besant [...].
>
> Mrs. Annie Besant visited Allahabad in those days [ca. 1902] and delivered several addresses on theosophical subjects. I was deeply moved by her oratory and returned from her speeches dazed and as in a dream. I decided to join the Theosophical Society, although I was only thirteen then. When I went to ask father's permission, he laughingly gave it; he did not seem to attach importance to the subject either way. I was a little hurt by his lack of feeling.

Great as he was in many ways in my eyes, I felt that he was lacking in spirituality. As a matter of fact he was an old theosophist, having joined the Society in its early days when Madame Blavatsky was in India. Curiosity probably led him to it more than religion, and he soon dropped out of it; but some of his friends, who had joined with him, persevered and rose high in the spiritual hierarchy of the Society.

So I became a member of the Theosophical Society at thirteen, and Mrs. Besant herself performed the ceremony of initiation [...]. I was thrilled. I attended the Theosophical Convention at Benares and saw old Colonel Olcott with his fine beard.

[...] I lost touch with theosophy [...] partly because I went to school in England [...]. But for Mrs. Besant I always had the warmest admiration.

In 1913, Besant launched the Theosophical Educational Trust in India, whose coordination work allowed for the creation of around thirty elementary and secondary schools. Before that, in 1911, she had allied with nationalist and educationalist Madan Mohan Malviya, with the goal of founding a Hindu University. The preamble of the petition for a Royal 'Charter of Incorporation creating the University of India' detailed Besant's aims:

[...] the placing in the first rank of Indian philosophy, history and literature and seeking in these, in the classical languages of India, the chief means of culture. While Western thought will be amply studied, Eastern thought will take the lead, and Western knowledge will be used to enrich but not to distort or to cripple, the expanding national life.

[...] the paying of special attention to [...] Indian arts and crafts, so as to revive these now decaying industries while bringing from the West all that can usefully be assimilated for the increasing national prosperity.[22]

The Benares Hindu University was inaugurated in 1916, after being approved by the British Parliament, and the Central Hindu College was

---

[22] Quoted in KUMAR, Raj, RAMESHWARI, Devi, and Romila PRUTHI. *Annie Besant: Founder of Home Rule Movement.* Jaipur: Pointer Publishers, 2003, pp. 94–5.

integrated into it. Malviya — four times president of the Indian National Congress — remained at the head of this university for over twenty years.

Because Robert Baden-Powell's Boy Scout Movement admitted only Europeans, Malviya also supported Besant's efforts to open scouting to Indian boys from 1913. Besant launched the Indian Boy Scout Association in Madras in 1916. She then asked Baden-Powell to recognize this Indian branch, but he refused. She answered to him and started a campaign with her article 'Why Not Indian Scouts?', published in the 13 October 1916 issue of her nationalist paper *New India*. By 1921, when Baden-Powell visited India, the Indian Boy Scout Association gathered 20,000 boys. This undeniable success led Baden-Powell to change his mind: not only did he make Besant Honorary Scout Commissioner for India, but he conferred upon her the highest Scout distinction: the Badge of the Silver Wolf, in 1932[23].

The Central Hindu College and the Benares Hindu University that Besant had pioneered were not places of religious and political indoctrination. On the contrary, as of 1908, in order to eliminate any sectarian tendencies, the CHC began to take non-Hindu students. That same year, when British authorities forbade Indian students to engage in political activities, Besant organized a mock Parliament at the CHC, modelled after that of Westminster, in order to encourage her students to discuss the political and social issues of their country, while favouring democratic and constitutional methods. The political context was quite tense then, for the Swadeshi movement[24] was fast spreading, and it attracted many of the young people who had been educated according to Besant's principles and values. Launched in reaction to the partition of Bengal, this national resistance movement advocated not only a boycott of British manufactured products in favour of locally handmade

---

[23] See 'Dr. Besant Receives "The Silver Wolf"'. *Theosophist* 54.3, December 1932, pp. 295–9.

[24] See SARKAR, Sumit. *The Swadeshi Movement in Bengal, 1903–1908*. Delhi: People's Publishing House, 1973.

ones[25], but also the creation of purely Indian educational and legal institutions, and it was accompanied by a wave of working-class agitation. Its founders were influential Indian nationalist figures, many of whom were Besant's close friends, especially Aurobindo Ghosh, Tilak Bipin Chandra Pal and Lala Lajpat Rai. For reasons that greatly differed from those of the British authorities, Besant — who had witnessed at first hand Bloody Sunday 1887 in Trafalgar Square — was opposed to her young students getting involved in such potentially dangerous active militancy, believing them to be insufficiently prepared. She founded the Sons, and then the Daughters of India, in 1908 in order to channel the energy of this young, educated generation into charitable or educational initiatives instead.

There was, however, some ambiguity at work in Besant's attitude when she presented the British Parliamentary system as a model to Indians. While India was the Mother of Spirituality, England remained for her the 'Mother of Parliaments', to borrow John Bright's 1865 expression. However, in this, Besant was not different from the first Indian nationalists, to whom she remained ideologically close, especially Mahadev Govind Ranade, Womesh Chunder Bonnerjee and above all Gopal Krishna Gokhale. Even though Gokhale came from a rather poor family, he had received an English education, like his mentor Ranade, and had graduated from Elphinstone College, one of the oldest of the University of Bombay. Bennerjee, for his part, had studied law in London. Their education and their perfect mastery of English gave them access to the subordinate administration of the Raj, as lawyers in the cases of Ranade and Bonnerjee, or civil servant in that of Gokhale. However, their education had also exposed them to British political thinkers: Gokhale admired Edmund Burke[26] and John Stuart Mill. Their criticism of the Raj and their desire to reform it ironically stemmed from their respect for British institutions and freedoms. The same paradox is obvious in this text written by Besant in July 1914:

[25] Imports of British products dropped twenty-five per cent in India between 1904 and 1908.

[26] Burke had sided with the colonies against his own government during the American War of Independence.

> They [the English] have given us of their best, and never will India forget that we owe to them the uplifting before Indian eyes of the ideals of Liberty and Self-Government, the inspiration of ordered Freedom, of National self-consciousness; we owe to them the training of the present generations of *vakils* [lawyers], doctors, great merchants, who founded and have carried on the National Congress, who formed Indian public opinion, the 'educated minority', regarded by The Times with a hatred born of fear, and by India as its present glory and its future hope.
>
> But we cannot sacrifice Indian Nationality on the altar of our gratitude to our English rulers. And that gratitude is best shown by carrying into practice what they have taught us [...].[27]

India and Ireland

Annie Besant, who was of Irish descent, had supported Irish nationalism since the trial and death sentence of the 'Manchester Martyrs', which she had attended with lawyer William Roberts in 1867[28]. She saw the same necessity to reform the Empire in the Irish and Indian nationalist causes. Besant was not the only one to connect the two: Charles Bradlaugh supported both, and so did the Indian nationalists close to Besant. Gokhale went to Ireland at the beginning of the 1890s, and with Dadabhai Naoroji, he convinced the Indian National Congress to make a symbolic gesture by electing Irish Protestant nationalist Alfred Webb as its president in 1894. Meanwhile, Naoroji, the first Indian MP, elected in 1892 for the London constituency of Finsbury, also stood for Irish rights in the House of Commons.

[27] Quoted in MORTIMER, Joanne Stafford. 'Annie Besant and India 1913–1917'. *Journal of Contemporary History* 18.1, January 1983, p. 65.
[28] See Chapter 1.

Among the Theosophists in Adyar, the link between India and Ireland was personified by James and Margaret Cousins[29]. Margaret came from a Protestant family in Derry. A musician, she had married the Celtic renaissance poet, playwright and literary critic James Cousins in 1903, also a Protestant, born in Belfast. They were both socialists and Theosophists and, after Margaret first met suffragettes at the 1907 Theosophical Society convention in London, she joined in their struggle. She started the Irish Women's Franchise League the following year. She was sent to jail for a month for taking part in the suffragettes' demonstrations in London in 1910. In 1913, she was sent to jail again, this time in Dublin, for having demonstrated in support of the Home Rule Bill. She demanded to be considered as a political prisoner, and when this was denied, she went on a hunger strike. Upon her release, she and James were forced into exile from Ireland. After a few months in Liverpool, they decided to leave for India. This did not come as a surprise: the Theosophical Lodge in Dublin, founded in 1886, had played a decisive role in the Celtic renaissance while spreading Eastern philosophy in Ireland, underlining the similarities between the two. William Butler Yeats, the most eminent member of the Dublin Lodge, shared this cultural point of view, and he had introduced the Cousins to his friend Rabindranath Tagore in 1913, the year Tagore was awarded the Nobel Prize in Literature.

Besant paid for James and Margaret Cousins' passage to India in 1915, where they immediately resumed their respective struggles. James Cousins became co-editor of *New India*, the nationalist paper launched by Besant, in which, in 1916, he openly supported the Irish Republicans' Easter Rising in Dublin, soon crushed by the British Army. Besant also entrusted him with the cultural section, confident in his ability to appreciate India's art,

[29] See CANDY, Catherine. 'Relating Feminisms, Nationalisms, and Imperialisms: Ireland, India and Margaret Cousins's Sexual Politics'. *Women's History Review* 3.4, 1994, pp. 581–94; and GAUDIN, Elisabeth. 'Margaret Cousins: De Dublin à Madras', in MOLINARI, Véronique, ed. *Droits des femmes, droits des autres. Des féministes britanniques face aux exclus de la citoyenneté (1860-1930)*. Presses universitaires Blaise Pascal, 2012.

music, and literature[30]. James Cousins became one of India's most respected art critics, as well as an eminent educationalist. Sri Aurobindo, who had written poems about Ireland in his youth, greatly admired him, to the point of publishing an essay with the same title as one of Cousin's books: *The Renaissance in India*, in which they each explored the similarities between the Celtic and Hindu cultures, and called for their synthesis. Margaret Cousins, for her part, was struck by the similarity of Irish and Indian women's conditions[31]. She taught at the Indian Women's University in Poona, then founded the Women's India Association with Besant and Dorothy Jinarajadasa in 1917, followed by the All India Women's Conference ten years later, which she led until 1936. In the meantime, she managed to become the first female magistrate of India in 1922, which did not, however, prevent her from being sent to jail once again, for protesting the state of emergency in 1932. James and Margaret Cousins lived long enough to see India's independence in 1947, and Prime Minister Nehru granted them a pension at the beginning of the 1950s.

Between Moderates and Extremists (1905–1915)

As for many Indian nationalists, the forced partition of Bengal in 1905 was a turning point in Annie Besant's struggle for the Indian cause, whose expression thereafter became more openly political. Her initial moderate position was that of Lala Lajpat Rai — whom she invited to address the students of the Central Hindu College in 1908 — and above all of Gokhale, to whom she was close. In 1905, Gokhale founded the Servants of India Society, whose educational aims were similar to Besant's. Gokhale too believed that political change could only come from a new generation of educated Indians, made aware of their civic and patriotic duties. Gokhale's Servants of India Society, which exists to this day, built elementary schools,

[30] CHATTERJEE, Dilip Kumar. 'Cousins and Sri Aurobindo: A Study on Literary Influence'. *Triveni*, April–June 1983.

[31] See 'Fights for Women's Rights in India' in Chapter 3.

organized evening classes for workers and launched travelling libraries.

Gokhale wanted Indians to get a greater share in the administration of their own country, so he had joined the Indian National Congress in 1889. As a reformist and a Moderate, he did not fight for complete Indian independence, but for a better understanding with British authorities, in order to bring them to respect Indians' rights. He earned the trust of the British Government, to the point of being invited to London by John Morley, the Liberal Secretary of State for India, in order to work with him and Viceroy Lord Minto on the so-called Minto-Morley Reforms. They became the Indian Councils Act 1909, which allowed Indians to be elected to the various legislative councils in India, to which only a few had been appointed thus far[32].

Besant first shared this cautious and pragmatic approach to India's Home Rule. The ideological conflict between Gokhale and the radical Bal Gangadhar Tilak, however, soon revealed tensions between Indian nationalists' principles and strategies, and Besant herself came to revise her point of view. In 1892, Gokhale, anxious to rid contemporary Hinduism of what he believed to be abuses and superstitions, came out in favour of the British Bill to raise the age of marital consent from ten to twelve years old — a position Besant shared. By contrast Tilak opposed any British intervention in Indian traditions, believing that these reforms, while necessary, had to be decided upon and carried out by Indians themselves, once independence had been won. After the partition of Bengal, Besant, contrary to Gokhale, supported the boycott implemented by the Swadeshi movement, of which Tilak was one of the main organizers. In doing so, she sided with radicals Bipin Chandra Pal and Lala Lajpat Rai, who, with Tilak, formed the 'Lal-Bal-Pal' triumvirate. During the 1907 Indian National Congress in Surat, Gokhale used all of his influence to block this triumvirate. The Congress ended up profoundly divided between the 'Maval Matavadi' faction of Moderates, who gathered around Gokhale, and the 'Jahal Matavadi' faction of Extremists, who followed Tilak, Pal, and Lajpat Rai. Despite managing

[32] The majority of the council members remained British Government appointments, however, and the electorate was limited to specific classes of Indians.

to reunite Bengal in 1912, the Extremists remained excluded from the INC until Gokhale's death at the early age of forty-eight, in 1915. Viceroy Lord Hardinge, who had agreed to reunite Bengal, moved the capital of India from Calcutta to Delhi. 'New Delhi' was designed by architect Edward Lutyens, the husband of Emily, Besant's Theosophist friend.

Plans for a Self-Governed India

From 1905, Annie Besant developed plans for a self-governed India in numerous articles, pamphlets, and lectures, collected in 1917 under the title *The Birth of New India*. In 'Federation', published in April 1914, Besant called for a transformation of the Empire into a 'Federation of Self-Governing Nations', drawing on the concept of 'Home Rule', i.e. the form of autonomy the Liberals had proposed for Ireland from the 1880s. This 'Federation' would be headed by an Imperial Council, symbolically presided over by the British Sovereign, and a Parliament, wherein all the nations of the Empire would be equally represented and would enjoy the same rights.

In 'Indian Self-Government', published in 1915, Besant explained how a self-governed India could be organized as a hierarchy of assemblies. The first level would be the village *Panchayat*, with neighbourhood councils in cities. Immediately above them, there would be district councils, representing several villages or neighbourhoods, allowing for cooperation in agriculture, health and education, and serving as intermediaries with provincial parliaments in charge of the budget. Those provincial parliaments would be overseen by a national one, which would control the army, the post office and the railways, all essential to the country's unity. India could then take its rightful place in the Imperial Federation. To this hierarchy of assemblies would correspond a form of gradual democracy. Besant did not reject universal suffrage, but advocated it at the level of the *Panchayat* only: 'the fathers and mothers of the village, above the age of twenty-one years, form a natural electorate', she said. The council members at the levels above would be elected by those of the assembly immediately beneath them, as well as by male and female voters whose age and education requirements would be higher with each level: 'Thus might complete Self-Government come about, built from below upwards into a secure and stately edifice.'

This elitist approach is often used against Besant. It was analysed in its original context by Carla Risseeuw in 1999[33]. Risseeuw explained that there is today a confusion between 'fraternity' and 'equality', but Besant knew and made a difference: she promoted 'fraternity', wherein 'elder brothers and sisters' — 'elder' by education and spiritual evolution — had to take on the responsibility of helping their 'younger siblings' to progress in their own rights. Besant believed that the ancestral Indian traditions of local democracy and cooperation had been forgotten by the rural population. In April 1914, in Bombay, in her 'National Education' lecture, she once again called out to her privileged audience, which she herself defined as 'the English-educated class of Indians', saying: 'it is to [you] that India must look for the building up of these village units into Self-Government.' One year later, while she did not think the immediate and simultaneous implementation of all the levels of her institutional edifice was possible as yet, she already believed that: 'The Village Councils should be instituted at once [...] the District Boards should quickly follow. [...] Then, when the War is over, steps should be taken to establish Provincial Autonomy, and the time for the establishment of a National Parliament fixed.'

Political Struggle for Indian Home Rule[34]

By 1914–1915, when Annie Besant published the articles and gave the lectures mentioned above, she had become a well-known figure of the

[33] See RISSEEUW, Carla. 'Thinking Culture through Counter-Culture: The Case of Theosophists in India and Ceylon and their Ideas on Race and Hierarchy (1875–1947)', in COPLEY, A. ed. *Gurus and their Followers: New Religious Reform Movements in Colonial India*. Oxford University Press, 2000, pp. 180–205.

[34] See MORTIMER, Joanne Stafford. 'Annie Besant and India 1913–1917'. *Journal of Contemporary History* 18.1, January 1983, pp. 61–78.

nationalist movement. In January 1910, she had written an open letter to the Raj authorities, accusing them of covering up some of their officers' racism, after a former Central Hindu College student had been insulted on a train. She concluded it thus: 'we [...] who love India, and hope to see her a self-governing part of this mighty Empire, we appeal to the Government of India not to allow this work of love and service be wrecked by brutality and folly.' This open letter had a considerable impact. Viceroy Lord Minto placed the CHC under surveillance and delayed the creation of the Hindu University. Gokhale then wrote to Besant: 'the insult and vexations you have had to endure will be repaid a hundredfold by the gratitude of the Indians for the way you have spoken out'[35].

Besant joined Gokhale as a member of the Indian National Congress in 1913. With the Theosophical Society, she had already launched the Brothers of India, whose members had to pledge to work not only toward India's spiritual unity, but also for the social and political reforms necessary for its autonomy. The foundation of the Brothers of India was marked by a series of lectures given by Besant in Madras in September and October 1913, gathered under the unequivocal title *Wake Up, India: A Plea for Social Reform*. She showed herself to be increasingly irritated by the moderation and the lack of initiative of the INC, from which Extremists had been excluded since 1907. In October 1914, she wrote in her paper *New India*: 'Congress raises little enthusiasm among Indians since it continues in the same groove, passing year after year similar resolutions and making little substantial progress'[36].

Besant decided to resort to the strategies she had adopted in the 1880s as a socialist. With *Our Corner*, and above all the *Link*, she had already founded periodicals from which to conduct her political struggles. She

---

[35] Letter and answer quoted by KUMAR, Raj, RAMESHWARI Devi and Romila PRUTHI. *Annie Besant: Founder of Home Rule Movement*. Jaipur: Pointer Publishers, 2003. pp. 78–9.

[36] *New India*, 17 October 1914, quoted in BEVIR, Mark. 'Theosophy as a Political Movement', in COPLEY, A., ed. *Gurus and their Followers: New Religious Reform Movements in Colonial India*. Delhi: Oxford University Press, 2000.

therefore launched *Commonweal*[37], *'A Journal of National Reform,'* in January 1914. She then bought the *Madras Standard*, which she renamed *New India*, a daily that she symbolically launched on 14 July 1914 (Bastille Day). She saw it as a tribute to the newspaper *Vande Mataram*, founded at the time of Bengal's partition by Bipin Chandra Pal. In the issue of *New India* on 23 July, Besant summarized her stance by calling for India to become 'a Self-Governing community in the great Federated Empire'. A few months earlier, she had already clarified her position in the first issue of *Commonweal*: 'We stand, then, for Union among All Workers in the National Cause, and ask only to be allowed to serve it in any of the four great departments [...] religion, education, social reform, and politics.' Significantly, the order in which these 'four great departments' were announced exactly matches Besant's gradual involvement in India's cause. However, for her, one type of involvement did not replace nor contradict another: Besant added them in an all-encompassing and coherent struggle.

Home Rule League (1915–1919)[38]

Besant was unable to leave India for the entirety of the First World War and, as a consequence, she became even more involved in nationalist politics, refining her plan for India's self-government in a long series of articles and lectures. In his biography of Besant[39], published in 1941, Sri Prakasa, later the first Indian ambassador to Pakistan, emphasized the importance of the

[37] As an obvious homage to utopian socialist William Morris, Besant gave her weekly the same title, *Commonweal*, as the one he had chosen in 1885 for the paper of his Socialist League.

[38] See BEVIR, Mark. 'The Formation of the All-India Home Rule League'. *Indian Journal of Political Science* 52.3, 1991, pp. 341–56; and OWEN, Hugh F. 'Towards Nationwide Agitation and Organisation. The Home Rule Leagues: 1915–18', in LOW, Donald Anthony, ed. *Soundings in Modern South Asian History*. University of California Press, 1968.

[39] SRI PRAKASA, *Annie Besant: As Woman and As Leader*. Adyar: Theosophical Publishing House, 1941.

war to explain Besant's growing influence:

> These years were also the years of Mrs. Besant's most intense work for India's political freedom. The war had thrown all Indian politics and politicians off their guard and out of gear. They did not know exactly what to do and how to do it. Politics and personalities go together the world over — in India even more than elsewhere. The liberals the great leaders of moderate Indian politics were for every assistance being given to England and support afforded to Government in every way. But Mrs. Besant suddenly came out with the slogan: 'The moment of England's difficulty is the moment of India's opportunity' [...].

The Indian National Congress of December 1914 was still dominated by the Moderates, and Besant did not manage to have it readmit Lokamanya Tilak[40], whose point of view she shared by then. The radicalism of Besant's position must be underlined: Tilak had just served a six years' detention in exile in Burma, for having presented Khudiram Bose as a martyr in his newspaper *Kesari*. The eighteen-year-old Bengali had been sentenced to death for attempting to kill Douglas Kingsford, the chief magistrate of the Presidency Court of Alipore, in 1908, and accidentally killing two English women instead. Kingsford was hated by Indians for having two teenagers caned for singing 'Vande Mataram'[41], India's national anthem. Just after Khudiram Bose's sentencing, Tilak had published an article entitled 'The Country's Misfortune', in the 12 May 1908 issue of *Kesari*, in which he wrote:

> [...] under these circumstances, no one in the world, except the white officials, inebriated with the insolence of authority will think that not even a very few of the people of Bengal should become turn-headed and feel inclined to

[40] See WOLPERT, Stanley A. *Tilak and Gokhale: Revolution and Reform in the Making of Modern India*. Oxford University Press, 1990 (1962).

[41] 'Vande Mataram', meaning 'I pray / bow down to thee, Mother', is the title of an 1882 poem by Bankim Chandra Chattopadhyay that became a hymn to India, the 'Mother Land'.

commit excess. Experience shows that even a cat shut up in a house rushes with vehemence upon a person who confines it there and tries to kill it.

When he was sentenced to jail, Tilak replied: 'In spite of the verdict of the jury I maintain that I am innocent. There are higher powers that rule the destinies of men and nations and I think it may be the will of the Providence that the cause I represent may be benefited more by my suffering than my tongue and pen'[42]. It was doubtlessly this ideal that drew Besant to Tilak. He used his time in prison to write an exegesis of the Bhagavad Gita, entitled the *Gita Rahasya*, stressing the importance of *Karma Yoga*, the path of action. Tilak renounced violence upon his release, having come to the conclusion that it only delayed India's liberation. Gokhale's death in 1915 allowed Extremists to re-enter the Congress. Tilak then agreed to take the oath written by the Moderates, to obtain 'by strictly constitutional means [...] the attainment by India of self-government similar to that enjoyed by the self-governing members of the British Empire.'

In the meantime, Besant, disappointed by the Congress' timidity, had launched the idea of a Home Rule League in September 1915, when India's economic and social situation was disastrous because of the war, and over one million Indians had been sent to fight on the various fronts. Since the Congress refused to campaign for Home Rule, Besant officially founded her League on 3 September 1916. It immediately allied itself with Tilak's, launched in April 1916, to form the All-India Home Rule League. According to Besant's supporter Sri Prakasa: 'her Home Rule League became a power to be reckoned with; and her *New India* became the most popular and influential paper.' Besant was elected president of the All-India Home Rule League, and the British branch was entrusted to her friends Labour George Lansbury and Theosophist Emily Lutyens. Based in Delhi, the All-India Home Rule League, which attracted a

[42] See KELKAR, N. C., ed. *Full & Authentic Report of the Tilak Trial (1908). Being the Only Authorised Verbatim Account of the Whole Proceedings with Introduction and Character Sketch of Bal Gangadhar Tilak, Together with Press Opinion*. Bombay: Indu-Prakashi Press, 1908.

significant number of Congress members, soon became influential in Bombay, Calcutta and Madras too. Besant and Tilak spent the autumn of 1916 touring India, often in precarious conditions, in order to recruit Muslims and Hindus, Extremists and Moderates, to their League. After Besant's house arrest in June 1917, Motilal Nehru, the Prime Minister's father, organized a huge rally in Allahabad, while the petition in support of the League gathered some 700,000 signatures. This petition recalled the League's five objects, the first of which being Indian Home Rule. The others were subordinate to it, especially that to develop political education and debate, in order to break up the people's inertia and help them regain self-confidence. The League also explained that, while it was organizing political action outside of the Indian National Congress, it still respected it.

In his autobiography, Prime Minister Nehru saw a turning point for the nationalist struggle in Besant's and Tilak's allying and in their League, and he underlined the influence of Besant's political actions at this time:

> Gradually political life grew again. Lokamanya Tilak came out of prison, and home rule leagues were started by him and Mrs. Besant. I joined both, but I worked especially for Mrs. Besant's league. Mrs. Besant began to play an ever-increasing part in Indian politics. The annual sessions of the Congress became a little more exciting and the Moslem League began to march with the Congress. The atmosphere became electric, and most of us young men felt exhilarated and expected big things in the near future. […] The home rule leagues were attracting not only all the old Extremists who had been kept out of the Congress since 1907 but large numbers of newcomers from the middle classes.

In a year, the League managed to gather 60,000 members. Gandhi, who then admired Besant's work, said: 'she has made Home Rule a *mantram* in every cottage.'

Among the 'big things' expected by the young Nehru to which Besant contributed, there was the Lucknow Pact[43], signed by the All-India Muslim

[43] See DATAR, Abhay. 'The Lucknow Pact of 1916: A Second Look at the Congress-Muslim League Agreement'. *Economic & Political Weekly (EPW)* 47.10, March, 2012.

League and the Congress taking place in Lucknow in December 1916. Besant was fighting for a self-governing but also a unified India. She therefore worked incessantly to bring Moderates and Extremists closer together, and to get them to rise above religious differences. This was how she had succeeded in bringing together the All-India Home Rule League with the All-India Muslim League. Led by Moderate Muhammad Ali Jinnah — who was to become Pakistan's first governor-general in 1947 — the Muslim League, based out of Lucknow, had been founded in 1906, following the partition of Bengal. Already aware of the power of such an alliance, when religious tensions served British interests, Besant had published an article in 1910, entitled 'Islam in the Light of Theosophy':

> In this country of India, where so large a proportion of Indians belong to the great faith of the Prophet Muhammad, there are some seventy million people who regard Him as the chief messenger of God. Here naturally Theosophy comes in to help all those who follow that faith.

In December 1916, largely thanks to Besant, the Congress and Jinnah's Muslim League, the two most influential nationalist movements, jointly presented British authorities with a list of reforms to be implemented at the end of the war. Gandhi had returned to India for good the previous year, after having spent over two decades in South Africa, where he had fought for the rights of the Indian community. In his biography of Besant, Sri Prakasa, recalled that as early as 1916:

> It was clear that Mrs. Besant and Gandhiji could not work together. Mrs. Besant joined hands with Mr. Tilak, whose name was as yet greater than Gandhiji's in Indian politics; whose programme was more intelligible; whose ideals were more practical. The Indian public had no direct personal experience and knowledge of Gandhiji. He was to them a legend and a mystery. At the Lucknow Congress of December 1916, Mr. Tilak and Mrs. Besant had their way more or less; the Congress-Muslim League pact was also sealed, Mrs. Besant appealing to the Hindus to yield and sacrifice to their Muslim brethren for the country's sake.

Among the reforms proposed by the Congress for better representation of Indians within the country's institutions, there was the official recognition of a Muslim electorate and a well-defined role for Muslims in Indian institutions.

House Arrest (June–September 1917)[44]

The Raj authorities promptly reacted, and unwillingly confirmed Annie Besant's influence in India at the time. At the beginning of 1917, the new Viceroy, Lord Chelmsford, publicly condemned Besant's activities and writings. Her letters and telegrams were thereafter intercepted and censored, and she was forbidden to travel to Bombay and to the Central Provinces. Chelmsford wrote to Austen Chamberlain, then Secretary of State for India: 'I hate all this suppression but India is in too inflammable a state to admit of lighted sparks about. If she misbehaves further, the Madras Government will be asked to place [Annie Besant] out of communication with her paper and politics'[45]. After a policeman was murdered in Calcutta, Chelmsford asked the governor of Madras to put Besant under house arrest as of 15 June 1917, in Ootacamund (called Ooty for short), a small town high up the Nilgiri Hills, in the southwest of India. Besant's first action upon arriving there was to fly the red and green flag of the All-India Home Rule League, one of the precursors of the current Indian flag. She was sent to Ooty with two faithful friends: George Arundale, who was the secretary of the Home Rule League, and B. P. Wadia, founder of the Madras Labour Union, one of the first Indian trade unions, and co-editor of *New India*.

British authorities justified Besant's house arrest by the fact that *New India* campaigned for the League and thus, according to them, incited violence; and Besant was sentenced according to the repressive terms

[44] See ROBB, Peter. 'The Government of India and Annie Besant'. *Modern Asian Studies* 10.1, 1976, pp. 107–30.
[45] Quoted by WOLPERT, Stanley. *A New History of India*. Oxford University Press, 2004 (7th ed), p. 294.

of the Press Act 1910. The Act, promulgated only in India, imposed censorship, so as to limit the reach of nationalist movements. Implemented in an even more ruthless fashion during the war, the Press Act demanded heavy financial securities from newspaper owners, whose amounts were arbitrarily decided upon by magistrates. Customs officers and postmen were allowed to confiscate or prevent the distribution of any publications, the printing of which could be suspended or banned by the authorities. The Act defined as offences not only attempts to incite murder, disorder or racial and religious hatred, but also insults to the Army or Navy, contempt of the Government or of local princes, intimidation of public officials, and even discussion of ongoing trials. British authorities had repeatedly used the Press Act against *New India*, first demanding a ridiculously high security in May 1916, then, when Besant managed to pay it, seizing all copies of the newspaper in August. True to herself, Besant fought this decision at the High Court of Madras, and all the way up to the Privy Council, which contributed to spreading awareness of her Home Rule League. However, in 1917, she could do nothing against the Defence of India Act 1915, thanks to which a state of emergency was declared and Habeas Corpus suspended.

The news of Besant's house arrest provoked a wave of indignation throughout India, but also among British socialists, and a revived boycott of British products. All the main nationalist leaders assured her of their support, including Nehru, Gandhi and Jinnah. Besant went on fighting for the unification of India beyond political and religious rifts while under house arrest, and she managed to rally new supporters to her cause, including Motilal Nehru, as his son recalls in *Toward Freedom*:

> Mrs. Besant's internment added greatly to the excitement of the intelligentsia and vitalized the home rule movement all over the country. It stirred even the older generation, including many of the Moderate leaders. [...] Mrs. Besant's internment also resulted in my father and other Moderate leaders joining the Home Rule League. [...] My father remained in it and became the president of the Allahabad branch. [...] The episode of Mrs. Besant's internment and subsequent events influenced him considerably.

The counter-productive aspect of Besant's house arrest did not escape British authorities, and they had to compromise: Liberal Edwin Montagu, whom Besant had met in 1913, was appointed Secretary of State for India. In his first speech in this post in the House of Commons, in August 1917, Montagu called for a 'gradual development of self-governing institutions with a view to the progressive realisation of responsible government in India as an integral part of the British Empire.' This declaration, though cautious, was sufficiently similar to Besant's plans to make the idea of her house arrest absurd. After a power struggle between Montagu and the local government of Madras, Besant was eventually released on 17 September. Lord Chelmsford wrote to Montagu in October regarding Besant: 'It would be asking too much of human nature, especially her nature, to expect her to refrain'[46].

President of the Indian National Congress of December 1917

Thanks to her house arrest, Annie Besant became the living symbol of the Indian nation, and she was acclaimed all the way back to Adyar with cries of 'Vande Mataram!'. In Calcutta, where the Congress was held in December, she received an ovation by a crowd of some 300,000. On 26 December 1917, boosted by such popular support, Besant, then seventy years old, was elected President of the INC by a vast majority of the 4700 delegates. A few weeks later, Lord Chelmsford exclaimed: 'no-one who had experience of the results of interning Mrs. Besant last year wants to repeat the mistake'[47].

Besant's long inaugural speech as president of the Congress, 'The Case for India', began with these words: 'To-day let me: Western-born but in spirit Eastern, cradled in England but Indian by choice and adoption: let me stand as the symbol of union between Great Britain and India: a union of hearts and free choice, not of compulsion.' Besant once again dwelt

[46] Quoted by ROBB, Peter. 'The Government of India and Annie Besant'. *Modern Asian Studies* 10.1, 1976, p. 127.

[47] Ibid., p. 129.

on the past glory of India, before detailing its contemporary economic, educational, health and social difficulties, directly calling the governance of the Raj into question: 'All we say in the matter is: You have not succeeded in bringing education, health, prosperity, to the masses of the people. Is it not time to give Indians a chance to work for their own country?', and she added: 'What shall a Nation give in exchange for its Soul? Better hardship and freedom, than luxury and thraldom. This is the spirit of the Home Rule movement.'

In his autobiography, Gandhi, who spoke of 'Dr. Besant's brilliant Home Rule agitation', said he believed that in 1917, she stood 'among some of the most powerful leaders of public opinion' in India. Incidentally, Sri Prakasa emphasized Besant's ideological influence on Gandhi:

> When we come to think of it, it might almost be said that Mahatma Gandhi, who had been the undisputed leader of the Indian National Congress and as such of a major portion of political India since 1920, only intensified the programme that had been chalked out by Mrs. Besant in the days when she led the extreme wing in Indian politics. She seems in a way to have heralded Mahatmaji's non-co-operation.

Nehru, however, proved more critical in his memoir, emphasizing the social limits of the movement launched by Besant, Tilak and their supporters, including his own father: '[The Home Rule Leagues] did not touch the masses', he explained, adding that the movement was also divided when it came to deciding upon tactics, and failed to attract the attention of the British Government in any significant way.

The Government of India Act and the Rowlatt Act (1919)

Despite what Nehru wrote about the British Government and the All-India Home Rule League, Secretary of State for India Edwin Montagu met Annie Besant, along with other nationalist leaders, during his Indian tour in 1917–1918. His and Viceroy Lord Chelmsford's *Report on Indian Constitutional*

Reform[48] was presented to the Government in the spring of 1918. They proposed gradual reforms: as had Besant, they advocated 'complete popular control' at the local level, and demanded that 'measures of responsibility' be immediately conceded at the provincial one, with 'complete responsibility' as the final objective, but only 'as soon as conditions permit'[49], leaving some doubt on the date of India's real autonomy, while, incidentally, avoiding the use of the term 'Home Rule'.

The Montagu-Chelmsford Reforms were embodied in the Government of India Act that introduced a diarchy in Indian provinces: agriculture, health, education and local administration were transferred to enlarged provincial assemblies, but defence, foreign affairs and communications remained under the control of the Viceroy. At the provincial level, executive councils were placed under the control of governors, appointed, like council members, by the Secretary of State for India. The Imperial Legislative Council also was reformed, to become a two-tiered enlarged legislature: the Legislative Assembly being the lower house, and the Council of States the upper one, with a mix of elected and appointed members in both cases

The Government of India Act was nevertheless immediately followed by the implementation of the recommendations of the Rowlatt Commission, named after its chairman, judge Sidney Rowlatt. The Commission, appointed before the end of the war, had the explicit mission of evaluating terrorist threats in India, especially in Bengal and Punjab, as well as possible links between Indian nationalists and Germany, the United States or Bolsheviks. The Commission continued its investigation after the Armistice, at a time of social unrest in India, as textile workers in Bombay went on strike, and riots broke out in Punjab — while the Spanish flu pandemic resulted in the death of twelve million Indians. Sidney Rowlatt did not find evidence of any link between Indian nationalists and Bolsheviks, but he believed they had been in contact with Germany. His conclusion offered the British

[48] See MONTAGU, Edwin Samuel. *Report on Indian Constitutional Reform*. Calcutta: Superintendent Government Printing, India, 1918.
[49] Quoted by WOLPERT, Stanley. *A New History of India*. Oxford University Press, 2004 (7th ed.), p. 298.

Government the necessary pretext not only to extend the state of emergency beyond the end of the war, but also to reinforce it, with the Anarchical and Revolutionary Crimes Act 1919, known as the Rowlatt Act. The Indians soon nicknamed it the Black Act, for it gave 'extraordinary powers' to the Viceroy, including direct censorship of the press, and the right to arrest and detain political activists without a trial. The Black Act was also perceived by the new generation of Indian nationalists as the failure of those leaders who, like Besant, had tried to negotiate reforms with the British Government.

Gandhi's Takeover of the Nationalist Movement in 1919

In response to the Black Act, Tagore symbolically renounced the knighthood King George V had bestowed upon him in 1913, when he had won the Nobel Prize in Literature. As for Gandhi, he began to formulate his strategies of civil disobedience (*satyagraha*) and passive resistance (*ahimsa*). Sri Prakasa recalled:

> Suddenly burst upon the scene Mahatma Gandhi, with all the halo and glamour that surrounded him on account of his South African work, with his strange archaic personal habits, with his stranger notions of right and wrong, and strangest of all, his ideals of solving all the ills of mankind by unheard-of remedies. Mrs. Besant and he came nearest together in many aspirations and ways of doing things. Only Mrs. Besant was more human, and Mahatma Gandhi seemed far away from the mundane creation.

Sri Praksa believed that Annie Besant was the first to confer the title of Mahatma, 'Great Soul', onto Gandhi: 'Mrs. Besant herself had said somewhere that the only "Mahatma" she recognised in politics was Gandhiji. "Mahatma", in Theosophical parlance, stood for Great Spiritual Being: those who looked after the wellbeing of the world.' Despite her respect for Gandhi, Besant came out against his strategies in 1919, for she deemed them dangerous and irresponsible. In 1910, she had explained in 'India's Awakening':

> Those who are trained in politics, as in my past life I've been [...] make it, as we made it, one of the rules of political life never to tell [...] a procession to go where there was danger, unless we walked in front, so that we should be the first people on whom the blows fell. [...] it means playing with the lives of men. Leaders in the political arena have to remember all that, when they take the responsibility of calling men to action.

In April 1919, Gandhi launched a general strike (*hartal*) in Delhi, but he failed to control his supporters, who attacked peddlers who continued to sell their goods in the train station. British troops intervened to stop the riot, firing into the crowd and killing several people. Besant wrote an 'I told you so' sort of article, which, taken out of context, was used against her by Gandhi, especially this passage: 'before a riot becomes unmanageable, brickbats must inevitably be answered by bullets.' Besant, who knew only too well how British authorities could resort to violence, had used the verb 'must' to express her certainty as to this; her opponents alleged that she had meant 'must' as an injunction, and that she supported these repressive methods.

To make matters worse, Gandhi's supporters suggested that Besant had written these lines several days later, in reaction to the massacre at Amritsar. On 10 April 1919, Satya Pal and Saifuddin Kitchlew, who had answered Gandhi's call for civil disobedience, were arrested in Amritsar. Some 50,000 gathered to demand their release, and the British troops of Colonel Reginald Dyer fired at the crowd, killing at least twenty protestors. In retaliation, three Europeans were lynched and several others attacked, and a general strike was called. Dyer therefore declared martial law and forbade all gatherings. Three days later, on 13 April, some 10,000 to 20,000 people came together nonetheless in Jallianwala Bagh Park, around the Golden Temple, for the traditional Sikh harvest festival of Baisakhi. Dyer's soldiers once again opened fire, this time killing between 400 and 1000 unarmed men, women and children, taken completely by surprise. The news of the massacre had a considerable impact, and the confusion about Besant's attitude was disastrous for her reputation among Indians. Hardly eighteen months after her triumphal election as President of the Indian

National Congress, Besant was forced to step down from her presidency of the All-India Home Rule League, and was succeeded by Gandhi.

During the Congress symbolically organized in Amritsar in December 1919, its president, the until-then Moderate Motilal Nehru exclaimed: 'if our lives and honour are to remain at the mercy of an irresponsible executive and military, if the ordinary rights of human beings are denied to us, then all talk of reform is a mockery.' The Congress therefore adopted the strategy of civil disobedience advocated by Gandhi. The first national *satyagraha* was launched on 1 August 1920, the day Tilak died. Besant left the Congress, predicting a bloodbath. She only attended two of the subsequent Congresses: in Belgaum, in 1924, the only one presided over by Gandhi — for which he had decreed that only members who had spun enough cotton on the *charkha*, the small traditional spinning wheel, and were dressed in *khadi*, a handmade local fabric, would have the right to vote. Besant also attended the Congress in Calcutta in 1928, once again presided over by Motilal Nehru.

The British Side of Besant's Struggles for Indian Home Rule[50]

Gandhi had side-lined an embarrassing ally, on account of Besant's reformist approach, her sex and her ethnic origins, but in doing so, he had deprived himself of her influence on the British Government. Indeed, some among the Fabians and other socialists alongside whom she had fought in the 1880s, were now MPs and sometimes Cabinet members. Besant herself then wrote: 'My old political work is now full of help for me.'

In the spring of 1913, Besant and an Indian nationalist delegation, that included Lala Lajpat Rai, Jinnah, Chettur Sankaran Nair, Gokhale and Sarojini Naidu, went to London to defend their cause to Lord Crew, the Liberal Secretary of State for India. Besant gave a noteworthy lecture at the

[50] See GUPTA, Partha Sarathi. *Imperialism and the British Labour Movement, 1914–1964*. London & Basingtoke: Macmillan, 1975; and OWEN, Nicholas. *The British Left and India: Metropolitan Anti-Imperialism, 1885–1947*. Oxford University Press, 2007.

Queen's Hall on this occasion: *India's Plea for Justice*, after which her old socialist friends Henry Mayers Hyndman and James Keir Hardie joined her in criticizing the Raj. Besant also had a powerful ally in Labour MP and later Opposition Leader, George Lansbury[51]. Working-class Lansbury was initially close to the Liberals, especially Montagu, whom he regarded as his mentor. In the 1890s, disappointed by the Liberals' lack of support for women's vote, Lansbury, who later fought alongside the suffragettes, joined the Social Democratic Federation, to which Besant had belonged, then the Labour Party, and in 1912 launched the *Daily Herald*. Lansbury, who was a Christian socialist, joined the Theosophical Society in 1914, out of admiration for Besant, as he explained in his 1928 autobiography. It was largely thanks to his influence that Ramsay MacDonald, who had visited India before the war to audit its public services, and who became Prime Minister in 1924, declared: 'Dominion status for India is the idea and the ideal of the Labour Government.' Furthermore, speaking before the University Labour Federation, Josiah Wedgwood, a member of MacDonald's Government, asserted, in January 1924: 'The Labour Party hopes to overcome the difficulties by accelerating the conversion of India into a self-governing dominion' [52].

The Labour Party had asked Besant to run in the December 1918 General Election — the first for which women could stand — but her telegram accepting the offer was intercepted by British authorities, and only made it to Britain after the deadline for candidate applications had passed. Besant, returning to London after five years, officially joined the Labour Party in July 1919, and on that occasion gave a lecture entitled 'Socialism in India' to the Fabian Society. During this 1919 visit, she attended all of the Parliamentary committee meetings on the government of India. She denounced the repressive measures that they advocated before some 6,000 people in the Royal Albert Hall, and expressed her conviction that only a swift implementation of Indian Home Rule could put an end to violence.

---

[51] See LANSBURY, George. *My Life*. London: Constable & Co., 1928.

[52] Quoted by ROY, M. N. 'India and the British Labour Government'. *Labour Monthly* 6.4, April 1924, pp. 200–10.

Fight for an Indian Constitution (1924–1925)

At the end of 1921, Gandhi called a general strike during the official visit of the Prince of Wales, later Edward VIII. Violent riots broke out in Bombay, leading to the arrest of some 20,000 Indians. Gandhi himself was sentenced to six years in jail in 1922 for inciting violence. He was released in 1924, officially for health reasons, but mostly because he had renounced political agitation in favour of social action — a promise that he kept until 1929.

Annie Besant took advantage of Gandhi's absence from the political scene to call for an Indian constitution in 'Advance, India', published in *New India*. The *London Magazine* then wrote: 'Gandhi's only rival in India is a woman — perhaps the most remarkable of living women.' In 1924, Besant had reasons to be optimistic: the Labour Party had just come into power for the first time, and Ramsay MacDonald was Prime Minister, with the support of the Liberals. MacDonald was an old acquaintance of Besant's, having taken part with her in the Bloody Sunday 1887 demonstration in Trafalgar Square. Moreover, he had chosen another old friend of Besant's, Fabian Sydney Olivier, as Secretary of State for India. This appointment could not but please Besant, for Olivier, as opposed to Josiah Wedgwood, the other prospective candidate for the post, did not support Gandhi in his demand for a totally independent India, even though he had him released from jail that year. However, Olivier proved even more cautious than Besant had hoped, no doubt because of the political vulnerability of the minority Labour Government. In any case, the Conservatives won the October 1924 General Election, held four days after the publication by the *Daily Mail* of the 'Zinoviev letter', a forgery calling for a Communist revolution in Britain.

While the Indian nationalist leaders had not as yet reacted to Besant's call for an Indian constitution, they adopted her idea of an all-party conference, held in January 1925 in Delhi. The Indian National Convention met in Cawnpore in April, with Besant as its general secretary. As such, she drafted a Commonwealth of India Bill. Sri Prakasa recalled that Besant 'was always keen also on India becoming a self-governing partner in the British Commonwealth of Nations', and asserted that she had been 'the first person who used the word "Commonwealth" in this connection instead of "Empire". While, today, Besant's demands sound conservative, it must be recalled how radical it was to believe that India and Britain could sit *as equals* in a Commonwealth assembly. The Convention agreed to demand that India be accorded dominion status, the Viceroy only keeping responsibility over defence and foreign policy for a transitional period. A Bill of Rights was included in the Commonwealth of India Bill, in which Besant's influence and experience of a lifetime of social and political struggles is obvious: the Bill provided for protection of individual rights, including religious freedom and freedom of expression, as well as sex equality.

In July 1925, Besant left for London to present the Bill to Parliament. George Lansbury, who had been returned to the House of Commons in 1924, introduced the Bill in December, but it was rejected in its first reading by the Conservative majority.

The Nehru Commission (1928)

In 1928, Annie Besant, then eighty-one years old, was invited to sit on a new all-party commission, organized by Motilal Nehru, of which his son Jawaharlal was secretary. What became known as the Nehru Commission only had nine members, two of whom Muslim, and the fact that Besant was part of it shows that she had remained a leading figure of Indian nationalism. Incidentally, that year, the *New York Times Magazine* included her in their list of 'Great Women […] who Play Heroine Parts in the Life of the World Today'[53]. The Nehru Commission decided to report on the way India had been governed since the 1919 Acts. It was meant as a response to the Simon Commission, unanimously rejected by the Indians.

[53] [LUDWIG Emil] 'Ludwig Beholds Great Women; From Far Scattered Lands and Widely Differing Fields of Endeavor the Biographer Selects a Notable List of Workers Who Play Heroine Parts in the Life of the World Today'. *New York Times Magazine*. 26 February 1928, p. 76.

The Simon Commission — appointed by the Conservative Government at the end of 1927 — was nicknamed the 'White Seven', for all its members were British MPs. Considering this an insult to Indians, the Indian National Congress, meeting in Madras in December 1927, as well as Jinnah's Muslim League, decided to boycott the Commission, sent to India to evaluate the possibilities of constitutional reforms. Chaired by Liberal Sir John Simon, it included Labour Clement Attlee who, ironically, as Prime Minister, would grant independence to India in 1947. Their report, published in May 1930, called for more responsibility, especially at the provincial level, and for a constitution that could naturally evolve toward Home Rule. However, the context in which the 'White Seven' had worked cast doubts on the validity of their recommendations even before the report was published. They had been greeted by crowds of demonstrators brandishing black flags on their arrival in Bombay in February 1928, and the same happened in every city they visited, while Gandhi called a general strike. In October, the Commission reached Lahore, where demonstrations were organized by Lala Lajpat Rai, who fell under the *lathi*s, the batons used by the local police, and died from his injuries on 17 November.

In the meantime, Besant co-authored the Nehru Report, published in August 1928. It proposed once again that India attain Dominion status, and included a Bill of Rights, demanding sex equality and religious freedom. The Report, concerned with minority rights, provided for provinces drawn according to linguistic criteria, but not for a separate Muslim electorate: Jinnah therefore refused to approve it. Jawaharlal Nehru, for his part, left to found the Socialist Independence League for India. Supported by Gandhi. Nehru became the youngest president of the Indian National Congress in 1929 in Lahore. He made the Congress adopt the motto '*purna svaraj*' (total independence), and India's independence was unilaterally proclaimed on 26 January 1930. A few weeks later, Gandhi began his widely publicized 'Great Salt March', which earned him, as well as Nehru, six months in jail.

Besant returned to Britain in 1930 to defend the Nehru Report, and to give lectures. This visit proved her last major political action, but also a failure. The Nehru Report was discussed beside the Simon Commission

Report during the three round tables of 1930–1932 on India, but the Government of India Act 1935 was almost exclusively inspired by the Simon Commission's recommendations. It only granted the right to vote to fourteen per cent of the Indian population, and did not include the Bill of Rights so dear to Besant. In 1931, shortly after Motilal Nehru's death, and while Gandhi was participating in the round table in London, Besant expressed her concern that ethnic and religious tensions were such by then in India, that any constitution had become impossible, and she predicted the country's partition. That year, she presided over the All-India Humanitarian Conference in response to these tensions, and was consequently nominated for the Nobel Peace Prize.

Death, Funeral and Tributes

Annie Besant passed away in Adyar on 20 September 1933. When news of her death reached the Indian National Congress, a minute of silence was suggested, but Jawaharlal Nehru replied: 'We had better talk of Mrs. Besant.' Sri Prakasa, who was in attendance, recalled: 'He paid a warm tribute to Mrs. Besant.' The Bombay stock market did not open the day of Besant's funeral. A ceremony also took place at the Benares City Hall, where it was decided that the road between the headquarters of the Theosophical Society and the Central Hindu College in Adyar would bear Besant's name.

Besant's body, draped over with a flag in India's colours, was placed on a traditional pyre in Adyar. She had asked her friend, Theosophist and nationalist Bhagavan Das, that her funeral pyre be erected in 'Kashi', as Benares was called in the Rigveda, by the Ganges River: 'the wish of an old Hindu woman', Sri Prakasa commented. This could not be arranged, but an urn containing some of Besant's ashes was carried in procession by Sri Prakasa's father, from the Theosophical Hall in Benares to the river. They were scattered in the Ganges from a small boat, where her closest friends were seated. Besant's funeral was her final homage to the culture and spirituality of India, for which she had fought for over forty years.

Afterword

While researching and writing this biography of Annie Besant, I kept wondering why she had fallen into relative obscurity, at least among the general public, and I came to a few — non-mutually exclusive — conclusions.

First of all, Besant's conversion to Theosophy still remains poorly understood, and has even been ridiculed by those researchers who underestimate the scope of the late-Victorian spiritual and occult revival, in which the Theosophical Society played a critical part. Some historians even lose interest in the second half of Besant's life, or evaluate her earlier struggles with scepticism in light of this conversion.

Conversely, though the Theosophical Society has done a remarkable job in preserving, making available and discussing Besant's Theosophical writings, many Theosophists remain unfamiliar with Besant's life prior to her conversion — although therein lie many of the sources of her interpretation of Theosophy.

Sadly, Besant's having been a woman may also have prevented her from passing into our historical consciousness. She worked and fought alongside a number of talented men in a spirit of brotherhood, but their memory has often eclipsed that of their female comrade. Because of this, Besant's influence on British secularism and socialism are just beginning to be re-evaluated.

Then, in a climate of understandable post-colonial guilt, the role that this British woman played in India is an embarrassment to some Western historians, who tend to minimize it. Thus her presidency of the Indian National Congress in 1917 has been almost completely forgotten in the West — even though Indians themselves have preserved the memory of Besant as one of their freedom fighters. Streets in Chennai, Mumbai and indeed many other places in India bear her name, and a prominent golden statue of Besant stands on the Chennai seafront alongside monuments to other influential Indian leaders. Despite the criticism of her cautious reformist approach that was expressed in her lifetime by more radical nationalists — including Gandhi — and that is occasionally repeated by Indian historians, Besant remains sufficiently well-known for the State Bank of India to have used her name and image in a publicity campaign in the early 2010s, with a slogan proudly proclaiming: 'The Banker to this Indian'.

Finally, Besant seems to have become a victim of trends in historical research that increasingly favour highly specialized and circumscribed studies. As a result, apart from a couple of biographies whose flaws I underlined in my foreword, most non-theosophical academic research centred on Besant has been limited to a few specific struggles only, especially her pioneering fight in 1877 for the right to information on birth control, and her support of the matchgirls' strike of 1888.

Admittedly, Annie Besant embarked on a number of different struggles during her long life, but all of them were part of the same never-ending quest — and there are no better words to conclude this biography than her own:

> I ask no other epitaph on my tomb but
> 'SHE TRIED TO FOLLOW TRUTH'.[1]

[1] *Why I Became a Theosophist*. London: Freethought Publishing Co., 1889.

Bibliography

By Annie Besant (in chronological order)[1]

[By the Wife of a Beneficed Clergyman]. *On the Deity of Jesus of Nazareth. An Enquiry into the Nature of Jesus by an Examination of the Synoptic Gospels.* Edited and prefaced by Rev. Charles Voysey. London: T. Scott, 1873.

On the Political Status of Women. Lecture of August 25, 1874: Co-operative Hall, Castle Street. London: Charles Watts, 1874.

The True Basis of Morality. London: Freethought Publishing Co., 1882 (1874).

Landlords, Tenant Farmers, and Labourers. London: Freethought Publishing Co., 1880 (1874).

Civil and Religious Liberty: With Some Hints Taken from the French Revolution. London: Charlcs Watts, 1875.

Liberty, Equality, Fraternity. London: Charles Watts, 1875.

The Marriage Question. London: Charles Watts, 1875.

Auguste Comte; His Philosophy, His Religion and His Sociology. London: Charles Watts, 1875.

History of the Great French Revolution in Six Lectures. London: Charles Watts, 1876.

'The Legalisation of Female Slavery in England'. *National Reformer,* 4 June 1876.

English Republicanism. London: Charles Watts, 1877.

Is the Bible Indictable? Being an Inquiry Whether the Bible Comes within the Ruling of the Lord Chief Justice as to Obscene Literature. London: Freethought Publishing Co., 1877.

The Law of Population: Its Consequences and Its Bearing upon Human Conduct and Morals. London: Freethought Publishing Co., 1877.

Marriage, As It Was, As It Is, and As It Should Be: A Plea for Reform. London: Freethought Publishing Co., 1882 (1878).

My Path to Atheism. London: Freethought Publishing Co., 1885 (1878).

The Story of Afghanistan: Or, Why the Tory Government Gags the Indian Press. A Plea for the Weak against the Strong. London: Freethought Publishing Co., 1879.

Malthusian Tract No. 10: The Social Aspects of Malthusianism. London: Malthusian League, 1879.

[1] Kurt Leland compiled an exhaustive bibliography of Annie Besant's published writings, online at: http://www.kurtleland.com/annie-besant-shrine

God's Views on Marriage, As Revealed in the Old Testament. London: Freethought Publishing Co., 1881.
The Transvaal. London: Freethought Publishing Co., 1881.
Labour and Land: Their Burdens, Duties and Rights. London: Freethought Publishing Co., 1881.
The Landlords' Attempt to Mislead the Landless. London: Freethought Publishing Co., 1881.
Egypt. A Criticism of British Policy, 1875–1882. London: Freethought Publishing Co., 1882.
Coercion in Ireland and Its Results. A Plea for Justice. London: Freethought Publishing Co., 1882.
The Story of Soudan, London: Freethought Publishing Co., 1884.
Autobiographical Sketches. London: Freethought Publishing Co., 1885.
Woman's Position According to the Bible. London: Freethought Publishing Co., 1885.
'Ganga, the River Maid', in *Legends and Tales*. London: Freethought Publishing Co., 1885.
The Evolution of Society. London: Freethought Publishing Co., 1886.
Why I Am a Socialist. London: Freethough Publishing Co., 1886.
The Socialist Movement. London: Freethought Publishing Co., 1887 (1886).
Radicalism and Socialism. London: Freethought Publishing Co., 1887.
'Among the Adepts: Madame Blavatsky on The "Secret Doctrine"'. *Pall Mall Gazette*, 25 April, 1889, p. 3.
'The Evolution of the Universe'. *National Reformer*, 23 June 1889.
Why I Became a Theosophist. London: Freethought Publishing Co., 1889.
'Practical Work for Theosophists'. *Lucifer* 4:271, June 1889, pp. 271–4.
'Industry under Socialism', in SHAW, George Bernard, ed. *Fabian Essays in Socialism*. Garden City, New York: Doubleday, 1961 (1889).
The Trades Union Movement. London: Freethought Publishing Co., 1890.
Theosophy and the Law of Population. London: Theosophical Publishing Society, 1896 (1891).
1875 to 1891: A Fragment of Autobiography. London: Theosophical Publishing Society, 1891.
Annie Besant: An Autobiography. London: T. Fisher Unwin, 1893.
'Thought-Forms'. *Lucifer* 19, September 1896, pp. 65–75.
'India, Her Past and Her Future', in *Essays and Addresses*, vol. 4: *India*. London: Theosophical Publishing Society, 1913 (1893).
'India's Mission Among Nations', in *Essays and Addresses*, vol. 4: *India*. London: Theosophical Publishing Society, 1913 (ca. 1894).

'The Means of India's Regeneration', in *Essays and Addresses*, vol. 4: *India*. London: Theosophical Publishing Society, 1913 (1895).
The Path of Discipleship. Benares: Theosophical Publishing Society, 1899 (1895).
The Ancient Wisdom: An Outline of Theosophical Teachings. London: Theosophical Publishing Society, 1897.
The Three Paths to Union with God. London: Theosophical Publishing Society, 1913 (1897).
Evolution of Life and Form. London & Benares: Theosophical Publishing Society, 1900 (1898).
Dharma; or The Meaning of Right and Wrong. London & Benares: Theosophical Publishing Society, 1899.
Some Problems of Life. London & Benares: Theosophical Publishing Society, 1900.
Avataras. London & Benares: Theosophical Publishing Society, 1900.
Esoteric Christianity; or, The Lesser Mysteries. London & Benares: Theosophical Publishing Society, 1901.
Ancient Ideals in Modern Life. London & Benares: Theosophical Publishing Society, 1901.
'The Indian Nation. An Address Delivered to the Hindu College Boarders' Debating Society', in *The Birth of New India: A Collection of Writings and Speeches on Indian Affairs*. Adyar, Madras: Theosophical Publishing House, 1917 (ca. 1902).
'Widow-Remarriage', in *The Birth of New India: a Collection of Writings and Speeches on Indian Affairs*. Adyar, Madras: Theosophical Publishing House, 1917 (1903).
'The Education of Indian Girls', in *The Birth of New India: a Collection of Writings and Speeches on Indian Affairs*. Adyar, Madras: Theosophical Publishing House, 1917 (1904).
The Bhagavad-Gita (translation from Sanskrit). London & Benares: Theosophical Publishing Society, 1905.
'The Place of Phenomena in the Theosophical Society', in *London Lectures of 1907*. London & Benares: Theosophical Publishing Society, 1907.
The Future Socialism. Adyar: Theosophical Publishing House, 1916 (1908).
'The Work of the T. S. in India', in *The Birth of New India: a Collection of Writings and Speeches on Indian Affairs*. Adyar, Madras: Theosophical Publishing House, 1917 (1909).
'Islam in the Light of Theosophy', in *The Birth of New India: a Collection of Writings and Speeches on Indian Affairs*. Adyar, Madras: Theosophical Publishing House, 1917 (1910).
A Study in Karma. Adyar: Theosophical Publishing House, 1917 (1911).
Giordano Bruno: Theosophy's Apostle in the Sixteenth Century, a Lecture Delivered in the Sorbonne at Paris, on June 15, 1911. Adyar: Theosophist Office, 1913.

Essays and Addresses, vol. 1: *Psychology*. Madras: Theosophical Publishing Society, 1911.
Initiation: The Perfecting of Man. London: Theosophical Publishing Society, 1912.
Education in the Light of Theosophy. Adyar: Theosophist Office, 1912.
Essays and Addresses, vol. 2: *The Spiritual Life*. Madras: Theosophical Publishing Society, 1912.
Essays and Addresses, vol. 3: *Evolution and Occultism*. Madras: Theosophical Publishing Society, 1913.
'India's Awakening', in *Essays and Addresses*, vol. 4: *India*. Madras: Theosophical Publishing Society, 1913.
Wake Up, India: A Plea for Social Reform. Adyar, Madras: Theosophical Publishing House, 1913.
Mysticism. London: Theosophical Publishing Society, 1914.
'Federation', in *The Birth of New India: A Collection of Writings and Speeches on Indian Affairs*. Adyar, Madras: Theosophical Publishing House, 1917 (1914)
'Indian Self-Government', in *The Birth of New India: A Collection of Writings and Speeches on Indian Affairs*. Adyar, Madras: Theosophical Publishing House, 1917 (1915).
'Why Not Indian Scouts?'. *New India*. 13 October 1916.
'The Case for India', in *Congress Speeches of Annie Besant*. Madras: Commonweal Office, 1917.
'Girls' Education', in *The Birth of New India: A Collection of Writings and Speeches on Indian Affairs*. Adyar, Madras: Theosophical Publishing House, 1917.
The Theosophical Society and the Occult Hierarchy: Three Lectures Delivered in the Kensington Town Hall, London, to Fellows of the Theosophical Society, October 1925. London: Theosophical Publishing House, 1925.
'On the Watch-Tower: A Jubilee Function'. *Theosophist*, September 1927, pp. 650–1.
LELAND, Kurt, ed. *Invisible Worlds: Annie Besant on Psychic and Spiritual Development*. Wheaton, Ill.: Quest Books, Theosophical Publishing House, 2013.
SAVILLE, John, ed. *A Selection of the Social and Political Pamphlets of Annie Besant*. New York: Augustus M. Kelley, 1970.

With Charles Bradlaugh

'Preface' in [KNOWLTON, Charles.] *The Fruits of Philosophy: An Essay on the Population Question*. London: Freethought Publishing Co., 1877.

With Charles W. Leadbeater

Thought-Forms. Adyar: Theosophical Publishing Society, 1905.

Occult Chemistry: A Series of Clairvoyant Observations on the Chemical Elements. London: Theosophical Publishing House (revised edition edited by A. P. Sinnett, 1919) (1908).

Man: Whence, How and Whither, a Record of Clairvoyant Investigation. Adyar: Theosophical Publishing House, 1913.

The Lives of Alcyone: A Clairvoyant Investigation into the Lives throughout the Ages of a Large Band of Servers (2 vol). Adyar: Theosophical Publishing House, 1924.

Primary sources

Books

Report of Her Majesty's Commissioners Appointed to Inquire into the Revenues and Management of Certain Colleges and Schools, and the Studies Pursued and Instruction Given Therein: With an Appendix and Evidence. London: G. E. Eyre & W. Spottiswoode, for H. M. Stationery Office, 1864.

The Government Organisation of Unemployed Labour. Report Made by a Committee to the Fabian Society and Ordered to be Printed for the Information of its Members. London: George Standring, 1886.

What Socialism Is. Fabian Tract No. 4. London: George Standring, 1886.

The Religious Census of London: Reprinted from the British Weekly. London: Hodder & Stoughton, 1888.

ALCYONE [J. Krishnamurti], *At the Feet of the Masters.* Adyar: Theosophist Office, 1910.

BESTERMAN, Theodore. *Mrs. Annie Besant: A Modern Prophet.* London: Kegan Paul, 1934.

BLAVATSKY, H. P. *Isis Unveiled: A Master-Key to the Mysteries of Ancient and Modern Science and Theology.* New York: W. J. Bouton, 1877.

——. *The Secret Doctrine: The Synthesis of Science, Religion and Philosophy.* London: Theosophical Publishing Co., 1888.

——. *The Key to Theosophy: A Clear Exposition in the Form of Question and Answer of the Ethics, Science, and Philosophy for the Study of Which the Theosophical Society Has Been Founded.* London: Theosophical Publishing Co., 1889.

BRADLAUGH, Charles. *The Autobiography of Mr Bradlaugh. A Page in His Life.* London: Austin, 1873.

BRADLAUGH-BONNER, Hypatia. *Charles Bradlaugh: A Record of His Life and Work by His Daughter with an Account of His Parliamentary Struggle, Politics and Teachings by John M. Robertson, M.P.* (2 vols). London: T. Fisher Unwin, 1895.

BUCKLE, George Earle, ed. *The Letters of Queen Victoria. Volume 5: 1870–1878.* Cambridge University Press, 1926.

BUTLER, Josephine E. *The New Abolitionists: a Narrative of a Year's Work*. London: Dyer Brothers, 1876.
CONWAY, Moncure Daniel. *My Pilgrimage to the Wise Men of the East*. Boston & New York: Houghton, Mifflin & Co., 1906.
COUSINS, James Henry, ed. *The Annie Besant Centenary Book, 1847–1947*. Adyar: Besant Centenary Celebrations Committee, 1947.
DARWIN, Charles. *On the Origin of Species by Means of Natural Selection, or the Preservation of Favoured Races in the Struggle for Life*. London: John Murray, 1859.
——. *The Descent of Man, and Selection in Relation to Sex*. London: John Murray, 1871.
DARWIN, Francis, ed. *The Life and Letters of Charles Darwin, Including an Autobiographical Chapter*. 3 vols. London: John Murray, 1887.
DESPARD, Charlotte. *Theosophy and the Woman's Movement*. London: Theosophical Publishing Society, 1913.
DRYSDALE, George. *The Elements of Social Science; or, Physical, Sexual, and Natural Religion. An Exposition of the True Cause and Only Cure of the Three Primary Social Evils: Poverty, Prostitution, and Celibacy*. London: E. Truelove, 1854.
FOOTE, George W. *Mrs. Besant's Theosophy: A Candid Criticism*. London: Progressive Publishing Co., 1891 (1889).
——. *Secularism and Theosophy. A Rejoinder to Mrs. Besant's Pamphlet*. London: Progressive Publishing Co., 1891 (1889).
FRAZER, James. *The Golden Bough: A Study in Comparative Religion* (retitled *The Golden Bough: A Study in Magic and Religion* in its second edition). New York & London: Macmillan, 1894 (1890).
GANDHI, Mohandas K. *An Autobiography; or, The Story of My Experiments with Truth* (translated from the Gujarati by Mahadev Desai). Ahmedabad: Navajivan Publishing House, 1993 (1927–1928).
GEORGE, Henry. *Progress and Poverty: An Enquiry into the Cause of Industrial Depression and of Increase of Want with Increase of Wealth*. London: Paul Kegan, 1881 (1879).
GUEST, L. Haden. *Theosophy and Social Reconstruction*. London: Theosophical Publishing Society, 1912.
HOLYOAKE, George Jacob. *The Principles of Secularism*. London: Austin & Co., 1871 (3rd ed.).
HUGO, Victor. *L'Homme qui rit*. Paris: Gallimard, 2002 (1869).
HYNDMAN, Henry Mayers, & BRADLAUGH, Charles. *Will Socialism Benefit the English People? Verbatim Report of a Debate between Henry M. Hyndman and Charles Bradlaugh Held at St. James' Hall on April 17th, 1884*. London: Freethought Publishing Company, 1884.

JINARAJADASA, C, ed. *The Golden Book of the Theosophical Society: A Brief History of the Society's Growth 1875–1925*. Adyar, Madras: Theosophical Publishing House, 1925.

JUDGE, William Q. *Issues in the T.S.: Articles by William Q. Judge*. William Q. Judge Series 27. Bangalore: Theosophy Company, nd.

JUPP, William. *The Religion of Nature and Human Experience*. London: P. Green, 1906.

KANDINSKY, Wassily. *Concerning the Spiritual in Art* (translated by Michael T. H. Saddler, 1914). New York: Dover, 1977 (original in German, 1910).

KELKAR, N. C., ed. *Full & Authentic Report of the Tilak Trial (1908). Being the Only Authorised Verbatim Account of the Whole Proceedings with Introduction and Character Sketch of Bal Gangadhar Tilak, Together with Press Opinion*. Bombay: Indu-Prakashi Press, 1908.

KINGSFORD, Anna (with MAITLAND, Edward). *The Perfect Way; or, The Finding of Christ*. London: Field & Tuer, 1882.

[KNOWLTON, Charles.] *The Fruits of Philosophy, or The Private Companion of Young Married Couples. By a Physician*. New York: self-published, 1832.

KRISHNAMURTI, Jiddu. *The Collected Works of J. Krishnamurti, 1933–1967* (17 vol). Ojai: Krishnamurti Foundation of America,1992.

LANSBURY, George. *My Life*. London: Constable & Co., 1928.

LOTI, Pierre. *L'Inde (sans les Anglais)*. Paris: Calmann-Lévy, 1903.

——. *India* (translated from the French by George A. F. Inman). New York: Duffield, 1913.

MALTHUS, Thomas Robert. *An Essay on the Principle of Population and Other Writings*. London: Penguin Classics, 2015 (1798).

MANN, Tom. *Memoirs*. London: Labour Publishing Co., 1923.

MILL, John Stuart. *On Liberty*. London: Penguin, 2010 (1859).

——. *De la liberté*, (trad. Laurence Lenglet). Paris: Gallimard, 1990 (1859).

——. 'The Subjection of Women', in *On Liberty and The Subjection of Women*. London: Penguin Classics, 2006 (1869).

——. *Principles of Political Economy. A Selected Edition with Chapters on Socialism*. RILEY, Jonathan, ed. Oxford University Press, 1998 (1848–1871).

MONTAGU, Edwin Samuel. *Report on Indian Constitutional Reform*. Calcutta: Superintendent Government Printing, 1918.

MUDIE-SMITH, Richard, ed. *The Religious Life of London*. London: Hodder & Stoughton, 1904

NEHRU, Jawaharlal. *Toward Freedom: The Autobiography of Jawaharlal Nehru*. New York: The John Day Co., 1941.

NIETZSCHE, Friedrich. *Beyond Good and Evil* (translated by Helen Zimmern, 1906). New York: Dover, 1997 (original in German, 1886).

PEASE, Edward Reynolds. *The History of the Fabian Society*. London: A. C. Fifield, 1916.

SHAW, George Bernard. *An Autobiography, 1856–1898. Selected from His Writings.* WEINTRAUB, Stanley, ed. London: Reinhardt, 1969.

——. ed. *Fabian Essays in Socialism*. Garden City, New York: Doubleday, 1961 (1889).

——. et al. *Dr. Annie Besant: Fifty Years in Public Work,* London: Privately Printed, 1924.

SINNETT, Alfred Percy. *The Occult World*. London: Trübner & Co, 1881.

——. *Esoteric Buddhism*. London: Trübner & Co, 1883.

SMILES, Samuel. *Duty, with Illustrations of Courage, Patience & Endurance.* London: John Murray, 1880.

SNELL, Henry. *Men, Movements and Myself*. London: J.M. Dent & Sons, 1936.

SRI PRAKASA, *Annie Besant: As Woman and As Leader.* Adyar: Theosophical Publishing House, 1941.

STEAD, W. T. *The M. P. for Russia: Reminiscences & Correspondence of Madame Olga Novikoff*. London: A. Melrose, 1909.

SUNDARAM, V. A., ed. *Benares Hindu University 1905–1935*. Benares Hindu University, 1936.

TYNDALL, John. *Address Delivered Before the British Association Assembled at Belfast, With Additions*. London: Longmans, Green & Co., 1874.

VOYSEY, Charles. *The Sling and the Stone*. London: Williams & Norgate, 1865.

WEDDERBURN, William. *Allan Octavian Hume: Father of the Indian National Congress, 1829 to 1912*. London: T. Fisher Unwin, 1913.

WEST, Geoffrey [Geoffrey Harry Wells]. *Mrs. Annie Besant*. London: Gerald Howe, 1929.

WILLIAMS, Gertrude M. *The Passionate Pilgrim: A Life of Annie Besant.* London: John Hamilton, 1932 (1931).

WOLLSTONECRAFT, Mary. *A Vindication of the Rights of Woman*. London: Penguin Books, 2004 (1792).

ZIRKOFF, Boris de, ed. *H. P. Blavatsky's Collected Writings* (15 vol.) Wheaton, Ill: Quest Books, 1933–1990.

Articles

Chapter 6 'Girls' Schools', in *The Schools Inquiry Commission Report* vol.1. London: Her Majesty's Stationery Office, 1867–8, pp. 546–70.

'The Workmen's Congresses in London'. *St James's Gazette*, 17 July 1889.

'The International Congress of Workers. The Closing Sitting'. *Pall Mall Gazette*, 23 July 1889.

'Why I Became a Theosophist: Mrs Besant Offers an Explanation to Her Secularist friends'. *Pall Mall Gazette*, 12 August 1889, p. 6.
'The Great Strike'. *Morning Post* (London), 31 August 1889, p. 5.
'The Taylors' Strike'. *Globe* (London), 28 September 1889, p. 7.
'The Hyde Park Meeting'. *London Evening Standard*, 5 May 1890, p. 3.
'By a Special Contributor'. 'From the Radical Benches: The Peers and Women'. *Reynolds's Newspaper*, 15 June 1890, p. 5.
'Theosophy in Relation to the Problems of Modern Life'. *Women's Penny Paper* 92, 26 July 1890, p. 471.
'The Democratic World'. *Reynolds's Newspaper*, 14 September 1890, p. 8.
'London School Board'. *South London Press*, 7 March 1891, p. 8.
'Madame Blavatsky Died Yesterday'. *London Daily News*, 9 May 1891, p. 5.
'The Prophetess of the Buried Tea Cup'. *Pall Mall Gazette*, 9 May 1891, p. 1.
'Mrs. Besant to Retire from the School Board'. *Pall Mall Gazette*, 25 June 1891, p. 4.
'Mrs. Besant's New Mission'. *St James's Gazette*, 26 June 1891, p. 9.
'I Believe in Madame Blavatsky'. *Pall Mall Gazette*, 13 July 1891, pp. 1–2.
'Mrs. Besant and the Secularist Society'. *Pall Mall Gazette*, 1 September 1891, p. 6.
'Mrs. Besant's "*Apologia Pro Vita Sua*." Curious Statement'. *Pall Mall Gazette*, 31 August 1891, p. 6.
'Mrs. Besant's Farewell Address to Secularism'. *Reynolds's Newspaper*, 6 September 1891, p. 5
'Mrs Besant v. Mrs Bishop'. *Woman's Signal*, 12 April 1894.
'Dr Annie Besant, President of the Theosophical Society, Laying the Foundation Stone for the Adyar Synagogue'. *The Jewish Theosophist* 1.4, July 1927, p. 3.
'Dr. Besant Receives "The Silver Wolf"'. *Theosophist* 54.3, December 1932, pp. 295–9.
HODGSON, Richard et al. 'Report of the Committee Appointed to Investigate Phenomena Connected with the Theosophical Society', in *Proceedings of the Society for Psychical Research* 3. London: Kegan Paul, Trübner & Co, 1885, pp. 201–400.
JUDGE, William Q. 'Convention Reports of the TS American Section. April 22–23, 1894', in *Issues in the T.S.: Articles by William Q. Judge*. William Q. Judge Series 27. Bangalore: Theosophy Company, nd.
LANSBURY, George. 'Annie Besant as a Politician', in *Dr. Annie Besant: Fifty Years in Public Work*. London: privately printed, 1924.
[LUDWIG, Emil] 'Ludwig Beholds Great Women; From Far Scattered Lands and Widely Differing Fields of Endeavor the Biographer Selects a Notable List of Workers Who Play Heroine Parts in the Life of the World Today'. *New York Times Magazine*, 26 February, 1928. p. 76.
MEAD, G. R. S. '*The Quest* — Old and New: Retrospect and Prospect'. *Quest Reprint Series* 1 April 1926. *Psypioneer Journal* 11.3, March 2015, pp 97–107.

MORRIS, William. 'How We Live and How We Might Live', in MORTON, A. L. *Political Writings of William Morris.* London: Lawrence & Wishart, 1973 (1884).
PODMORE, Frank. 'Madame Blavatsky and the Theosophical Society'. *Good Words*, February 1892, pp. 82–86.
[RIGBY, Elizabeth.] '*Vanity Fair* and *Jane Eyre*'. *Quarterly Review* 84.167, December 1848, pp. 153–85.
ROY, M. N. 'India and the British Labour Government'. *Labour Monthly* 6.4, April 1924, pp. 200–10.
SHAW, George Bernard. 'Radicals and Social-Democrats'. *Pall Mall Gazette*, 17 September 1890, p. 2.
——. 'Mrs. Besant as a Fabian Socialist'. *Theosophist*, October 1917, pp. 9–19.
STEAD, W. T. 'Mrs. Annie Besant'. *Review of Reviews*, 4 October, 1891, pp. 349–67.
[WALTER, Arthur.] 'Law Report: High Court of Justice, June 21. Queen's Bench Division. The Queen v. Bradlaugh and Another'. *The Times*. 22 June 1877.

Secondary sources

Books

ARNSTEIN, Walter. *The Bradlaugh Case: A Study in Late Victorian Opinion and Politics*. Oxford University Press, 1965
BANKS, Olive. *Becoming a Feminist: The Social Origins of 'First Wave' Feminism.* Brighton: Wheatsheaf Books, 1986.
BELLAMY Joyce M. & John SAVILLE, eds. *Dictionary of Labour Biographies.* London: Macmillan, 1979.
BEVIR, Mark. *The Making of British Socialism*. Princeton University Press, 2011.
BROWN, Richard. *Sex, Work and Politics: Women in Britain, 1780–1945.* CreateSpace, 2014.
BUISINE, Andrée. *La Franc-maçonnerie anglo-saxonne et les femmes.* Paris: Trédaniel, 1995.
CAMPBELL, Bruce F. *Ancient Wisdom Revived: A History of the Theosophical Movement*. University of California Press, 1980.
CAPRA, Fritjof, *The Tao of Physics: An Exploration of the Parallels between Modern Physics and Eastern Mysticism*. Boston: Shambala, 2000 (1975).
CHALLINOR, Ray. *A Radical Lawyer in Victorian England: W. P. Roberts and the Struggle for Workers' Rights*. London: I. B. Tauris, 1990.
CHANDRASEKHAR, Sripati. *'A Dirty, Filthy Book': The Writings of Charles Knowlton and Annie Besant on Reproductive Physiology and Birth Control and an Account of the Bradlaugh-Besant Trial*. University of California Press, 1981.

CLAVIER, Paul. *Qu'est-ce que la théologie naturelle.* Paris: Librairie philosophique J. Vrin, 2004.

COSTE, Bénédicte, ed. *Believing in Victorian Times, Cahiers victoriens et édouardiens* 76. Montpellier: Presses Universitaires de la Méditerranée, October 2012.

DESCHAMPS, Yannick & Suzy HALIMI, ed. *Orthodoxie et hérésie dans les îles britanniques, Revue française de civilisation britannique* 18.1, Spring 2013.

DIXON, Joy. *Divine Feminine: Theosophy and Feminism in England.* Johns Hopkins University Press, 2001.

DROZ, Jacques. *L'Internationale ouvrière de 1864 à 1920.* Paris: Centre de documentation universitaire, 1965.

FLANDERS, Judith. *The Victorian House: Domestic Life from Chidbirth to Deathbed.* London: Harper Perennial, 2003.

GODWIN, Joscelyn. *The Theosophical Enlightenment.* Albany: State University of New York Press, 1994.

GOZARD, Manon. *Annie Besant's Emblematic Struggle to Obtain a University Degree in London in the Mid-1880s.* Master I dissertation (n.p.), University of Paris-Sorbonne, Paris 4, 2012.

GLEADLE, Kathryn. *British Women in the Nineteenth Century.* Basingstoke: Palgrave Macmillan, 2001.

GRATTAN-GUINNESS, Ivor. *Psychical Research: A Guide to Its History, Principles and Practices.* London: Aquarian Press, 1982.

GUPTA, Partha Sarathi. *Imperialism and the British Labour Movement, 1914–1964.* London & Basingtoke: Macmillan, 1975.

HANAGRAAF, Wouter J.; FAIVRE, Antoine; van den BROEK Roelof & Jean-Pierre BRACH, eds. *Dictionary of Gnosis & Western Esotericism.* Leiden & Boston: Brill, 2005.

HARRIS, Philip S., general ed. *The Theosophical Encyclopedia.* Manila: Theosophical Publishing House, 2006.

HIBBERT, Christopher. *Edward VII: The Last Victorian King.* Basingstoke: Palgrave Macmillan, 2007.

HOLLIS Patricia. *Ladies Elect: Women in English Local Government, 1865–1914.* Oxford University Press, 1987.

HOUGHTON, Walter E. *The Victorian Frame of Mind, 1830–1870.* Yale University Press, 1957.

HUXLEY, Aldous. *The Perennial Philosophy.* London: Chatto & Windus, 1946 (1945).

JUNG, Carl Gustav. *Modern Man in Search of a Soul* (translated by Cary F. Baines). Oxford: Routledge Classics, 2001 (1933).

KUMAR, Raj. *Annie Besant's Rise to Power in Indian Politics, 1914–1917.* New Delhi: Concept Publishing Co., 1981.

KUMAR, Raj, RAMESHWARI Devi & Romila PRUTHI. *Annie Besant: Founder of Home Rule Movement*, Jaipur: Pointer Publishers, 2003.

LARSEN, Timothy. *Crisis of Doubt: Honest Faith in Nineteenth-Century England.* Oxford University Press, 2006

LAVOIE, Jeffrey D. *The Theosophical Society: The History of a Spiritualist Movement.* Boca Raton, Fla.: Brown Walker Press, 2012.

LEDBETTER, Rosanna. *A History of the Malthusian League 1877–1927*. Ohio State University Press, 1976.

LÖWITH, Karl. *Meaning in History: The Theological Implications of the Philosophy of History*. Chicago University Press, 1949.

LUTYENS, Mary. *Krishnamurti: The Years of Awakening.* London: John Murray, 1975.

MACKAY, Carol Hanbery, ed. BESANT, Annie. *Autobiographical Sketches* (1885). Peterborough, Ont.: Broadview Press Ltd, 2009.

MANVELL, Roger. *The Trial of Annie Besant and Charles Bradlaugh.* London: Pemberton, 1976.

MASLOW, Abraham. *Religions, Values, and Peak-Experiences.* London: Penguin, 1994 (1964)

McLEOD, Hugh. *The Religious Crisis of the 1860s.* Oxford University Press, 2007.

MEADE, Marion. *Madame Blavatsky: The Woman Behind the Myth.* New York, G. P. Putnam's Sons, 1980.

NETHERCOT, Arthur Hobart. *The First Five Lives of Annie Besant.* University of Chicago Press, 1960.

——. *The Last Four Lives of Annie Besant.* University of Chicago Press, 1963.

OPPENHEIM, Janet. *The Other World: Spiritualism and Psychical Research in England, 1850–1914.* Cambridge University Press, 1985.

OWEN, Alex. *The Darkened Room: Women, Power and Spiritualism in Late Victorian England.* University of Chicago Press, 2004 (1989).

——. *The Place of Enchantment: British Occultism and the Culture of the Modern.* University of Chicago Press, 2004.

OWEN, Nicholas. *The British Left and India: Metropolitan Anti-Imperialism, 1885–1947.* Oxford University Press, 2007.

PELLING, Henry M. *The Origins of the Labour Party, 1880–1900.* Oxford University Press, 1966 (1954).

PERT, Alan. *Red Cactus: The Life of Anna Kingsford.* Watson Bay, NSW: Books and Writers, 2006.

PILCHER-DAYTON, Ann. *The Open Door: the History of the Order of Women Freemasons 1908–2008.* London: Order of Women Freemasons, 2008.

PORTER, Andrew, ed. *The Oxford History of the British Empire: the Nineteenth Century.* Oxford University Press, 1999.

RAINE, Kathleen. *Blake and Tradition* (2 vols). London: Routledge & Kegan Paul, 1969.

RAW, Louise, *Striking a Light: The Bryant and May Matchwomen and their Place in History*. London: Continuum, 2009.

ROBINSON, W. Sydney. *Muckraker: The Scandalous Life and Times of W. T. Stead: Britain's First Investigative Journalist.* London: Robson Press, 2012.

ROWBOTHAM, Sheila. *Edward Carpenter: A life of Liberty and Love.* New York: Verso (New Left Books), 2009.

ROYLE, Edward. *Radicals, Secularists and Republicans: Popular Freethought in Britain, 1866–1915.* Manchester University Press, 1980.

SARKAR, Sumit. *The Swadeshi Movement in Bengal, 1903–1908.* Delhi: People's Publishing House, 1973.

SAVILLE, John & Joyce M. BELLAMY, then Keith GILDART & David HOWELL, eds. *Dictionary of Labour Biography* (13 vols), Basingstoke: Palgrave Macmillan, 1972–2010.

SCHWARTZ, Laura. *Infidel Feminists Secularism, Religion and Women's Emancipation in England, 1830–1914.* Manchester University Press, 2013.

SMITH, Harold L. *The British Women's Suffrage Campaign, 1866–1928.* London: Longman, 2009 (2nd ed.).

SMITH, Warren S. *The London Heretics 1870–1914.* London: Constable, 1967.

de SOUZENELLE, Annick. *Le Féminin de l'être: pour en finir avec la côte d'Adam.* Paris: Albin Michel, Col. Spiritualités vivantes, 2000.

STACK, David. *The First Darwinian Left: Socialism and Darwinism 1859–1914.* Cheltenham: New Clarion Press, 2003.

STEINBACH, Susie. *Women in England 1760–1914: A Social History.* London: Weidenfeld & Nicolson, 2004.

SHEARMAN, Hugh. *Charles Webster Leadbeater: A Biography.* London: St. Alban Press, 1980.

TAYLOR, Anne. *Annie Besant: a Biography.* Oxford University Press, 1992.

TAYLOR, Barbara. *Eve and the New Jerusalem: Socialism and Feminism in the Nineteenth Century.* London: Virago, 1983.

TERRIER, Marie. *La Contribution théorique et militante d'Annie Besant (1847–1933) au renouveau socialiste des années 1880 en Grande-Bretagne. Genèse et prolongements.* PhD dissertation (n.p.). Université Sorbonne-Nouvelle, Paris 3, 2015.

THOMPSON, F. M. L. *The Rise of Respectable Society: A Social History of Victorian Britain, 1830–1900.* London: Fontana, 1988.

TILLETT, Gregory. *The Elder Brother: A Biography of Charles Webster Leadbeater.* London: Routledge & Kegan Paul, 1982.

TORT, Patrick. *L'Effet Darwin. Sélection naturelle et naissance de la civilisation.* Paris: Editions du Seuil, 2008.

TURNER, Frank M. *Contesting Cultural Authority. Essays in Victorian Intellectual Life.* Cambridge University Press, 1993.

WALKOWITZ, Judith. *Prostitution and Victorian Society: Women, Class, and the State.* Cambridge University Press, 1980.

WALLACE, Alan B. *Choosing Reality: A Contemplative View of Physics and the Mind.* Boston: Shambala, 1989.

WINDERGERDEN, Sophia A. *The Women's Suffrage Movement in Britain, 1866–1928.* London: Palgrave, 2003.

WILSON, Colin. *Rudolf Steiner: The Man and His Visions.* London: Aeon Books, 2005 (1985).

WOLFE, Willard. *From Radicalism to Socialism: Men and Ideas in the Formation of Fabian Socialist Doctrines, 1881–1889.* Yale University Press, 1975.

WOLPERT, Stanley A. *Tilak and Gokhale: Revolution and Reform in the Making of Modern India.* Oxford University Press, 1990 (1962).

——. *A New History of India.* Oxford University Press, 2004 (7th ed.).

Articles

ALDERMAN, Geoffrey. 'Hartog, Numa Edward (1846–1871)', in *Oxford Dictionary of National Biography.* Oxford University Press, 2004.

ARNSTEIN, Walter L. 'Gladstone and the Bradlaugh Case'. *Victorian Studies* 5.4, June 1962, pp. 254–69.

ANDERSON, Nancy Fix. 'Bridging Cross-cultural Feminisms: Annie Besant and Women's Rights in England and India, 1874–1933'. *Women's History Review* 3.4, 1994, pp. 563–80.

BANKS, J. A. & Olive. 'The Bradlaugh-Besant Trial and the English Newspapers', *Population Studies* 8.1, July 1954, pp. 22–34.

BANTMAN, Constance. 'Du *lib-labism* à la grande fièvre ouvrière: les *trade unions* entre libéralisme, travaillisme et action directe', in MOTARD, Anne-Marie, ed. *Les Syndicats britanniques: déclin ou renouveau? Revue française de civilisation britannique* 15.2, 2009, pp. 45–57.

BENSIMON, Fabrice. 'Le Chartisme', in PIGENET, Michel & Danielle TARTAKOWSKY, eds. *Histoire des mouvements sociaux en France de 1814 à nos jours.* Paris: La Découverte, 2012, pp. 79–89.

BEVIR, Mark. 'The Formation of the All-India Home Rule League'. *Indian Journal of Political Science* 52.3, 1991, pp. 341–56

——. 'The West Turns Eastward: Madame Blavatsky and the Transformation of the Occult Tradition'. *Journal of the American Academy of Religion* 62.3, 1994, pp. 747–67.

——. 'Annie Besant's Quest for Truth: Christianity, Secularism and New Age Thought'. *Journal of Ecclesiastical History* 50.1, 1999, pp. 62–93.

——. 'Theosophy as a Political Movement', in COPLEY, Antony, ed. *Gurus and their Followers: New Religious Reform Movements in Colonial India*. Oxford University Press, 2000, pp. 159–76.

——. 'Theosophy and the Origins of the Indian National Congress', in *International Journal of Hindu Studies* 7.1/3, 2003, pp. 99–115.

BLYTH, Caroline. 'Unhappy Anniversary: Women, Marriage and the Biblical Law in the Writings of Annie Besant', in CALVERT-KOYZIS, Nancy & Heather E. WEIR, eds. *Strangely Familiar: Protofeminist Interpretations of Patriarchal Biblical Texts*. Williston, Vt.: Society of Biblical Lit, 2009, pp. 121–37.

BOUCHER-RIVALAIN, Odile. 'Harriet Martineau (1802–1876), from Unitarianism to Agnosticism', in COSTE, Bénédicte, ed. *Believing in Victorian Times, Cahiers victoriens et édouardiens* 76. Montpellier: Presses Universitaires de la Méditerranée, October 2012, pp. 27–43.

BRANDSER KALSEM, Kristin. 'Law, Literature, and Libel: Victorian Censorship of "Dirty, Filthy" Books on Birth Control'. *William and Mary Journal of Women and the Law* 10.3, 2004, pp. 533–68.

BROWN, Lyn, MP. 'Out of the Shadows: the Women who Sparked the Labour Movement'. *The Guardian*, 4 November 2013.

BURFIELD, Diana. 'Theosophy and Feminism: Some Explorations in Nineteenth Century Biography', in HOLDEN, Pat, ed. *Women's Religious Experience*. London: Croom Helm, 1983, pp. 27–56.

CANDY, Catherine. 'Relating Feminisms, Nationalisms, and Imperialisms: Ireland, India and Margaret Cousins's Sexual Politics'. *Women's History Review* 3.4, 1994, pp. 581–94.

CHATTERJEE, Dilip Kumar. 'Cousins and Sri Aurobindo: A Study on Literary Influence'. *Triveni*, April–June 1983.

CROW, John L. '*Thought Forms*: A Bibliographic Error'. *Theosophical History* 16.3–4, July–October 2012, pp. 126–7.

DAVENPORT-HINES, Richard. 'Blavatsky, Helena Petrovna (1831–1891)', in *Oxford Dictionary of National Biography* (online ed.). Oxford University Press, 2011 (2004).

DATAR, Abhay. 'The Lucknow Pact of 1916: A Second Look at the Congress-Muslim League Agreement'. *Economic & Political Weekly (EPW)* 47.10, March 2012.

DUNNINGHAM-CHAPOTIN, Diana. 'The Theosophical Order of Service', in HARRIS, Philip S., general ed. *The Theosophical Encyclopedia*. Manila: Theosophical Publishing House, 2006.

FARNELL, Kim. 'A Brief Biography of Alan Leo', skyscript.co.uk, August 2006.

FORBES, Geraldine. 'The Politics of Respectability: Indian Women and the Indian National Congress', in LOW, D. A., ed. *The Indian National Congress: Centenary Hindsights*. Oxford University Press, 1988, pp. 55–97.

GAUDIN, Elisabeth. 'Margaret Cousins: De Dublin à Madras', in MOLINARI, Véronique, ed. *Droits des femmes, droits des autres. Des féministes britanniques face aux exclus de la citoyenneté (1860–1930)*. Presses universitaires Blaise Pascal, 2012.

GEOFFROY, Sophie. 'Darwin et les féministes: Annie Besant (1874–1933) et la question du contrôle des naissances ou *The Descent of Man* versus *The Fruits of Philosophy* (1832 réimp. 1877)', in GEOFFROY, Sophie & Michel PRUM, eds., *Darwin dans la bataille des idées*. Paris: L'Harmattan, 2012, pp. 63–100.

———. 'Une *New Woman* théosophe aux origines du Droit Humain britannique: Annie Besant (London 1847–Adyar 1933)', in RÉVAUGER, Cécile, ed. *Les Femmes et la franc-maçonnerie des Lumières à nos jours*. Bruxelles: La Pensée et les Hommes, 2012, pp. 121–46.

HALIMI, Suzy. 'Sir Moses Montefiore (1784–1785), défenseur de la foi', in DESCHAMPS, Yannick & Suzy HALIMI, eds. *Orthodoxie et hérésie dans les îles britanniques, Revue française de civilisation britannique* 18.1, printemps 2013, pp. 151–60.

HALL, Kathleen. 'Theosophy and the Emergence of Modern Abstract Art'. *Quest* 90.3, May–June 2002.

HARRIS, Philip S. 'Blavatsky, Helena Petrovna (1831–1891)', in HARRIS, Philip S., general ed. *The Theosophical Encyclopedia*. Manila: Theosophical Publishing House, 2006.

HOBERMAN, Ruth. 'Women in the British Museum Reading Room during the Late-Nineteenth and Early-Twentieth Centuries: From Quasi- to Counterpublic'. *Feminist Studies* 28.3, Autumn 2002, pp. 489–512.

HOBSBAWM, Eric. 'The Lesser Fabians', in MUNBY, Lionel M., ed. *The Luddites and other Essays*. London: Michael Katanka, 1971, pp. 231–44.

HUSS, Boaz. '"A Jew Living in an Ashram": The Spiritual Itinerary of S. S. Cohen'. *Journal of Indo-Judaic Studies* 15, 2015.

LACHMAN, Gary. 'Kandinsky's Thought Forms and the Occult Roots of Modern Art'. *Quest* 96.2, March–April 2008.

LAMBS, Luc. 'Préface', in BESANT Annie & Charles LEADBEATER. *La Chimie occulte: Série d'observations faites sur les éléments chimiques au moyen de la clairvoyance* (Translated by René Allendy). Paris: Adyar, 2004 (1908).

LANGER, William L. 'The Origins of the Birth Control Movement in England in the Early Nineteenth century'. *Journal of Interdisciplinary History* 5.4, Spring 1975, pp. 669–86.

LARSEN, Timothy. 'The Bible and Belief in Victorian Britain', in COSTE, Bénédicte, ed. *Believing in Victorian Times, Cahiers victoriens et édouardiens* 76. Montpellier: Presses Universitaires de la Méditerranée, October 2012, pp. 11–26.

MACKAY, Carol Hanbery. 'Confounding or Amazing? The Multiple Deconversions of Annie Besant'. *Quest* 90.2, March–April 2002, pp. 50–6.

MOORE, Robin J. 'Imperial India', in PORTER, Andrew, ed. *The Oxford History of the British Empire: the Nineteenth Century*. Oxford University Press, 1999, pp. 422–45.

MORTIMER, Joanne Stafford. 'Annie Besant and India 1913–1917'. *Journal of Contemporary History* 18.1, January 1983, pp. 61–78.

MOULTON, Edward C. 'Allan O. Hume and the Indian National Congress: a Reassessment'. *South Asia* 8.1–2, June–December 1985, pp. 5–23.

NASH, David S. 'Unfettered Investigation: The Secularist Pressand the Creation of Audience in Victorian England'. *Victorian Periodicals Review* 28.2, 1995, pp. 123–35.

——. 'Charles Bradlaugh, India and the Many Chameleon Destinations of Republicanism', in NASH David & Antony TAYLOR, eds. *Republicanism in Victorian Society*. Stroud: Sutton, 2000, pp. 106–24.

——. "The Credulity of the Public Seems Infinite": Charles Bradlaugh, Public Biography and the Battle for Narrative Supremacy in Fin-de-siècle England'. *Journal of Victorian Culture* 7.2, 2002, pp. 239–62.

——. 'Reassessing the "Crisis of Faith" in the Victorian Age: Eclecticism and the Spirit of Moral Inquiry'. *Journal of Victorian Culture* 16.1, 2011, pp. 65–82.

OWEN, Hugh F. 'Towards Nationwide Agitation and Organisation. The Home Rule Leagues: 1915–18', in LOW, Donald Anthony, ed. *Soundings in Modern South Asian History*. University of California Press, 1968.

PAINTER, Kate. 'Wife Rape in the United Kingdom', Paper presented at the American Society of Criminology 50th Anniversary Meeting, November 20–23, 1991, San Francisco. http://www.crim.cam.ac.uk/people/visitors/kate_painter/wiferape.pdf

PAXTON, Nancy L. 'Feminism under the Raj: Complicity and Resistance in the Writings of Flora Annie Steel and Annie Besant'. *Women's Studies International Forum* 13.4, 1990, pp. 333–46.

PECASTAING-BOISSIERE, Muriel. 'Annie Besant', in *Le Maitron: dictionnaire biographique du mouvement ouvrier et social* (maitron-en-ligne.univ-paris1.fr), 2011.

——. 'Les Luttes féministes d'Annie Besant (London, 1847 – Madras, 1933)'. *Bulles de Savoir*, 13 July 2013. http://bullesdesavoir.com/2013/07/13/les-luttes-feministes-dannie-besant-londres-1847-madras-1933.

——. 'W. T. Stead's Character-Sketch of Annie Besant in the *Review of Reviews* of October 1891'. *Revue Française de Civilisation Britannique* 20.1, 2015, pp. 89–100.
——. 'Annie Besant: un incontro tra scienza e veggenza'. *Rivista Italiana di Teosofia* 71.4–5, April–May 2015, pp. 2–7 & pp. 5–10.
——. 'Annie Besant: Povezovanje znanosti in duhovnosti'. *Teozofska Knjiznica in Bralnica Alme M. Karlin*. Ljubljana: Octobre 2015 (http://www.jivatma.si/annie-besant/).
——. 'Annie Besant and Charles W. Leadbeater's "Key to the Meanings of Colours" in *Thought-Forms*', in RIBEYROL, Charlotte, ed. *The Colours of the Past in Victorian England*. Oxford: Peter Lang, 2016, pp. 205–33.
PRESCOT, A. 'Builders of the Temple of the New Civilisation: Annie Besant and Freemasonry', in HEIDLE A. & J. SNOEK, eds. *Women's Agency and Rituals in Mixed and Female Masonic Orders*. Leiden: Brill, 2008, pp. 359–92.
PRICE, Leslie. 'Did Mr Wallace Join the Theosophical Society?' *Psypioneer Journal* 8.6, June 2012, pp. 193–4.
——. 'The Hodgson Report (Theosophy)', in *Psi Encyclopedia*, 2016 https://psi-encyclopedia.spr.ac.uk/articles/hodgson-report-theosophy.
RIDLEY, Jane. 'Lutyens, Lady Emily (1874–1964)', in *Oxford Dictionary of National Biography* (online ed.). Oxford University Press, 2004.
RIVIÈRE, Jean. 'La Face cachée de Newton: antitrinitarien et alchimiste', in DESCHAMPS, Yannick & Suzy HALIMI, eds. *Orthodoxie et hérésie dans les îles britanniques. Revue française de civilisation britannique* 18.1, printemps 2013, pp. 73–9.
RISSEEUW, Carla. 'Thinking Culture through Counter-Culture: The Case of Theosophists in India and Ceylon and their Ideas on Race and Hierarchy (1875–1947)', in COPLEY, A, ed. *Gurus and their Followers: New Religious Reform Movements in Colonial India*. Oxford University Press, 2000, pp. 180–205.
ROBB, Peter. 'The Government of India and Annie Besant'. *Modern Asian Studies* 10.1, 1976, pp. 107–30.
ROBERTS, M. J. D. 'Morals, Art, and the Law: The Passing of the Obscene Publications Act, 1857'. *Victorian Studies* 28.4, Summer 1985, pp. 609–29.
ROYLE Edward. 'Harriet Teresa Law (1831–1897): Feminist, Secularist, Radical', in BELLAMY Joyce M. & John SAVILLE ed., *Labour Biographies*, vol. 5. London: Macmillan, 1979.
——. 'Bradlaugh, Charles (1833–1891)', in *Oxford Dictionary of National Biography* (online ed.). Oxford University Press, 2004.
SANTUCCI, James A. 'Blavatsky, Helena Petrovna', in *Dictionary of Gnosis & Western Esotericism*. Leiden & Boston: Brill, 2005.

SIMÉON, Ophélie. 'Robert Owen, père du socialisme britannique?'. *La Vie des idées*, 2 septembre 2012, http://www.laviedesidees.fr/Robert-Owen-pere-du-socialisme.html.

TERRIER, Marie. 'Le Néomalthusianisme d'Annie Besant (1877–1891) et la volonté d'"améliorer la race humaine"', in PRUM, Michel, ed. *Racialisation dans l'aire anglophone*. Paris: l'Harmattan, 2012, pp. 51–68.

TURNER, Frank M. 'The Crisis of Faith and the Faith that was Lost' & 'The Secularization of the Social Vision of British Natural Theology', in *Contesting Cultural Authority. Essays in Victorian Intellectual Life*. Cambridge University Press, 1993.

WHEELER, J. M. 'Scott, Thomas (1808–1878)' (revu par H. C. G. Matthew), in *Oxford Dictionary of National Biography* (online ed.). Oxford University Press, 2004.

WYLIE, Winifred. 'Montessori and the Theosophical Society'. *Quest* 96.2, March–April 2008, pp. 53–5.

YEO, Stephen. 'A New Life: The Religion of Socialism in Britain, 1883–1896'. *History Workshop* 4, Oxford University Press, Autumn, 1977, pp. 5–56.

YVARD, Jean-Michel. 'Agnosticisme, scepticisme et "voie négative" en Grande-Bretagne au dix-neuvième siècle', in COSTE, Bénédicte, ed. *Believing in Victorian Times, Cahiers victoriens et édouardiens* 76. Montpellier: Presses Universitaires de la Méditerranée, October 2012, pp. 28–45.

Acknowledgements

Not only did I find constant support and encouragement when I researched and wrote this biography of Annie Besant, but the project allowed me to meet some wonderful people, many of whom have become dear friends.

First of all, I would like to thank Dr Marie Terrier, who first contacted me as a post-graduate student in the autumn of 2009, when she discovered that we were both researching Besant. Our numerous long discussions over numberless cups of tea considerably enriched my own reflection, and I was happy to entrust her with the chapter on Besant's socialism — the topic of the PhD she passed with highest honours in 2015. I am also thankful for her proofreading the book at the various stages of its completion, both in French and in English.

I would next like to thank all of the colleagues who provided me with opportunities to give or to publish papers on Annie Besant as I was researching her life: Prof. Fabrice Bensimon at the Sorbonne, and the participants of his seminar on British history, especially the late Prof. Jean-Claude Sergeant; Prof. Ann Thomson and her research group on intellectual history at the University of Paris 8; the French Society of Victorian and Edwardian Studies (SFEVE); the research group 'Women's Voices and Paths' ('Voix et voies de femme') at the University of Lille 3; the Research Society on Women, Sex, and Gender (SAGEF); Dr Charlotte Ribeyrol at the Sorbonne and her seminar — and subsequent book — on 'the colours of the past in Victorian England'; the organisers of the symposium on W. T. Stead at the British Library in 2012; Trân-Thi Kim-Diêu and the organizers of the thirty-seventh congress of the Theosophical Society in Europe, held in Paris in 2013; Leslie Price, Prof. James Santucci and Janet Lee who organized the International Conference on Theosophical History in London in 2016; and the academic committee of the sixth European Society for the Study of Western Esotericism (ESSWE) Conference at Erfurt, Germany, in 2017 — where I met Prof. David Nash from Oxford Brookes University, who made a number of excellent suggestions concerning Chapter 3, 'Struggles for Freethought and Secularism'. I extend my thanks to Theosophists Sabine van Osta in Belgium, Enrico Stagni in Italy, Domen Kocevar in Slovenia, who either invited me to lecture on Annie Besant or published my papers.

I would also like to thank my post-graduate students Manon Gozard and Gaëlle Manika for sharing my fascination with Annie Besant. It was with great pleasure that I supervised their Master's dissertations on Besant in 2012 and 2014 respectively. The section in Chapter 3 entitled 'Struggle to Take a University Science Degree' is largely based on the research of Manon Gozard, who sadly passed away in 2014. This section is dedicated to her, as well as to her mother, the journalist Claudine Ducol, who also proofread the book in French.

I am of course most grateful to Trân-Thi Kim-Diêu and the Theosophical Society in France for their constant support: the original French version of the book could not have come into being without the Éditions Adyar and their director, Jeanne Leguay, to whom I am very grateful for trusting me when this biography was still nothing more than a detailed outline. Many thanks also to Peter Michel and Aquamarin Verlag for publishing a German translation of the book in 2017.

I was helped in translating the book into English by Keara Engelhardt, a language assistant at the Sorbonne-Nouvelle who holds a Masters in Translation from the University of Wisconsin-Milwaukee. Many thanks also to historian Richard Brown, who proofread my first draft translation of the biography. Richard made some invaluable comments and suggestions — and only asked for some crème brûlée in return.

This English translation of the biography was published thanks to tenacious help and support from Janet Lee and Tim Wyatt at the Theosophical Society in England (TSE). I am incredibly grateful to the TSE's educational charity, the Foundation for Theosophical Studies, who put up the capital to publish my book in English and as a result were persuaded into reviving the Theosophical Publishing House (London), making this book the first to be released under the new imprint — a completely unexpected honour. My thanks are further due to Tim Wyatt who oversaw the production of the finished manuscript and introduced us to the talented printer and designer Richard Aldred. Both Leslie Price and Kurt Leland did a fantastic job proofreading the book over the summer, so that it would be published just on time for Annie Besant's 170th birthday on 1 October 2017, and the International Annie Besant Conference that Kurt, Leslie, Janet and I jointly organized in London for that weekend.

Finally, I would like to thank my husband, the historian Cédric Pécastaing-Boissière from the University of Rennes 2, for his support, patience, numerous proofreadings and listening to my papers — and for sacrificing several summer holidays while I was researching, writing and translating the book.

Muriel Pécastaing-Boissière